Taxonomy of Behaviour Disturbance

Taxonomy of Behaviour Disturbance

D. H. Stott, N. C. Marston

and

Sara J. Neill

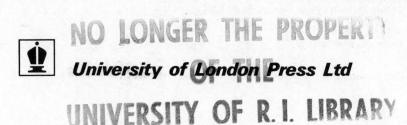

University of London Press Ltd

This book is about what on the American Continent is usually called emotional disturbance. This term has been abandoned as inaccurate. A person can be emotionally disturbed by a distressing experience without committing maladaptive acts. Similarly, some people can regularly commit maladaptive acts without being in the least emotionally disturbed, since they are unaware of the inappropriateness of their behaviour or are unconcerned about it.

Moreover, we have confined ourselves to the classification of observed behaviours. Emotions are feelings with physiological concomitants. That is to say, they are internal to the organism and unobservable unless they find expression in some behaviour. The classification of emotions would have to rely upon personal reports, and would entail a methodology quite different from that of the present study.

The research reported in this book was supported by grant No. 181 from the Ontario Mental Health Foundation and the Federal Health Grants of the Government of Canada.

ISBN 0 340 18856 1

University of London Press Ltd
St Paul's House, Warwick Lane, London EC4P 4AH

Printed in Great Britain by
Clarke, Doble and Brendon Ltd,
Plymouth

Computer Typesetting by Print Origination, Bootle, Lancs, L20 6NS.

93272

Contents

Guide to the Contents

This book describes the development of a typology of maladjustment by the analysis of the behaviour, as observed in school, of a large, randomly selected sample of students. Some readers may be interested chiefly in the methodology, and others in incidence and social-class, age and sex differences. Probably most, however, will wish to know to what extent our understanding of behaviour disturbance was furthered by new concepts and insights, and what value the types of maladjustment identified may have for the assessment and treatment of disturbed children and delinquents.

In any systematization of observations the methodology has to be discussed in detail if the new classification which results is to win acceptance. The reader interested chiefly in the more human aspects of the study may understandably be impatient of such reporting, and provided he is prepared to leave these technicalities to the methodologist and the statistician, may skip these sections of the book.

The following guide to the contents is given to enable those who take up this book to read selectively according to their interests.

Chapter One—discusses the methodological problems involved in the scientific treatment of behavioural data.

Chapter Two—is a critique of earlier attempts to achieve a typology of maladjustment.

Chapter Three—describes the history of the present typology, in particular the breaking down of the broad class of inhibited behaviour into three syndromes.

Chapter Four—reports the methodology of the classification through its various stages based on a random sample of school-age students. Those not interested in its technical passages can skip them in favour of the more general findings, such as the close association between Inconsequence and Hostility, and the lack of any syndromic cohesion in Norm Violation.

Chapter Five—describes the five core syndromes of maladjustment (Unforthcomingness, Withdrawal, Depression, Inconsequence and Hostility) induced from the statistical treatment, and discusses them as concepts. A second tier of non-syndromic groupings are shown to be compounds of the core syndromes. Deviant behaviour in particular is shown to be composite in character.

Chapter Six—discusses the rationale of the dichotomy of underreacting and overreacting behaviour and shows that it has a statistical foundation. It is then used as a basis for assessing the validity of the items as indications of each broad type of maladjustment.

Chapter Seven—demonstrates, first, that the greater amount of maladjustment among boys is accounted for by their being much more prone to overreacting behaviour; and, second, that in them this increases throughout the school years, while there is little change with age in underreacting behaviour for either sex.

Chapter Eight—examines the data to ascertain whether each of the types of maladjustment is expressed in the same phenotypic behaviours at different ages. They were found to do so to a surprising degree.

Chapter Nine—reports such social-class differences as were found, which were in overreacting behaviour. Analysis by age-groups suggested that this was due to congenital influences in girls but environmental in boys. Rural children were consistently better adjusted than those living in the industrial city. Children of Dutch origin, mostly urban dwelling, differed little from the city children.

Chapter Ten—reports the phenomenon of what is named the law of multiple congenital impairment—the tendency for many types of handicap, physical and behavioural, to occur in association with each other. The general reader will no doubt be satisfied with noting that all types of maladjustment obey this law, with its implication of a congenital/genetic factor strengthened by a differential sex pattern. For the specialist, because of the fundamental importance of this finding, its ramifications are demonstrated in detail.

Chapter Eleven—demonstrates an excess of motor impairment among the maladjusted, and conversely an excess of maladjustment among the motor-impaired thus affording further evidence of the law of multiple impairment and heightening the probability of a neurological factor in maladjustment.

Chapter Twelve—analyses the BSAG scores of the 133 members of the sample who became delinquent by number and type of offence, and discusses the results in the light of current theories of delinquency.

Chapter Thirteen—reports the results of a re-assessment of a sub-sample on the BSAG after one year in order to discover what changes occurred in the type and degree of maladjustment.

Chapter Fourteen—is a summary of the methodology, the findings and their implications.

1
The theoretical basis of classification

Physical descriptions uninformative—no agreed principles of classification—no agreed 'model' of the behavioural system—classification must have an aetiological basis—evolutionary value of behaviour—this gives a theoretical foundation for classification in terms of advantage to the organism—higher animals aim at general relationships of advantage—appraisal of the significance of situational changes—choice of executive behaviour.

Maladaptive behaviours classifiable by type of dysfunction—relation to motivation as the decision-making stage of behavioural process—the 'motives' of Bronfenbrenner and Riccuiti—Wright's insistence on the need for inferential descriptions—his three dimensions of classification—definition of 'intention'—dangers of the terms 'motive' and 'motivation'—ethological solution to the problem of inference—criteria for choice of descriptive terms—testing of the reliability and consistency of descriptions—definition of maladjustment—cultural values—incidence as a measure of disturbance—objectives of the present study.

Difficulties in the classification of behaviour

'For a phylogenetic comparison of behaviour, the problem of classification, of identifying the most meaningful and useful dimensions and descriptive units of behaviour, is of basic importance. Indeed, one may say it is *the* problem of psychology generally' (Nissen 1958).

The intractability of the problem derives from the intangible nature of behaviour. It defies definition in terms of primary sensory categories such as size, weight, shape or colour. Even before anything was known of atomic structure it was possible to identify gold, silver, copper, iron by stable physical characteristics. Plants can similarly be identified by physical descriptions which even the amateur botanist can follow. But physical acts are not the meaningful characteristics by which behaviours can be classified. 'Man lifting arm' leaves us relatively uninformed. To understand what is happening we need to know why he is lifting his arm. It may be to drink, to reach for something from a shelf, to hit someone. Even 'Man lifting his arm to drink' leaves us dissatisfied. He may be assuaging a basic physiological need for water, or he may be imbibing alcohol—but again for social reasons or for the neurophysiological effects, which (to carry the motivational probe one stage further) may be in pursuit of an emphemeral hedonistic pleasure or a general avoidance of life's realities.

Considering that the science of psychology has chiefly to do with behaviour it is logically astonishing that psychologists should in general have evaded the problem of its classification. Yet in view of the daunting complexities this is understandable. Not only are there at present no agreed principles of classification, there is also no generally accepted theory of behaviour, in the sense of a holistic conception of how the behavioural system works. In reporting an attempt at classification—even though it be of abnormal behaviour—we consequently find ourselves in a peculiar difficulty. There is a vast mass of knowledge in psychology about particular behavioural processes—that is to say, about the stages of the behavioural system—but no integration into an over-all model. Even the term 'behavioural system' is not in general use. Our difficulty, in short, is the lack of a *terra firma* upon which to build. We are forced back to first principles.

A biological evolutionary basis for classification

It can be at least agreed that scientific classification, to be meaningful, must be related to the reasons why different types or categories exist. Only then will there be a satisfactory array or clustering of characteristics which are specific to each type. Only then, also, will the classification have predictive value for the additional characteristics of each class which may emerge. There would not be much point, for example, in classifying plants by the colour of their flowers, for no other stable characteristics of each 'species' could be predicted from them, except for incidental reasons (e.g. white flowers are more likely to be sweet-scented because both whiteness and scent attract insects at night).

Among living things the reasons for the emergence of different types or species have to be sought in the evolutionary process. The botanical classification of Linnaeus turned out to be a good one because it was based upon the differentiation of the reproductive organs of plants, which represented evolutionary branching points.

The evolution of behaviour was the big breakthrough which differentiated animals from other organisms. To be sure, a few plants have the ability to respond to certain stimuli with a rapidity that suggests behaviour. The sundew closes its tendrils over its insect victims, and in a type of mimosa the leaves flatten themselves against the stem when touched, presumably so that rain drops can be guided directly to its roots. But behaviour implies a continuous, varied and adaptive interaction with the environment. It gave animals tremendous advantages in their struggle for survival. Nearly all animals can move about in search of food, or at least change their environment at different stages of their existence. They can escape from danger, and catch and eat other animals. By the evolution of yet other behaviours they have been able to build shelters and refuges.

As a simple extension of the above truism, it can be postulated that evolution of each and every behavioural pattern or disposition has depended upon the advantage which it conferred upon the behaving organism, or at least upon the species. We have here the foundation for a general theory of behaviour. To quote an earlier formulation of Nissen (1954): 'the integrating factor [in animal behaviour] . . . eventuates in consequences which provide near-optimum relations between the organism and its environment.' In sum, the *consequences* of behaviour, as seen in the changes which the organism is able to bring about in the relationships between itself and its environment, provide us with units of classification which are biologically meaningful. In discussing the cognate problem of defining conative tendencies, Murray (1954) arrived at a similar position: the actions from which dispositional concepts are induced 'can be defined most significantly in terms of the *kind* of satisfying effects which they (after a sufficient period of *learning*) are likely to produce'.

Classification by the relational change achieved

When it is a matter of ingesting food or drink, preserving body tissue from harm or maintaining an equable temperature, these 'satisfying effects' are easily recognised and classified. However, the behavioural systems of the higher animals achieve more complex relationships with the environment than mere response to nutritive or other purely organic stimuli. There is an obvious survival advantage in being able to choose general types of situation which make the satisfaction of these organic needs more probable. Woodworth (1958) instances the biological value of curiosity in putting the animal in a relationship of being informed about its environment. Being dominant within the group and holding territory also confer advantages when it comes to satisfying the primary organic needs. It has been argued (White 1959, Stott 1961) that any general relationship implying competence or effectiveness affords gratification, and hence reinforces behaviours which result in establishing such relationships.

This biological-evolutionary theory of motivation presents us with classes of results which are hard to describe in material terms. But this is not only a problem for us; it has also been a problem for behaving organisms in the course of their evolution. It was solved by the building into their genetic structure of a capacity to be reinforced by the attainment of those states which conferred strategic advantages. A primitive human being, in fashioning a tool by long and patient effort, is more likely to produce a finished and serviceable product if he is reinforced by feelings of achievement. The only common feature in the end-relationships towards which such behaviours are directed is that he brings some mental schema to realization. The next day he may achieve the same gratification by felling a tree or pulling home a heavy log. The classification of behaviour by results achieved, or the changes which the organism is able to effect, compels us, consequently, to recognize highly abstract classes of relationships—which, however, the higher animals are able similarly to recognize as being generally advantageous or disadvantageous.

Logically, this means that the organism, in its alert state, makes continuous appraisals of all phenomena reported through its senses in terms of their significance for its wellbeing. Owing to the mechanical complexities of carrying out such appraisals by general criteria of advantage or disadvantage, we have to suppose that they represent a not inconsiderable portion of higher brain function. As a corollary, if any part of the appraisal mechanism is in a state of dysfunction, the creature is unable to discern his advantage or disadvantage, and by definition his behaviour becomes maladaptive. We may follow this argument further. The prime value of the appraisal process is in signalling those situations which represent a threat to the organism. The latter then moves into a state of physiological arousal (or preparedness for action) and, normally, the situation is further assessed so that a decision can be taken about the most appropriate executive behaviour for the

3

re-establishment of a favourable relationship. Again, if this assessment- and decision-making process is in a state of dysfunction, the resulting behaviour, or lack thereof, will be maladaptive. The same processes occur when the situation is not optimally favourable even though not unfavourable in an absolute sense; an example is that of a child who does not demand candy until he sees other children enjoying such. Whether a failure to get the best out of a situation has to be regarded as maladaptive involves us in value judgments and cultural norms.

To the general theoretical proposition—that behaviours are best classified by the type of relationship which it seems the organism is seeking to establish—we can add the rider that maladaptive behaviours should be classified by the type of disadvantageous result which they have for the agent. And the word 'type' will have to be understood aetiologically in terms of the stage of the behavioural process—from perception through appraisal to executive response—which is the seat of the dysfunction. This is attempted in the course of the interpretation of the results reported in this monograph.

Inference of motivation as the 'intended' result

To relate this classificatory principle to the traditional terminology of psychology, we can say that we group behaviours according to their motivation. Once more we meet the difficulty in our exposition that there is no agreed definition or conception of motivation in contemporary psychology. The term 'motivation' is merely a name for that stage in the behavioural process at which decisions are taken about the need for action and the type thereof. Because this is an area of controversy and incomplete definition we have been compelled to make a broad outline-statement of our own concepts. The same applies to an even greater degree with regard to the motivation of maladjusted behaviour, which involves agreement about the classification of type of dysfunction. This part of our credo is, however, best left to a later stage, when it comes to the defence of our categories of maladjustment.

The assessment of motivation involves observer-judgment, and hence the risk of subjectivity. This risk can be avoided only if we limit ourselves to a phenomenological 'objectivity' which misses the point of the behaviour. To do so would amount to a renunciation of our task, and indeed that is what has generally happened in psychology. Some workers in this area have nevertheless faced up to the quandary. This is notably the case with Bronfenbrenner and Riccuiti (1960), whose threefold classification of personality characteristics will be used later in relation to the symptoms of behaviour disturbance which are the subject of the present study. All that need be noted here is that their second category of 'motives', based on a similarity of goal or end-state (despite different phenomenological behaviours), constitutes a classification by the 'intended' results.

Wright (1960) takes up an even more forthright position on the issue of meaningless objectivity versus meaningful subjectivity: 'Our discussion of reliability in observation has anticipated a need for partly inferential description in research on molar phenomena of child behaviour. Objectivity that rules out everything but palpable facts is unequal to the requirements of observing in such research. Behavioural categories that call for some degree of inference can nevertheless be objective in an important sense if the following is correct.' He divides current descriptive categories in child-behaviour studies into three 'dimensions'. The limitations of the first—*literal objectivity*—he illustrates from Arrington's category of 'physical contacts with persons'. This includes such psychologically disparate behaviours as taps on the shoulder, hostile blows and love pats. His second is *psychological specificity*, which carries the assumption that the ordinary observer has no difficulty in interpreting their motivation (or 'intended' end-result). As examples he quotes Heinicke's 'seeking affection' and 'seeking attention'. His third 'dimension' is that of *theoretical integration*—categories which are consistent with a theoretical standpoint but do not necessarily convey the same psychological message to the unsophisticated observer.

Barker and Wright (1955) neatly turn the tables on the 'objectivists' by arguing that: 'if one is to be objective in describing actions and psychological situations, one must break through a wall of directly observed conditions and events by inference, and must see things as the other person sees them from his viewpoint, and as they really are for that person'. In short, reality is the motivation or 'intention' of the agent.

Nonetheless, such a formulation needs to be stated in more precise terms, for it could open the flood gates of idiosyncratic interpretation. *'Intention' is therefore defined by us as the type of change by which reasonable inference is seen as the goal of the agent's behaviour.*

The terms 'motivation' and 'motives' have to be used circumspectly because of the reification to which they lend themselves. They are also contaminated by their everyday and legal use, as when the motive is sought for a crime. In psychology also there is considerable divergence in how the word 'motive' is used. At one extreme it denotes a conscious intention, at the other a fundamental behavioural disposition. A definition in terms of relational change which the organism can foresee, or to the probability of which he has become conditioned, at least circumvents the problem of consciousness or 'intention' as usually understood. Indeed the Gordian knot is cut if we work from the postulate that 'the *unconscious* grasping of relations is normal, with *conscious* thought as the special case . . . *all* thought is in the first place unconscious' (Stott 1950, pp.403-4). Lashley (1954), the neurologist, came to a similar conclusion; 'Our thoughts come in syntactical form, without effort and without knowledge of how that form is achieved. So in every case, that of which we are aware is an organized structure; the organizing is never experienced.' In short, we need no longer concern ourselves about the consciousness of an 'intention'. It is rather a question of classifying behaviours by the types of relationship which the agent sets out to achieve, whether this be consciously or unconsciously.

As Wright and Barker point out, such classification must nonetheless rest upon a process of inference. Left at that point, our position would have obvious methodological weaknesses. One has only to recall the bandying about of such terms as inferiority complex, insecurity, aggression, anxiety, guilt-feelings, or the markedly different interpretations of projective tests according to the theoretical standpoint of the particular psychologist, in order to appreciate the dangers of failing to control and define the processes of inference. We need an agreed basis for the interpretation of motivation. Put thus baldly, the task looks Herculean—none less than that of persuading our fellow psychologists forthwith to accept a general theory of behaviour.

5

The reading of attitude-signals

The ethologists offer us a solution. Tinbergen (1953) and Lorenz (1952) have pointed out that it is so important for animals of the same species to interpret each other's intentions that attitude-signals have been evolved for this purpose. Human beings are able to read the signals of domestic animals: we know what kind of relationship a dog is seeking to establish when it snarls or alternatively wags its tail, or a cat when it purrs or flicks its tail angrily from side to side. In birds such attitude-signals as the threat-postures or those of submission and begging can now be recognized, and the hand-sign language of the chimpanzee has recently been deciphered. The observations of the ethologists show that the characteristic signals are almost always recognized and interpreted correctly by other members of the species. We human beings can, for our part, make a reliable inference that a smile implies a desire for a friendly relationship (to such an extent that the mechanical smile of the politician who wishes to make people *think* he feels well towards them sometimes fails to carry conviction because it is not accompanied by the corresponding eye-behaviour). In certain social encounters the failure to smile conveys the opposite message. Other human attitude-signals are the exchange of meaningless verbalizing (enquiries about health, remarks about the weather, etc.) between people who are not on a footing of intimacy, which may be compared to the twittering of starlings seeking a roosting niche; and desultory conversation among intimates, which recalls the 'social talk' of budgerigars. Failure to verbalize in such situations would be interpreted as aloofness, moodiness or hostility. Unnecessary raising of the voice denotes anger, a whining voice or tears implies an appeal for sympathy or other consideration. Social signalling by eye-behaviour operates at a more subtle level which requires more sophisticated analysis, but can nevertheless be interpreted intuitively with fair reliability.

Criteria for choice of descriptive items

Every language has a wealth of terms which are descriptive of behaviour and personal attitudes. It is a matter of choosing those which give us the most reliable report of the behaviour and attitudes of the subject, while reducing extraneous variables to a minimum. Descriptive items of the following types, it is suggested, will be more likely to meet these requirements.

1 The inferences about attitude or intention must be limited to the attitude-signals which have been evolved in human beings, and which therefore reach the level of reliability characteristic of similar communication within infra-human species.

This criterion would exclude interpretations based upon current psychological theories and/or popular characterology. It is, for example, dubious to interpret a behaviour as indicating inferiority-feelings, insecurity or inadequate guilt-feelings (Hewitt and Jenkins 1946). Stott (1966a) drew attention to the ambiguities involved in accepting a statement that a child is 'aggressive', listing five disparate types of behaviour which commonly receive this description.

2 The description must be as independent as possible of the attitude of the rater to the subject.

Nearly all the names of traditional traits of character have approving-accepting or disapproving-rejecting overtones. Different words are used for the same behaviour according to the personal attitude of the speaker. A person may be 'angry', or 'in a temper', a child 'cheeky' or 'rude', 'unmotivated' or 'lazy'. To admit emotionally or morally charged descriptions is to invite 'halo' effect.

3 So far as is applicable, the description should be in relation to a stated stimulus-situation or human context.

Teachers tend to feel awkward, for example, in having to rate students on a scale for 'sociability' without reference to particular social relationships. A young person can be sociable with his peers, or with some of them, but unsociable towards others and towards adults. Similarly, a child may be submissive towards some people and dominant towards others. The same applies to general ratings of anxiety, to the difficulty of making which Bronfenbrenner and Ricciuti (1960) draw attention. Anxiety is a feeling which is aroused in a state of disadvantage when the subject can see no way of rectifying the unfavourable situation by an executive behaviour. It has evidently had evolutionary value in making continuance within the deprivation state highly unpleasant. It is therefore related essentially to some situation or class of situation.

The next stage must be the empirical testing of the reliability and consistency of the chosen descriptions. One can never be certain that particular forms of words mean the same thing when used, say, by teachers or psychologists, or by teachers in Britain and teachers on the American Continent. Differing types of social relationship may be rated as desirable, according to the cultural group or the age-level. In one sub-culture, at one age-level, friendly signals may be freely directed by normal children towards their teacher, in another age-group and sub-culture such may be frowned upon as a betrayal of peer-group cohesiveness. All this means that the descriptions of the attitude-signals, and to a lesser extent all the descriptions of the behavioural items, must be subjected to an analysis of their consistency as indicators of the inferred intention or motivation. A major part of the study to be reported was taken up with the testing of the consistency of the postulated descriptive items as indicators of inappropriate motivations, or more simply, types of maladjustment.

Definition of maladjustment

The present monograph reports a classification of maladjusted behaviour. Maladjustment can be defined in terms of the biological-evolutionary concept outlined at the beginning of this chapter. The value of behaviour was seen to consist in the establishment of more favourable relationships for the organism within its environment. Except for expressive acts—which come in a separate category—if a behaviour fails to yield such an advantage, or results in a net worsening of organism-environment relationships, it becomes maladaptive so far as the individual is concerned. In the language of every day, the person does not act in his own best interests. Some definitions of maladjustment (Underwood Report 1955) include harmful effects upon other persons. Unfortunately we do not live in a Utopia where such behaviour is always against the best interests of the evildoer. Nevertheless, in a limited environment of face-to-face relationships anti-social acts tend sooner or later to evoke retribution, and are consequently not in the best interests of the agent.

These interests have also to be conceived as integrated through time. A person may derive a here-and-now advantage, say, by physical or verbal injury to another, but at the cost of future disadvantages. Where an individual finds himself in a state of conflict, that is, where he can rectify one unfavourable relationship only by incurring some other disadvantage, he will normally choose a course of action which involves the least sacrifice. Obedience to this Law of Least Cost is one of the best differentiators between good and poor adjustment.

The individual's best interests for the purpose of our definition are as he interprets them in the light of the cultural values to which he subscribes. In a socio-economic group within which academic success is regarded as a primary goal, the boy or girl who fails to take advantage of academic opportunities may legitimately be regarded as acting against his or her best interests and hence as maladjusted. This would not apply to a young person brought up in a culture where educational achievement is hardly valued, and where the dominant value of acceptance by peers may entail an avoidance of any kind of socio-economic aspiration.

Prevalence as a test of abnormality

The incidence of a behaviour within a population is a good pragmatic measure of its 'normality'. Until this is known it is difficult to decide what diagnostic weight to place upon symptoms observed in clinical populations. Kanner (1957) points out that studies of clinical samples are biased because of the differential tolerance-thresholds of parents. The selectiveness of referrals from child-guidance clinics and juvenile courts 'has often resulted in a tendency to attribute to single behaviour items an exaggerated "seriousness" with regard to their intrinsic psychopathologic signifi-cance'. His point is well illustrated by Lapouse and Monk (1958), who arranged for the interviewing of mothers of 6-12-year-old children found at every 75th address in the Buffalo City Directory and environs. The mothers reported that 43 per cent of the children had seven or more worries and fears. 48 per cent lost their tempers twice a week or more, 28 per cent had nightmares, 49 per cent were described as overactive, 30 per cent as restless—and so on. One can draw the moral that check-lists of behavioural symptoms which are compiled for use in particular studies from *a priori* notions about what indicates maladjustment have little value.

Even more apposite is the study by Shepherd, Oppenheim and Mitchell (1966) of the relative severity of behaviour disturbance in clinical and non-clinical populations. They compared fifty children aged five to fifteen years attending child-guidance clinics (excluding cases suffering from psychosis, epilepsy or brain damage, and delinquency and attempted suicides), with matched controls who had never attended such a clinic. Case-material from which all references to clinical referral or treatment had been removed were rated independently on a five-point scale by severity of disturbance. Of the clinical group 74 per cent and of the controls 52 per cent were in the moderately or severely disturbed categories. By the chi^2 analysis used by the authors with two degrees of freedom this difference failed to reach the .05 level of significance, although re-calculation from their data using a dichotomous division with one degree of freedom shows that it does so ($chi^2 = 5.19$). The authors conclude that 'many so-called disturbances of behaviour are no more than temporary exaggerations of widely distributed reaction-patterns'. They point out that childhood behaviour 'cannot be deemed morbid without some knowledge about its frequency, intensity, duration, and association with other forms of behaviour, and the setting in which it occurs'. This describes the objectives of the present study.

2
Earlier classifications of behaviour disturbance

Critique of the methodology of Jenkins and his school: (*a*) pitfalls of clinical samples; (*b*) failure to achieve a comprehensive classification; (*c*) lack of specificity in the postulated syndromic clusterings—indeterminacy of classification by general trait-descriptions—call for a fresh start in classification—need for a conceptual basis to classification—dangers of classification by untested theoretical predilection.

Critique of the methodology of Jenkins and his school

a. Pitfalls of clinical samples. The most ambitious attempt to establish patterns of maladjustment in juveniles has been that of Hewitt and Jenkins (1946). They set out to establish syndromes of behavioural items which had 'similarity of meaning to the child' even though physically dissimilar, and to verify them statistically. Their work had the methodological disadvantages of being based upon clinic referrals, and furthermore upon descriptions of behaviour provided by parents, other relatives, teachers, medical doctors, social workers, psychologists, psychiatrists and other persons in the community. There could thus be no control or standardization of the form of the descriptions, and the lack of mention of a symptom had to be accepted as evidence of its absence. It is a matter of common observation by those who use data from case-files that referrants and teachers consulted tend to 'paint the child black (or white)' according to whether their own attitude is rejecting or accepting. This dichotomy of attitude could in itself produce 'syndromes' of statistically related items. An accepting attitude could notably cause the omission of bad traits, and rejection the omission of good traits.

To bring order into the heterogeneous descriptions used by so many different categories of informants, one of the authors and his wife 'transcribed' them into ninety-four problem behaviour traits. The elimination of those of too low or high frequency left forty-five. In the course of this transcription, and prior to statistical treatment, three behaviour syndromes were hypothesized, namely aggressive hostility, gang deviance and overinhibition.

b. Failure to achieve a comprehensive classification. The criterion for the inclusion of an item in a syndrome was a positive tetrachoric correlation of .30 or higher, and logical consistency with the remainder of the syndrome. Originally each syndrome consisted of ten to twelve items, but only six or seven were finally retained. Those cases in which at least three symptoms of any 'pattern' were present were grouped as representative of that pattern. The authors claimed that the existence of the three patterns as originally hypothesized was confirmed, and

10

that no others emerged. However, only 182 of the five hundred cases (when the thirteen overlaps are deducted)—or 36.3 per cent—proved classifiable. And only nineteen of the final list of forty-five behavioural items survived as syndrome members.

c. Lack of specificity in the postulated syndromic clusterings. As would be expected in a procedure by which items were grouped according to their joint appearance in a case, and cases were then grouped as showing a certain minimum number of such items, the frequencies of each of the items among the cases of their own 'pattern' were in excess of chance. Such an effect, being circular, could be produced from any array of randomly arranged characteristics.

A similar criticism can be made of the procedure for testing the exclusivity of the case-groupings. Eight of the fifty-two cases meeting the criteria for the 'unsocialized aggressive' syndrome overlapped with the seventy meeting those for 'socialized delinquency', giving a tetrachoric correlation of +.03. The overlap of five between the socialized delinquent group and the 'overinhibited' gave one of −.24. As would be expected there was no overlap between the unsocialized aggressive and the overinhibited groups. A certain overlap may be expected to occur by chance, and this can be expressed as $\frac{S_1 \times S_2}{n}$ where n equals the total number in the sample, and S_1 and S_2 the numbers in each group. Thus the expected chance overlap between the unsocialized aggressive and the socialized delinquent groups, in a sample of five hundred, would be 7.3, which is almost identical with the eight actually found. In short, despite a grouping of apparently associated items and the subsequent grouping of the cases *within the same sample*, the two groups of maladjusts were statistically not distinguishable by the behavioural items selected. The authors unwittingly confirm this result by their finding of a near-zero tetrachoric correlation between the two above groups. If they had been distinct there should have been a significant negative correlation.

Jenkins and Glickman (1947) treated data based on the records of three hundred delinquent boys in a Training School. They used somewhat similar traits: in the pattern of Unsocialized Aggressiveness, revengefulness and shamelessness were substituted for inadequate guilt-feelings; there were only three traits representing Socialized Delinquency; and there was an additional trait in the Emotionally Disturbed (counterpart of the Overinhibited). Between the groups of delinquents identified with the first two of the above patterns—of fifty-six and seventy-eight cases respectively—there was an overlap of eighteen, as against a chance expectation of 14.5; between groups identified with the latter two—of seventy-eight and sixty-three cases—there was an overlap of twenty as against a chance expectation of 16.3. These worse than chance results are confirmed by the low positive correlations of .11 and .12 reported by the authors.

Lorr and Jenkins (1953) carried out a factor analysis of the hundred traits for which Ackerson (1942) had worked out intercorrelations, using a sample of 5000 clinic referrals. They chose five traits which appeared central to each cluster, transferring those common to two clusters to that giving the higher correlation. This was done separately for boys and girls; of the twenty five traits fourteen were common to both sexes. Five factors emerged, consisting of the three found in earlier studies by Jenkins, plus 'brain damage' and 'schizoid'. However, these factors, as conceptualized from their component traits, are relatively uninformative.

11

It is hardly surprising that, in the factor of Socialized Delinquency, truancy from home, truancy from school, staying out late nights, police arrest and stealing will have elements of intercorrelation. The same can be said of violence, fighting, quarrelsomeness, disturbing influence in school and destructiveness, which comprise the five components of the factor of Unsocialized Aggressiveness in boys. One must also question the emergence of a 'Schizoid' syndrome from such near-normal traits as inefficiency at work or play, lack of initiative, listlessness or indifference, daydreaming, and absentmindedness. It is hard to know how to interpret the sixth, 'Queerness'.

Some twenty years later Jenkins re-treated the Hewitt-Jenkins data by computer, and in a preliminary report (1964), published the relative incidence of the traits in the three 'Superclusters' which emerged. This was useful in showing what degree of specificity there was in the characteristics of each type. It is immediately apparent from the percentage incidence in the cases classed as Undomesticated (formerly the Unsocialized Aggressive) and in those classed as Socialized Delinquent that several traits are common to both. For example, 'Defiance of authority' occurs in 60 per cent of the former and in 57.6 per cent of the latter. If chi^2 values are calculated for the thirteen 'Undomesticated' traits with a total incidence of fifty or more in the above two Superclusters, it will be found that five are non-significant, and two are significant only at the .05 level. Of the four which were significant at the .001 level, two ('Temper outbursts' and 'Quarrelsomeness') were members of the Unsocialized Aggressive syndrome which emerged from the treatment by Jenkins and Glickman of Ackerson's data, and were synonymous with traits in the same syndrome derived from Jenkins's own data. They were thus among the criteria for classifying the cases in the type bearing this name; their preponderance among the type was therefore to be expected. The third, 'Inability to get along with other children', was a negative criterion for the Socialized Delinquent, and hence also relatively preponderant among the Unsocialized Aggressive. The chi^2 values of the relative incidence within the same Superclusters of the six 'Socialized Delinquent' traits with combined frequency of fifty or more show that two are non-significant, and these figure among the seven core-traits of the syndrome.

Two years later Jenkins (1966) published fuller results of this cluster analysis. There emerged two 'Inhibited' groups of symptoms, between which there was an unspecified amount of overlap, the first being termed Shy-Seclusive and the second Overanxious-Neurotic. The three Aggressive groups which appeared were named Hyperactive-Distractible, Undomesticated and Socialized Delinquent. The cases were classified under these headings if they showed at least three out of the six symptoms of which each syndrome was composed. On this occasion 291, or 58 per cent of the five hundred, met this criterion. As previously, the syndromes are relatively uninformative. The six of the Shy-Seclusive include three—seclusive, shyness-timidity and absence of close friendships—which would be expected to go together, and would act as a qualification for type-membership of a case.

Jenkins is frank in admitting large overlaps even across the broad Inhibited/Aggressive dichotomy. Of the Overanxious-Neurotic, 65 per cent are also Hyperactive. Quarrelsomeness was found in 54 per cent of the Hyperactive and 55 per cent of the Undomesticated. Nervousness—an Overanxious-Neurotic symptom—occurred in 49 per cent of the Hyperactive and 38 per cent of the Undomesticated.

Using as subjects two hundred boys of age-range six to fifteen years referred to child-guidance centres in Tokyo, Kobayashi *et al.* (1967) analysed sixty-eight behavioural items, most of which were taken from the above cited studies of Jenkins. They were grouped in three levels—primary symptoms, consisting of three which intercorrelated at +.30 or more: secondary symptoms, which correlated at the same level with more than half of the primary; and peripheral, which correlated similarly with one or more of the primary or secondary. They identified Jenkins's three patterns and an additional one characterized by a lack of concentration, hyperactivity, mischievousness, etc. Following the methods of statistical analysis used by Jenkins, they correlated the behavioural items with cases which had been classified by manifestation of the behaviours in question, and obtained correlations which duly reflected the circularity of the procedure.

In reviewing the results of Jenkins and his associates one cannot escape the conclusion that no fundamental classification of disturbed behaviour could emerge from the very general trait-descriptions drawn from the reports of diverse informants and unrelated to specific situations. If any general and consistent finding emerges from their statistical analyses, it is that of a dichotomy between the overreacting and the 'overinhibited' (or underreacting) patterns. Whereas there was considerable overlap between the three overreacting (unsocialized aggressive, socialized delinquent and hyperactive-distractible), and again between the two overinhibited (Shy-Seclusive and Overanxious-Neurotic), there was very little between the two main divisions.

Indeterminacy of classification by general trait-descriptions

Peterson (1961) culled the fifty-eight most-mentioned 'problems' from the case-records of 427 referrals to a guidance clinic, as reported by teachers, caseworkers, probation officers, parents, etc. These he transcribed into mostly single-word trait-descriptions as traditionally used in factor analyses. Many contained a questionable degree of inference or interpretation: Negativism, Impertinence, Uncooperativeness could tell as much of the attitude of the reporter as of that of the subject; Dislike of School and Feelings of Inferiority are too inferential. The result of his factor analysis of the fifty-five items with adequate frequency was that only two factors, Conduct Problem and Personality Problem, were retained for rotation. He admitted that the names of these dimensions were grossly inappropriate, since both were expressions of personality and both affected conduct. Empirically, inferences about 'personality' can be made only from the observation of the tendencies of individuals, in given situations, to behave in a consistent and therefore predictable way. The data from which personality traits are induced consist of behaviour. Therefore, to use 'conduct' and 'personality' as the basis for a dichotomous classification constitutes what in logic is termed a category-error. However, despite these unfortunate names for his two dimensions, which he retained in order to remain in conformity with Himmelweit (who had used 'conduct-problem'), he made it clear that he had in mind the broad dichotomy of 'turned-out' and 'turned-in' reaction: 'In one case, impulses are expressed and society suffers; in the other case, impulses are evidently inhibited and the child suffers.' His results revealed the ambiguity which arises from the use of single-word trait-names. In each factor the first fifteen traits showed appreciable and significantly different loadings; but this left nine of the twenty-four Conduct

Problems and sixteen of the thirty-one Personality Problems unclassified, amounting to a failure to classify 45 per cent of those treated.

Quay and Quay (1965) obtained teacher-ratings on Peterson's scale of problem behaviour for 518 seventh- and eighth-grade children. Once again—presumably owing to low frequencies—less than half of the fifty-eight items were retained for statistical analysis. In each of the samples Peterson's two factors accounted for over 80 per cent of the total communality, in other words the usual dichotomy of underreacting and overreacting behaviour makes itself apparent. In addition, the authors tentatively identify a third factor among the eighth-graders which they name Inadequacy-Immaturity, but the items show high coefficients of factor similarity (from .55 to .70) with the two main factors of Conduct and Personality. Using the same trait list with 441 emotionally disturbed pupils in special classes Quay, Morse and Cutler (1966) also identify a third factor, consisting of sluggishness, laziness, lack of interest, preoccupation, dislike for school, and inattentiveness. While claiming an affinity for it with the factor of Inadequacy-Immaturity which was noted in earlier studies, they suggest that it may be associated with autism or a pre-psychotic condition. A more parsimonious interpretation would be an avoidance of the teaching-learning situation with an admixture of depression. The fundamental criticism of their methodology, which can be made of most analyses based upon general traits, is that it is not actual observations of behaviour but the interpretations of the observers which are being statistically related to each other. It is hard to know what kinds of behaviour teachers subsume under a heading of 'feeling of inferiority' or from what indications they infer 'dislike of school'. The behaviours which some teachers see as 'laziness' or 'lack of interest' could spring from a variety of motivations, from depression, avoidance or unconcern for the approval of adults to a cultural rejection of or indifference to education. We are thrown back upon the necessity of securing data which are objectively descriptive of behaviours and emotional expression, and as free as may be from pre-classification by the informant. Because attention has been directed more upon the perfection of statistical techniques than upon the quality of the data to be treated, factor analysts often find themselves having to give names to factors whose items are conceptually incompatible. Yet the whole purpose of the exercise is vitiated if it does not result in an advance in our understanding. Attempts to fit the incongruous findings into a traditional conceptual mould are epistemologically irresponsible.

In his studies of delinquent boys (1964, 1966) Quay meets the above difficulty once again when he attempts to interpret a third factor consisting of 'shortness of attention, easily flustered, shyness, lack of interest, laziness and day-dreaming', and it hardly helps us conceptually to identify this factor as Inadequacy-Immaturity. Moreover, three of the eight items with loadings of more than .50 in this factor among the pre-adolescent delinquents have very nearly the same loadings in the 'psychopathic unsocialized' factor, i.e. the conduct-problem category; and among the adolescent delinquents only two of five items meeting this criterion have loadings which are twice as high as in either of the other two factors. One of the five, 'Inattentiveness to what other say' has a loading, among the pre-adolescent delinquents, of .52 in this third factor but .50 in factor I (and similarly .58 and .46 respectively among the adolescent delinquents). Quay's third factor of Inadequacy-Immaturity does not therefore emerge unambiguously as a distinct grouping.

Unfortunately, in the Manual of their Behavior Problem Checklist, Quay and

Peterson (1967) do not give the loadings of its items in other than the factor in which each is placed, and so it is impossible to judge the over-all validity of their four factors or the specificity of their component items. This is especially to be regretted in respect both of Inadequacy-Immaturity, in which the loadings are low, and of Socialized Delinquency (Sub-cultural Delinquency) in view of the failure of Jenkins to establish this latter as a distinct pattern.

Call for a fresh start in classification

From his review of attempts at the classification of psychiatric symptoms in children, Rutter (1965) concluded that: 'A generally acceptable classification of psychiatric disorders which occur in childhood is urgently needed and the lack of such a classification has been a severe obstacle to progress in child psychiatry . . . . The classification of adult mental disorders is unsatisfactory, but the situation in child psychiatry is worse.' Because of the need for *some* working classification, Rutter tentatively proposes that below, which, however, he does not claim as detailed or complete; indeed he emphasizes that the categories may require further subdivision, and may be superseded with the advent of new data.

  1 Neurotic disorders
  2 Anti-social or conduct disorders
  3 Mixed group (where neither of the above symptoms predominate)
  4 Developmental disorders (sometimes called habit disorders)
  5 The hyperkinetic syndrome
  6 Child psychosis
  7 Psychosis developing at or after puberty
  8 Mental subnormality
  9 Educational retardation as a primary problem
 10 Depression
 11 Adult-type neurotic illnesses.

This classification is more a summary of contemporary psychiatric diagnoses than the basis for a fresh start in taxonomy, and perpetuates some of the conceptual stereotypes which have stood in the way of progress. Notably it retains the false distinction between inner-person illness (neurosis) and maladjustment seen in social relationships; the terms 'neurosis, neurotic, neuroticism' are so variously used, and so ill-defined, as to be only a drawback in a fresh empirical classification. When it comes to mental subnormality or educational retardation, no one with experience in these fields would regard such categories as exclusive of behaviour disturbance; and there are reasons for believing that much learning disability may be attributed not in the main to cognitive but to temperamental handicaps (Chess, Thomas and Birch 1959).

Need for a conceptual basis to classification

Rutter's article is nevertheless of value in drawing attention to the need for a determined effort at a classification working from stated principles. His second and third principles can be readily accepted: these are that the classification must be relevant to the clinical situation and have predictive value; and the aim must be to

15

classify disorders, not children, the latter being a recurrent source of confusion and circularity in the work of Jenkins and his school. In his first principle he touches upon a key issue upon which anyone undertaking a classification has to clarify his position. A classification, he maintains (with formal correctness), must be based on 'observable behavioural signs, not concepts'. In the previous chapter it was argued that any classification, if it is to be meaningful and have predictive value, must reflect the reasons for the existence (or in the case of organisms, the evolution) of the differentiating characteristics. At some stage, therefore, a conceptual basis has to be provided for the categories if they are to have any scientific value. But whether—or to what degree—one starts with concepts or with naive observations is a chicken-and-egg problem. Our culturally transmitted categories of behaviour and personality must have originated in empirical observations on the part of our ancestors. Whether recognized or not, this heritage of concepts is the starting point of everyone's thinking, and it is unrealistic even to attempt to make a completely fresh start from a *tabula rasa*. Moreover, the concepts in the mind of the scientist at any one time determine the kind of observations he makes, and run the risk of being self-confirmatory. On the other hand, to set out to make observations without any concepts about the structuring of the phenomena, and hence to have no idea of how to select what is relevant, would result in triviality and bewilderment. The scientist has no infallible defence against this danger of his own ultimate conceptual subjectivity. The best he can do is continually and self-consciously to query his current ideas, heeding in particular his all-too-easily repressed uneasiness when faced with discordant or unclassifiable observations, and bearing in mind that the progress of science depends upon the destruction of old concepts as much as upon the birth of new. Basically, an exercise in classification cannot but be initiated from a conceptual position, but thence must proceed inductively by a progressive testing and modification of the categories until the best possible arrangement, with the time and resources available, is obtained. In effect, taxonomy is central to the empirical method of science. To prevent ourselves being run off our feet by untested theorizing we need to remind ourselves of the principle of parsimony (or minimal conclusion). On the other hand mere phenomenological inventories have no value in science. Gains are measured in concepts.

Dangers of classification by untested theoretical predilection

Rutter criticizes the classification of childhood psychopathological disorders drawn up by the Group for the Advancement of Psychiatry (1966) for falling into the errors of both phenomenology and theoretical assumption. Since this Report springs from an authoritative source and is in a sense a credo of an important wing of psychiatry, it must be appraised in some detail even though the proffered classification was not subjected to any experimental test. One notes first that there is no consistency of taxonomic principle. Some of the main categories, such as those of the psychoneurotic and personality disorders, follow behavioural differences. But one—'Reactive disorders of early childhood'—centres around the child's situation, with the response varying from aggressive behaviour on the one hand to passive resistance, withdrawal, regression and pre-occupation with fantasy on the other. It can validly rank alongside the behavioural categories only on the assumption that children displaying such a range of behaviours are constitutionally normal individuals forced into maladaptive reactions by the abnormality of their environment—an assumption which in the present development of the aetiology of behaviour disturbance we are hardly justified in making. It would also assume that there is no significant environmental determinant in the psychoneurotic and personality disorders. The diagnostician is thus left to assign a disorder to one category or another according to his personal predilections about its origin. A further main category—brain syndrome of early childhood—although composed of behavioural indications—has a ready-made aetiology built into its title.

Even more subject to clinical predilection are the Psychoneurotic Disorders, since the key criterion is an assumption about their origin peculiar to one school of psychiatry. These disorders, it is postulated, are 'based on unconscious conflicts over the handling of sexual or aggressive impulses, which, though removed from awareness by the mechanism of repression, remain active and unresolved'. The symptoms are symbolic, that is to say, the result of interpretations along the above lines, and behavioural—though the latter, subdivided into six types plus an 'Other', are so varied as to be of little guidance to anyone who does not accept the symbolic signs.

As regards the Personality Disorders we are advised that, 'the total personality picture should be considered and not the presence of a single symptom or behavioural characteristic.' The most diverse personality-types fall under this rubric—from the 'well-organized with, for example, constructively compulsive traits or somewhat overdependent characteristics representing mild to moderate exaggeration of healthy personality trends [to] ... markedly impulsive, sometimes poorly organized personalities that dramatically come into conflict with society over their sexual or social patterns of behaviour.' The understandable reaction of the uninitiated is that 'you can't win'. There are thirteen sub-classes of Personality Disorders: Compulsive, Hysterical, Anxious, Overly Dependent, Oppositional, Overly Inhibited, Overly Independent, Isolated, Mistrustful, Tension-discharge, Sociosyntonic, Sexual Deviation, Other—some of which seem to be direct opposites. No lists of symptoms are given for any of these sub-classes, so that this taxonomy is not only untested but, by being untestable, falls outside the purview of empirical science. To forestall misunderstanding it should be mentioned that the comprehensive symptom list which forms the last part of the Report is an inventory arranged by areas of function such as 'Eating'. It bears no relation to the theoretically-based main classification.

3
Antecedents of the present study

Compilation of the Bristol Social Adjustment Guides—
classification by person- and task-relationship—threefold
subdivision of withdrawing behaviour—Unforthcomingness—
Hostility—item-validation in terms of maladjustment—
Inconsequence.

The primary observations

The precursor of the classification reported in the present monograph, that used in
the Bristol Social Adjustment Guides (Stott and Sykes 1956, Stott 1966a), met
Rutter's first condition that a classification of behaviour must be in terms of
'observable behavioural signs'. Stott composed a schedule of descriptions of
abnormal behaviour by observing the children in a series of small institutions, and
sitting with the house-parents in order to discuss the children's behaviour in
everyday situations. He subsequently submitted a similar schedule to groups of
teachers, with the invitation to modify or add to the descriptions so as to cover any
behaviour or emotional expression which picked a child out as being other than the
usual sort of happy, alert, companionable child or as suffering from a handicap or
peculiarity of temperament. The teachers were also free to add a description of the
child's behaviour at the end of the schedule in order to fill in any part of the
picture which did not emerge from the descriptive items. Care was taken not to give
any formal definition of maladjustment, or to suggest any types thereof. The
selection and classification of suitable items were carried out in a series of stages
with increased use of statistical means of evaluation as the items took shape. At
each stage, checked items which appeared to contradict the general impression of
the child were discussed with the teachers; in this way many ambiguities of wording
were revealed and corrected. A different group of teachers of children aged five to
fifteen years were then asked to choose three children from their classes, one being
a child whom they regarded as definitely disturbed in his behaviour, one mildly so
but who could not be described as a happy, thriving, effective child, and one who
could be described as such.

The schedule given to these teachers for checking consisted of 204 'maladjusted'
items, with some fifty normal counterparts. Since it bore little resemblance to the
standard type of forced-choice check-list or rating scale, a description of it is
required for the correct understanding of the nature of the operation. In the course
of his studies of Training School boys, Stott noted that contradictory results were
obtained if observers were asked to rate subjects on a scale of general traits or
descriptions without stipulating the precise context of the behaviour. Consequently
the teachers were asked to choose, from a series of statements, that (or those)

which best described the child's response to typical classroom situations or behaviour with respect to the school environment. For example, the first section of the schedule, headed 'Attitudes to Teacher', was broken up into fifteen small sub-sections with headings of which the following are examples:

Greeting teacher
Response to greeting
Helping teacher with jobs
Asking teacher's help
Contacts with teacher (other than verbal, such as bringing objects)
Liking for attention
Attitude to correction
Effect of correction

These sub-headings cued the teacher to report concretely about the child's responses or initiatives in detailed aspects of the child's interaction with him or her. The other main sections of the schedule were headed 'Attitude to School Work' broken up into five sub-headings, 'Games and Play' with four, 'Attitudes to other Children' with five, 'Personal Ways' (covering habit disorders, posture, appearance, punctuality, care for belongings, etc.) with thirteen, and 'Physique', covering general health and physical defects as observable by a class teacher. The last section was included so that the diagnostician had a complete picture of the child; its items were not treated as 'behaviour' or as indications of maladjustment.

The teacher was asked to underline any phrase which described the child's recent behaviour and attitudes. It was made clear that more than one item could be underlined under any sub-heading, but that none should be marked unless definitely true of the child. In no sense, therefore, were the statements within any series alternatives. To ensure that teachers clearly differentiated the procedure from the checking of the forced-choice scales to which they may have been used, they were told that they could ignore a sub-section if it seemed inappropriate. Moreover, at the end of each sub-section, to cover the eventuality that the teacher might not be sufficiently positive about the behaviour in question, were placed the letters 'n.n.' standing for 'nothing noticeable'. Further to remove any impression that the child was being forced into a preconceived mould, teachers were invited to add beside the underlining or at the end of the schedule any qualificatory remarks they thought necessary. These in fact proved useful in the subsequent re-wording of the items.

The order of the items in each series was scrambled in order to prevent a regular progression from 'good' to 'bad' which would have been conducive to mechanical underlining. Although it was impossible to disguise the fact that many of the items represented disturbed behaviour, no indication was given about how any item would be rated. Every sub-section, with the situational cue of its heading, was designed to induce the teacher to conjure up as concrete an image as possible of the child's actual behaviour or attitude. Beyond the recognition of emotional expression at the 'ethological' level (as described above) the teacher was asked to make no interpretation or judgment. This meant that all fashionable psychological trait-labels and similar terms had to be avoided, and the items phrased in teacher-language in so far as this described behaviour or attitudes without reflecting popular characterology. The 'popularization' of the language carried with it the risk

19

of ambiguity, but this was a matter for subsequent item-testing. It had the advantages that the recorders used only phrases which had a definite concrete meaning to them, and it gave them a feeling of competence in being able to respond meaningfully to the schedule. It was found, no doubt for this reason, that teachers liked completing it, in contrast to their general dislike—on grounds of artificiality—of marking forced-choice and, in particular, numerical rating scales.

The schedule was scored by overlaying transparent coding sheets which 'unscrambled' the items regarded as indicators of maladjustment. They were entered on the scoring form according to the groupings used at each stage of the classificatory process. The items regarded as 'normal' were left unscored.

The above form of the schedule and method of scoring have been retained in all subsequent editions of the Bristol Social Adjustment Guides.

Classification by overt act or inference of attitude

The first trial classification followed the principle of describing attitudes, as evidenced by emotional expression or other objectively recordable behaviour. The teacher or other observer who completed the schedule was called upon to make no further interpretations. The items were provisionally classified, as the first stage of a fairly long-term inductive procedure, for the most part by the type of relationship which the child, by his attitude and his emotional expressions, seemed to wish to establish. The only obvious instances of Wright's third taxonomic category, that originating in pre-existing concept or theory, were 'General inferiority manifestations' (based on an Adlerian interpretation of behaviour), and to a lesser extent, 'Anxiety for acceptance by other children'.

Induction of the concept of Unforthcomingness. The results for the 503 children upon whom this edition of the schedule was tested showed that the original groupings were inappropriate in two important respects. The investigator's concept of withdrawal, which included all inhibited behaviour, was based partly on current ideas of childhood schizophrenia and Bowlby's (1944) 'affectionless character', and partly on his experience of work with delinquent boys and institutionalized children.

Among both these groups it was genuine 'withdrawal' in the sense of a defensive self-isolation or an autistic indifference about social attachment. Among the schoolchildren now studied there was a large group who were unresponsive in a superficially similar way, but who were affectionate and helpful once they overcame their timidity and bewilderment. Such children would not be found in a Training School because they were the last people in the world to become delinquent; nor would they often be found in institutions, because they are acceptable in foster-homes. Children of this type are, moreover, seldom referred to a clinic because they present no behaviour 'problem' in the literal sense to the teacher, but are mostly regarded as dull children. Their omission from the classification served as an object-lesson in the dangers of working with pre-selected samples of maladjusted children. Fortunately the descriptive items that had been worked out in the meetings with the teachers or had been written in by them were sufficient for the establishment of a new grouping, which was named 'Unforthcomingness'.

The original item-validation. The second defect was that a number of attention-demanding items were over-marked for the normal and quasi-normal children. This was overcome by re-wording the items to render them more 'extreme', and to place beside them unscored items which represented a normal desire for adult attention and approval.

The validity of each item as an indicator of maladjustment was tested by comparing its frequency among the children scoring twenty or more items (the 'maladjusted') with that among those scoring nine or less (the stable and quasi-stable). By the chi^2 test, twenty-four items were more heavily represented among the maladjusted at the .01 level of significance, and 112 at the .05 level; five were doubtfully so or with too low a total frequency, and thirty-seven were not significant as discriminators.

The emergent syndromes

The most permanent aspect of this re-classification was the breaking up of the underreacting items into three syndromes: Unforthcomingness, Withdrawal and Depression. A new grouping, the 'K' syndrome of indifference to social attachments, was formed, which straddled the traditional underreacting/overreacting dichotomy. In its milder forms it appeared merely as unconcern about acceptance and approval, but in the severe forms as a deficiency of personal and social feeling and of moral compunctions. Although theoretically it may be described as an underreacting condition in that the affected child lacks the desire to establish social attachments, its actual manifestations can take the form of a release from social and moral inhibitions resulting in anti-social acts.

The separation of the 'K' items from the other negative (rejecting) reactions to adults brought into focus a grouping representing a more active and demonstrative hostility. This was conceptualized as a defence against the establishment of a good relationship or as a relationship-breaking mechanism. The hostile child was seen as committing acts which would annoy adults and thus secure his rejection, and as withholding the usual signals of friendliness in the form of smiling, speaking and helping. The symptoms were thus a mixture of provocatively deviant and defiant behaviour, and of sullenness.

The remaining groupings were: (1) 'Hostility to other children', which often went with hostility to adults and could hence be conceptualized as a transfer of a dominant attitude to other people, in the same way as hostility to a teacher is nearly always a transfer of a hostile reaction to loss of faith in parents. (2) 'Anxiety for adult affection and attention', consisting of a maladaptive seeking of notice, approval and sympathy. This was paralleled by (3) 'Anxiety for approval and acceptance by other children' manifested in showing off, bragging, being easily led into mischief, etc. The interpretation of these two attention-seeking syndromes in terms of anxiety was one more example of the dominance of contemporary concepts, and was later abandoned.

At this stage of the classification no formal test of the specificity of the syndromic groupings was made. Inspection suggested that zones of related behaviour rather than discrete syndromes were emerging. For example, the attitude of 'Hostility to Adults' tended either to be associated with 'Anxiety for Adult Attention' or with the 'K' (indifference) grouping. This was interpreted as representing different phases of Hostility. At the stage before the child has given up hope of establishing secure relationships with adults he would sometimes make desperate efforts to gain attention and affection, while easily reverting to the relationship-breaking mechanism when discouraged. At the second stage the Hostility would have become a set attitude merging into affectional isolation, with an absence of attempts to re-establish good relations.

There remained (4) the purely phenomenological grouping of 'Restlessness', which covered distractibility, hyperactivity, and the compulsive, substitutive activity generated by the pathological avoidance of traumatic memories (Stott 1950). A group of items resisted attempts at classification, while being evidently good indicators of maladjustment. And miscellaneous neurological symptoms were retained in a separate category as not being behavioural in the sense of being motivated.

Improved validity of the items as discriminators of maladjustment. After some of the non-significant items had been removed or modified to eliminate ambiguities, and additional items added to supplement groupings which had suffered losses, the schedule was re-tested on a further group of 613 children chosen by teachers, as before, in approximately equal proportions as maladjusted, unsettled and well adjusted. The validity of the items as indicators of maladjustment (consistency with total score) was again tested by chi^2 as described above. The improvements in the wording of many items resulting from the insights which had been gained into the nature of the maladjusted responses were reflected in higher levels of significance, as shown below:

Very good discriminators	$(p < .001)$	111
Good discriminators	$(p < .01)$	22
Doubtful discriminators	$(p < .05)$	22
Poor discriminators	(ns)	40
		195

The stage reached by the earlier classification

An appraisal may now be made of the progress that had been made by Stott and Sykes towards a classification of behaviour disturbance in children by the time of first publication of the BSAG. The most notable advance was in the breaking up of the broad spectrum of inhibited behaviour (variously termed neurotic, introverted, overanxious, shy-seclusive) into the three groupings of Withdrawal, Unforth-comingness and Depression. Despite the superficial similarity of the behaviour, these represent distinct motivations as defined in terms of the type of relationship that the agent seeks to establish. The subdivision of overreacting behaviour had not been so successful. As a concept Hostility had emerged clearly as a basic relationship-breaking mechanism, but too late to ensure the inclusion of the best obtainable indications. It merged with the 'K' grouping of indifference to social attachment and with attention-seeking. The motivation of the latter seemed ambiguous, possibly springing from anxiety and insecurity but also possibly being nothing more than a failure to inhibit a natural liking for attention and affection. Finally 'Restlessness' remained phenomenological and motivationally imprecise.

The formulation and testing of the concept of Inconsequence. In the course of a study of children discussed at case-conferences with the School Welfare Officers of the Glasgow Education Authority, Stott (1966a) was able to make a detailed study of a sample of hyperactive, behaviourally disorganized children. He came to the conclusion that their handicap lay in being unable to inhibit responses to stimuli at the primitive physical or instinctual level. The result is that such children do not give themselves time to monitor the consequences of a proposed behaviour. They may thus be termed 'Inconsequent' children. The normal child is able to inhibit response for long enough to be able to carry out a prior cognitive rehearsal, so that stupid or maladaptive plans for action can be rejected at the pre-behavioural stage without harm to anyone. The Inconsequent child carries out his trials in actual behaviour, so that he suffers from the bad consequences of the errors. Kagan (1965) described the problem-solving strategies of such impulsive children as having a shot-gun character. Several other authorities have drawn attention to a similar handicap in brain-damaged children. Göllnitz (1954) termed it Milieuan-fälligkeit—an inability to resist stimuli. Eisenberg (1964) described the brain-damaged child as having 'difficulty in focusing his attention selectively and sustaining it. In the extreme, he is at the mercy of every extraneous sight and sound in his environment.' In his view the basic impairment is one of inhibitional failure. Birch, Belmont and Karp (1964) concur in this view: 'the maintenance of normal behavioural functioning requires . . . effective insulation of the organism from other inputs, the latter occurring through the induction of inhibition'. It would be wrong to equate Inconsequence with brain damage, but it is characterized by a mild degree of inability to inhibit the first response that comes to mind, and might therefore be due to some form of brain dysfunction.

A number of items, falling mainly in the Restlessness and Attention-seeking syndromes, were reviewed as possible indications of Inconsequence, and thirteen of them were chosen to form the core of a new syndrome. Chazan (1968) tested it on a total of 907 children and identified forty who complied with the requirements that a minimum of six 'Inconsequent' items were marked and they made up at least half the BSAG score. He recommended that two of the items should be omitted because of their low frequency and two because they were too frequent among non-inconsequents. He proposed five additional items for the syndrome, but pointed out the relative rarity—as evidenced by the small number identified—of 'pure' Inconsequents. He cogently raised the question of the frequency with which Inconsequence was associated with other types of maladjustment. Stott sub-sequently chose thirty items in the published edition of the BSAG which had affinities with Inconsequence. These were tested (Marston and Stott 1970) on fifty children nominated by teachers after they had been provided with a general description of Inconsequence. Fifty randomly selected children served as controls. Twenty-two of the items reached significance at the .001 and four more at the .01 level. For an item-analysis the above one hundred were supplemented by fifty-six maladjusted and/or learning-disabled referred for remedial treatment, and the total sample was divided into three equal groups by their 'Inconsequent' scores. As good indicators of the syndrome those items were chosen which were well represented among children with high scores on the total of thirty 'Inconsequent' items, and sparsely represented among low-scoring children. Of the thirty items eighteen were significant at the .01 level in both directions by the chi^2 test, and seven others in one direction. Two others failed to reach significance because of their low frequency. With twenty-five or twenty-six indications of Inconsequence showing a satisfactory syndromic cohesiveness, it was concluded that they represented a basic type of maladjustment that should find a place in the BSAG.

With the clarification of the concept of Inconsequence it was realized that by no means the best possible range of items descriptive of this form of behaviour were included, since the schedule had been composed prior to its formulation. Accordingly observers were placed in classrooms containing known Inconsequents to make records of their behaviour, which were then discussed in a team conference and reduced to descriptive items.

These were incorporated in a general revision of the BSAG in preparation for the study reported in the present monograph. The opportunity was taken to insert further trial descriptions of Unforthcomingness and Hostility which reflected the progress in conceptualization since first publication.

4

The methodology of the classification and initial item-validation

The samples—validation of the items as indicators of maladjustment—syndromes as at the beginning of the study—
confirmation of Unforthcomingness, Withdrawal and Depression
as syndromes—items under 'Anxiety for Adult Attention' seen as
an aspect of Inconsequence rather than of anxiety—association
between Hostility and Inconsequence—establishment of a core
syndrome of Hostility—detailed analysis of interaction of Inconsequence and Hostility—two aspects of Hostility—a third
classification centred upon the core syndromes—dissolution of
the 'K' syndrome (Unconcern and Rejection)—'cultural' items—
questioning of the reality of a simple syndromic model—test of
consistency of items as indicators of type of maladjustment at
each age-level—test of specificity of items as syndrome-members
by sexes—an undifferentiated general underreacting group—
experimental formation and testing of three new overreacting
groupings (Norm Violation, Bad Peer Relations, Peer-Group
Deviance)—lack of syndromic grouping in Norm Violation—mixed
motivations in delinquency—theoretical distinction between the
core-syndromes and associated groupings—the sixth classification
—relationship of the associated groupings to the core syndromes.

The samples

In February 1969, teachers employed by the Board of Education of an industrial
city on the North American Continent were asked to complete the Day-School
edition of the BSAG, revised as described above, for all pupils born on the fifteenth
or sixteenth of any month in the year. A limitation to three per teacher was
established to avoid over-burdening and to ensure careful completion. Wherever a
teacher had more than this number of pupils in his or her class who met the
criterion, elimination was begun with those born on the sixteenth of a month
whose names occurred lowest in the alphabet. Thus no choice as to inclusion or ex-
clusion was left to the teachers (the limitation to three being carried out prior to the'
issue of the forms). The sample was thus a random one of pupils aged five to fourteen
years attending public schools, with a smaller proportion over fourteen years.

The City in question has a population of some 300,000, a considerable
proportion of which is supported by the steel and docking industries. Many of
those in the higher socio-economic groups live outside the City limits in a nearby
residential area, which was not included in the study. Nearly the whole of the City's

25

population was white, and its working population included a proportion of recent European, non-Anglo-Saxon immigrants, many of whom were Catholics. The Separate School system, which Catholic children would normally attend, was also outside the survey.

A month later a similar sample was obtained from the public schools in an adjoining rural area with an exclusively farming and small town population. In the spring a further similar sample was taken from twenty-nine of the thirty-five schools in the system administered by the Dutch Reformed Church, situated in both city and rural areas throughout Ontario. The sizes of the samples, with the numbers of children not assessed, were as follows:

	Total selected	*Number assessed*	*Number not assessed*	
			because > 3 per teacher	*because of change or illness of teacher*
City	2224	1940	267	17
Rural	333	291	37	5
Dutch Schools	296	296	–	–
		2527	304	

The proportion not assessed was considered within the limits of acceptability because the reasons for non-inclusion were not such as would bias the random nature of the samples.

Validation of the items as indicators of maladjustment

The first stage in the treatment of the data was to test the value of the items as indicators of maladjustment, and to eliminate those which did not meet the criteria. For this purpose the assumption was made that the majority of the items were reasonably good indicators, and hence that a total score would serve as a rough measure of the amount and degree of maladjusted behaviour. Individual items could then be evaluated, by their presence among high-scoring children and their absence among low scorers.

The sample was divided into the three standard adjustment categories of the BSAG, viz:

Stable and near-stable	(0-9 indications),	N= 1588
Unsettled	(10-19 indications),	N= 667
Maladjusted	(20 + indications),	N= 236
		2491*

*Records for thirty-six of the Dutch School pupils arrived too late for treatment at this stage. They were included in subsequent analyses.

Within each adjustment category the number and percentage of children scoring the items were calculated. The percentage in the worst-adjusted was divided by that in the best-adjusted, to give a ratio which served as a measure of the discriminatory value of each item as an indicator of maladjustment. The mean ratio for all the 150 items was 18.35—that is to say, on average the items were marked this number of times more frequently among the worst-adjusted compared with the best-adjusted children.

The distributions of the items were reviewed by:

i   inspecting the percentages to ensure that there was a satisfactory gradient from the well-adjusted to the maladjusted, as shown by the ratio.

ii   inspecting the number of 'Scorers' to ensure that no considerable number of well-adjusted children scored on the item, irrespective of the ratio.

iii inspecting the incidence to ensure that the item was scored a sufficient number of times to make its retention worthwhile.

In borderline cases the decision whether to accept or reject an item was deferred pending a review of its value as an indicator of a type of maladjustment. Twelve were rejected at this stage.

One of the objectives of the revision was to produce a shorter schedule that would be just as efficient as the earlier one in detecting severity and type of maladjustment. No rigid quantitative criterion for retention or rejection could be used for a reason that had an important bearing on the whole task of classification. Whereas overreacting children tended to accumulate a large number of scored items over a fair range of maladjustment, the underreactors tended—owing to the *absence* of response—to score fewer. This imbalance meant that higher percentages of scorers in the best-adjusted category, and a lower ratio as between the highest and the lowest, had to be accepted for some of the indications of underreaction. The mean ratios for each of the syndromes as they were at this stage are given in the second column of Table IV.1.

These ratios were only a rough measure of the diagnostic value of the items for another reason. There is such a great variety of maladjusted behaviours, and, as will be seen in Chapter Six, they tend to fall into two broad categories of underreaction and overreaction which correlate negatively with each other. There is thus strictly no general condition of maladjustment against which the items could be evaluated.

It was found that the chi^2 test did not act as a realistic yardstick for retention or rejection. Owing to the large numbers, high values were obtained, giving a $p > .001$, for items which on inspection could be seen to be marked too often among the best-adjusted.

The re-classification

With the incorporation of the Inconsequent (Q) syndrome the categories of behaviour disturbance as they existed at the beginning of the present study, with the number of items in each, are given in Table IV.1 overleaf.

The validation of the syndromes

The concept of a cluster or syndrome implies that the member-items are associated more frequently with each other than they are with non-member items.

TABLE IV.1 Numbers of items in the provisional groupings, and mean ratios of high/low scorer incidence

Syndromic grouping		Number of component items	Mean high/low incidence ratio
U	Unforthcomingness	22	5.34
W	Withdrawal	11	28.80
D	Depression	10	44.84
XA	Anxiety for Adult Attention and Affection	12	6.09
HA	Hostility	21	34.55
K	Unconcern about social attachments	22	21.17
Q	Inconsequence	40	10.84
MN	Miscellaneous neurological	8	13.37
M	Unclassified	4	17.02
		150	

Consequently the 'goodness' of the items as members of the above categories was measured by a Scorer/Non-Scorer ratio (S/N-S), calculated in the following way. The first step was to compute the mean number of other items in the syndrome with which the index-item was associated. The second step was to compute the mean number of the same items occurring in cases where the index-item was absent. The first mean was then divided by the second.

For the near-complete sample of 2491 cases, ratios were calculated for the 138 items which had survived the initial item-validation. A ratio of 2 or more was used as the criterion for retention in a syndrome. This meant that each of the cases scoring the item (i.e. in respect of whom the item was marked) had, on average, at least twice the number of same-syndrome items as the cases not scoring the item. The item was then hypothetically transferred to every other syndrome in turn, and the mean number of associated member-items for 'scorers' and 'non-scorers' calculated in the same way. Scorer/non-scorer ratios were calculated when it appeared on inspection that another syndrome might claim the item. Items not meeting the above criterion, or scoring a higher ratio in another syndrome, were reviewed, and transferred as indicated. This proved to be an exercise in induction which aided our understanding of the types of maladjustment and their inter-relationships. The syndrome of *Unforthcomingness* emerged with fourteen of its nineteen items meeting the criterion. For them the scorer/non-scorer ratios were not spectacular, averaging only 2.80, but this reflected the prevalence and quasi-normality of this form of behavioural handicap. However, in the other two underreacting syndromes, namely Withdrawal and Depression, the scorer/non-scorer ratios of these items were much lower. Thus Unforthcomingness appeared to be a type of behaviour disturbance distinct from other forms of underreacting behaviour. Of the remaining five original U items three were transferred to W, where their ratios were more than two while being less than two in U. These were:

Difficult to get a word out of him (*Talking with teacher*)
Timid, poor spirited; can't let himself go (*Team games*)
Shrinks from active play (*Informal play*)

Conceptually they could fit in either U or W, but at this stage of the re-classification it was important to follow strictly statistical criteria. In fact their S/N-S ratios for Withdrawal were far below those of the remainder of the items of that syndrome. This difficulty led us later to establish a small 'General Underreacting' grouping, of which they became members.

The eleven items of the *Withdrawal* syndrome emerged with very satisfactory S/N-S ratios, the lowest being 4.95 and averaging 8.24. They were also very specific in that most of their ratios were several times greater than those which they would have had in any other syndrome. Only one had what was later termed a specificity-ratio (ratio in own syndrome divided by that of the item in the nearest rival syndrome) of less than two, and it was 1.71. No changes were therefore needed in this syndrome.

The same applied to the eight items in *Depression*, except that 'Sometimes wanders off alone' had a somewhat higher ratio in W, even though it was much below the general ratio-values of the other W items. It was later transferred to the 'General Underreactors'. The other seven items for Depression tended to be synonymous in describing a lethargic condition. They had, however, to be retained, at the risk of apparent redundancies, because most of the items in the schedule described the responses of children in specified situations rather than being general out-of-context traits. A description covering lethargy had therefore to be included for each major situation or relationship. The repetition of the description at least prevented a lack of interest in a single area of function or situation being taken as indicative of depression.

As a syndrome *Anxiety for Adult Attention* fared badly. Four of the items obtained almost as high S/N-S ratios in Q, and three had higher or equal ratios in Q. This was interpreted to mean that the greater part of attention-seeking behaviour is not so much an indication of anxiety as a failure to inhibit natural urges for attention. In other words it can be conceptualized as an aspect of Inconsequence. The seven items in question were placed temporarily in a QX grouping. Only two items seemed genuinely representative of anxiety: one of these, 'Wants adult attention but can't put himself forward', actually had a low negative ratio for the X syndrome, that is to say, it was marked slightly more frequently along with other than X items. It met the criterion for U, and so was transferred to that syndrome. This is conceptually admissible because Unforthcoming children probably suffer more than any other type from a chronic high-anxiety level (even though all chronically anxious people are not Unforthcoming). But, as argued earlier, any assessment of anxiety based on observation rather than the subject's report involves inference which is tainted with popular notions about motivation. The other 'anxiety' symptom, 'Sidles up to or hangs around teacher' had a reasonably good S/N-S ratio for X, but since X itself had virtually ceased to exist this meant nothing. As the item was in any case only a moderate indicator of maladjustment it was deleted.

The syndrome of *Hostility* came out with ten very specific items, with S/N-S ratios ranging from 5 to 9 and averaging 8.42. The ratios of eight other items were also good, ranging from 3.9 to 8; but in all of them that for Q was a runner-up.

This association between Hostility and Inconsequence is theoretically instructive. From case-studies Stott (1966a) concluded that the 'pure' Inconsequent type of child is found only when he is lucky enough to have parents of supranormal capacity for affection and patience. The more usual state of affairs is that, from an early age, the child's inhibitional impairment—seen in enterprising meddlesomeness, thoughtless experimentation, inability to persevere with one activity, resistance to correction and other forms of social learning—exceeds the tolerance-limit of one or both parents. Response to intolerable stress takes the form either of attack or avoidance, or that mixture of both which constitutes hostility. Thus parents tend to react adversely and develop rejecting attitudes towards Inconsequent children on account of their tiresomeness. The natural response to such rejection on the part of the child is to destroy the unrewarding love-relationship by summoning up hatred and indulging in hostile acts. Hence Hostility often arises as a secondary complication of primary Inconsequence. Other authors have made similar observations. Eisenberg (1964) has also drawn attention to the vicious circle of worsening child-parent relationships originating in the uncontrollability of the neurologically impaired child. Chess (1969) speaks of the 'progressive worsening of the behaviour of parents and child, increasing familial disorganization and conflict and the eventual inability to retain the child within the family setting'. The appearance of Hostility and Inconsequence in conjunction with each other in the present analysis is consistent with the above hypothesis, and explains why so few pure 'Inconsequent' items are found.

The ten 'Hostile' items less contaminated with Q all described some aspect of moodiness, sullenness or uncooperativeness, that is to say, a relationship-avoiding rather than a relationship-breaking form of response. This is admittedly too narrow a concept of Hostility, but since the validity of the method of re-classification depended upon a willingness to break up syndromes in order to let other possible groupings emerge, it was decided to retain only the ten moody-type items as a core-grouping of hostile behaviour and to place the remainder in a provisional H/Q group.

The K syndrome of *Unconcern and Rejection* presented the same problem. Only three items stood out with S/N-S ratios in K which were not challenged by other syndromes. Six others had the highest ratios in K, but those in Q or H were nearly as high, and in nine of the K items the ratio in Q or H actually exceeded that in K. These fifteen were added to the provisional HQs to form an HQK group. This statistical association between K, H and Q might be interpreted theoretically along rather similar lines to the QH association. As an alternative to hostility, some Inconsequent children may develop a relationship of estrangement towards rejecting parents. It could be equally argued that Inconsequence and an indifference to social attachments are associated congenital impairments of the behavioural system, producing the classical hyperactive psychopath. Be this as it may, the fact remained that, as far as observation by teachers in Ontario day-schools are concerned, insufficient indications of a hypothetical syndrome of Unconcern and Rejection are obtainable to justify a grouping. In a residential setting, where many more facets of inter-personal behaviour are visible, it could be a different matter: one may have to have intimate and prolonged dealings with the 'psychopath' to get a measure of his indifference to social acceptance and social obligations.

Examination of the syndrome of Inconsequence (Q) confirmed its association with Hostility (H). Only four of the items in the original Q grouping, and one from the 'Neurological', came out with S/N-S ratios twice as high in Q as in any other syndrome. Theoretically even more revealing was that twelve Q items had nearly as high ratios in H as in their own syndrome, *even though conceptually the behaviour was not typical of hostility.* This finding is so significant for the appreciation of the dynamics of the overreacting types of behaviour disturbance that the items in question are given in Table IV.2 together with their S/N-S ratios in Q and the runner-up syndrome (which in all but one is H).

TABLE IV.2 Inconsequent items highly associated with Hostility

Item	Situation	S/N-S ratio in Q	S/N-S ratio in H
Gets up to all kinds of tricks to gain attention	Seeking attention or approval	4.40	3.77
Misbehaves when teacher is engaged with others	Classroom behaviour	4.15	4.02
Responds momentarily but it doesn't last long	Effect of correction	4.52	3.87
Never gets down to any solid work (flips over pages of book without reading it)	Working by himself	3.94	3.68
Never really gets down to job and soon switches to something else	Manual tasks or free activity	3.96	3.41
Has a hit-and-miss approach to every problem	Facing new learning tasks	3.28	2.61
Inclined to fool around	Team games	3.97	3.39
Shows off (clowns, strikes silly attitudes, mimics)	Ways with other children	4.15	3.56
Foolish or dangerous pranks when with a gang	Physical courage	3.89	3.88

(table continues overleaf)

31

Item	Situation	S/N-S ratio in Q	S/N-S ratio in H
Careless, often loses or forgets books, pen	Belongings	3.32	3.25
Twists about in his seat, slips on to floor, climbs about on desk, etc.	Sitting in desk	3.81	3.19
Constantly restless (raps with pencil or ruler, shuffles with his feet, changes position)	Nervous habits, fidgets, etc.	4.35	3.91

The following, previously unclassified item, should be included in the above list:

Item	Situation	S/N-S ratio in Q	S/N-S ratio in H
Doesn't seem to understand that he should keep in his seat	Sitting in desk	3.01	3.00

There were even five items which obtained the highest S/N-S ratios in Hostility even though descriptively they contained no suggestion of a hostile or aggressive attitude. They are given below in Table IV.3.

TABLE IV.3 Items statistically within the Hostility syndrome without being descriptive of Hostility

Item	Situation	S/N-S ratio in Q	S/N-S ratio in H
Behaves badly as a means of getting attention	Classroom behaviour	4.76	4.94
Can't resist playing to the crowd	Effect of correction	4.26	4.41
Slumps, lolls about	Sitting in desk	3.43	3.88
Plays the hero, tries to show he doesn't care	Attitude to correction	3.10	3.58
Attends to anything but his work (talks, gazes around, plays with things)	Paying attention in class	4.45	3.86

Little imagination is needed to appreciate that a child who displays a repertoire of behaviour such as described in the above eighteen items will be a source of not inconsiderable irritation to his teachers, and, if he behaves in the same way at home, to his parents. It is not surprising, therefore, that he will evoke adverse reactions from the adults around him, including threats and gestures of rejection. The expected response to these is hostility. As an alternative explanation it might be argued that the parental rejection and the resulting hostility came first, and that the above symptoms are those of anxiety. There are several reasons for rejecting this explanation. First, the behaviours in question are also found in children whose parents show a permissive tolerance with no suggestion of rejection (Stott 1966a). Second, anxiety presupposes apprehension about the nature and furture development of a situation, in other words, a foreseeing of consequences which is not typical of the Inconsequent child. Thirdly, anxiety arises when no solution to the unfavourable situation can be discerned; as soon as a rectifying executive-behaviour, of however forlorn a type, is initiated, anxiety vanishes. The only element of plausibility in the attribution of the above behaviours to anxiety is that they are displacement activities, that is to say, are motivated by substitutive excitements which enable the person to avoid anxiety-creating memories. But the young person under the compulsions of avoidance-excitement resorts to a far more hectic and serious type of deviant behaviour than the petty disruptiveness described in the above items. His substitutive acts make him over-active to the extent that people say he does 'sudden mad things', but he does not normally show off or clown, or otherwise thoughtlessly exploit his environment to gain a momentary re-inforcement as does the Inconsequent child (Stott 1950). Typically, the Inconsequent is a carefree nuisance; if only he had a greater capacity for anxiety he would be easier to manage.

Phenomenologically, hostile behaviour can be divided into two types. The first is the moodiness and surliness described above, which in terms of the basic executive-reactions can be characterized as a refusal to exchange the routine social-attachment signals of smiling, greeting, willingness to help or to participate in a common purpose. This is either a defence against the establishment of good inter-personal relationships or a signal of a negative type, indicating that such a relationship is rejected. The second consists of initiatives taken to worsen or destroy a relationship: the person provokes rejection by committing acts calculated to alienate sympathy and to make the other person angry. Of the twenty-one original indications of Hostility, ten were of the first type and eleven of the second. Examples of the latter, with their H and Q S/N-S ratios, are given in Table IV.4 overleaf.

This aspect of Hostility is more in accordance with the impulsive behavioural release of the Inconsequent temperament than is the first, moody-sullen aspect. When the Q child is motivated to respond by hostility to the bad feeling that his tiresomeness generates, he does so in an aggressive, enterprising way. It is not surprising, therefore, that the second aspect of Hostility shows high runner-up Q S/N-S ratios.

Cognate with the aggressive hostility of the Q child is his inability to inhibit primitive attack-responses in frustrating situations or in attempts to get his own way. A group of such behaviours, included in the schedule as indications of Q, actually obtained higher S/N-S ratios in H. This was partly due to the use of the fairly wide Hostility syndrome which included eleven items of the aggressive aspect;

33

TABLE IV.4 Expressions of provocative Hostility

Item	Situation	S/N-S ratio in H	S/N-S ratio in Q
Seems to go out of his way to earn disapproval	Seeking attention or approval	8.02	5.30
Openly does things he knows are wrong in front of teacher	Classroom behaviour	5.65	4.68
Aggressive defiance (screams, threats, violence)	Attitude to correction	6.62	4.21
May spoil his work purposely	Manual tasks or free activity	5.06	4.60
Damage to personal property	Other deviant behaviour	3.92	3.30
Uses bad language which he knows will be disapproved of	Other deviant behaviour	5.89	4.72

but more fundamentally it could be an extreme form of the nuisance-rejection-hostility dynamic described above. The items in question are listed in Table IV.5

Only two items resisted classification at this stage. One of these was truancy, which was similarly found in the original classification to be spread over a wide range of maladjusted behaviour. The other, 'Plays childish games for his age', was so little reported as to be of doubtful value. One previously unclassified, 'Attacks other children viciously' fell into place in the aggressive-hostile-inconsequent grouping with H and Q ratios of 6.97 and 4.57. 'Destructive, defaces with scribbling' (Belongings) showed itself as another HQ item with ratios of 5.34 and 4.83.

The four surviving *Neurological* symptoms (easily startled, involuntary hand movements, tics, bad nailbiting) were not behaviours in the sense that there was a presumed intention to effect a change in a person-environment relationship. None had significant S/N-S ratios in any other syndrome, and so were retained as a separate grouping.

The subsequent treatment covered the near-total sample of 2491 including the Rural County and most of the Dutch Reformed Church Schools. As a preliminary to closer examination all items were classified within the syndrome giving the highest ratio, as follows:

U	15	Q	35
W	15	K	3
D	13	N	4
H	47	Unclassified	2

TABLE IV.5 Indications of failure to inhibit aggressive responses

Item	Situation	S/N-S ratio in H	S/N-S ratio in Q
Resentful muttering or expression for a moment or two	Attitude to correction	7.31	3.32
Tries to argue against teacher	Asking teacher's help	4.31	3.05
Bad loser (creates a disturbance when game goes against him)	Team games	5.24	3.79
Tries to dominate and won't cooperate when he can't get his own way	Informal Play	3.27	2.64
Squabbles, makes insulting remarks	Ways with other children	5.55	3.48
Flies into a temper if provoked	Physical courage	6.24	3.71

The U, W and D syndromes stood up well, with little change. K lost one marginally to D; the original three remaining K items showed only moderate power in discriminating between the maladjusted and the stable/near-stable groups, having scorer/non-scorer ratios, calculated between these as for the syndrome ratios, of 3.9, 4.6 and 5.8. The items in question were:

Not shy but never comes for help
    (*Asking teacher's help*)
Avoids teacher but talks to other children
    (*Talking with teacher*)
Avoids any such contact but not reticent
    with other children
    (*Contacts with teacher*)

Their common theme—an exclusiveness as against the teacher—suggested a cultural or quasi-normal developmental factor. It could be that in certain school-environments, especially among teenagers, there is a peer-sanction against too great a familiarity with the teacher on pain of being thought to curry favour; and

35

exclusiveness is one way of emphasizing the peer-group cohesion which is typical of adolescents. Since these items added little to the instrument as regards the detection of maladjustment, and it was thought important to minimize cultural factors, they were deleted, which meant the disappearance of the K syndrome.

The classification on the basis of highest ratio remained unsatisfactory, not only because of the excessive number of H items, but also because it disguised the continued tendency for the H and Q items to be associated. It remained to be seen whether this large group of eighty-two items could be subdivided into groupings of a more manageable size.

Is the syndromic model realistic?

At this stage, also, the question was asked whether a syndromic classification of manifestations of behaviour disturbance is in accord with reality. Were we, in short, attempting something impossible? For a group of symptoms regularly to occur in association with each other, and to occur only at a significantly lower frequency apart from the syndrome, presupposes a disease-entity arising from some such cause as a viral infection or dysfunction of a particular organ. This could be the case with certain types of behaviour disturbance, if, for example, they originated in lesion or dysfunction of some part of the neural organization of the behavioural system. It may be, for example, that Unforthcomingness reflects a dysfunction of those mechanisms which monitor the individual's situation by the criterion of 'coping' or effectiveness (Stott 1961). Similarly, dysfunction of the inhibitory mechanisms should produce an Inconsequent syndrome. We run into difficulties, however, when a primary dysfunction generates secondary complications, because we no longer have to deal with a unitary aetiology or disease-entity but with the result of an interaction between the affected individual and his environment. It has been suggested above that the extent to which an Inconsequent child develops hostility depends upon the degree to which he exhausts the tolerance of adults and provokes rejecting attitudes to which he responds in like measure. The extent to which he indulges in aggressive responses to frustration or makes aggressive bids for dominance may be a function of the permissiveness of his upbringing. In short, multiple determination of a condition may preclude a neat syndromic arrangement of symptoms. On the other hand, it may be possible to achieve a structured classification which reflects the dynamic of the development of maladjustment.

The empirical method of science requires that arrangement and structuring should be induced from the phenomena themselves rather than by the adoption of a preconceived model derived from the classification of other types of data. The syndromic model, in short, may not be the one which most accurately reflects the real state of affairs in the area of behaviour disturbance. We decided that our methodology must be to accept whatever classification or structuring fitted the facts best, without attempting to impose any model.

For the re-computing of the scorer/non-scorer ratios in preparation for a third classification it was decided to establish a number of core syndromes consisting only of those items with unambiguous syndrome-membership in the above classification. These, with the number of items in each, were as given in the final column of Table IV.2—except that the nine items in the provisional XQ grouping, since they had S/N-S ratios which were specific to Q, were added to the remaining five 'pure' Qs to give a core-Q of fourteen items; and the unwieldy group of 56 items of the HQK were held in limbo in order to see how they grouped themselves around the new 'cores'.

Consistency of the 'syndromes' at different ages. Up to this stage the analysis had been carried out for both sexes and all age-groups combined. It had not been ascertained whether there are different patterns of maladjustment for boys and girls in general, or for children at different ages.

The consistency of the syndrome-membership of the items was first tested by age-groups. The sample was divided into four categories by age at the time of the survey, as follows:

	Number
5th to 8th birthday	717
8th to 11th birthday	828
11th to 14th birthday	781
Over 14 years	165
	2491

The object, in simple language, was to find out whether each item indicated the same type of maladjustment in children of all ages within the limits of the sample. This was done by calculating the scorer/non-scorer ratios by age-groups and seeing whether these were consistently the highest in the same syndromes in each age-category. The residual K syndrome had already been eliminated; and the neurological symptoms were also left out of account because, as explained above, they are not motivated behaviour.

The degree of consistency shown by this analysis is summarized in Table IV.6 below. It omits the last age-category, first, because the numbers are often too small and, second, because pupils of fourteen years and older who are still in the elementary school would include a disproportionate number of those who had had to repeat grades, and these would not be typical as regards social adjustment. Those items with too low a frequency in any age-category to give reliable results are analysed separately.

It is seen that the great majority of the items showed a satisfactory, and indeed a surprising consistency over the age-range for which they were tested. This meant that the exercise in classification could proceed for the whole sample irrespective of age. Theoretically it encouraged us to hypothesize that the groupings, even at the stage that they were then, represented fundamental forms of dysfunction of the behavioural system.

Syndrome-specificity. The comparison of the scorer/non-scorer ratios for each item within each of the core syndromes was now formalized into a further ratio of *syndrome-specificity* (S-S). It was obtained by dividing the highest S/N-S ratio which the item obtained in any syndrome by that in the next-best syndrome. Thus an S-S ratio of 2 for U means that the item is twice as good an indicator of Unforthcomingness as it is, say, of Withdrawal if the next highest S/N-S ratio were in that syndrome.

The items were now grouped by syndromes according to their S-S ratios. This left unresolved the large number of items in H and Q, which were marginally acceptable to either syndrome (i.e. with S-S ratios near to unity in each).

TABLE IV.6 Consistency of items by type of maladjustment over the age range 5th — 14th birthday

Consistency rating	Adequate frequency (at least 10 cases scoring item in each age-group)		Inadequate frequency (less than 10 cases scoring item in one or more age-groups)	
	No. of items	%	No. of items	%
1 Completely consistent (same syndrome gives highest scorer/non-scorer ratio in all three age-categories)	78	75.0	11	52.4
2 Reasonably consistent (same syndrome gives highest ratio in two, and is second highest in the third)	23	22.1	3	14.3
3 Partly consistent (same syndrome has highest ratio in two, but is not second highest in the third)	2	1.9	5	23.8
4 Inconsistent	1	1.0	2	9.5
	104	100.0	21	100.0

Consistency as between the sexes. Preparatory to the fourth classification the S-S ratios were calculated for each sex separately, as shown in Tables V.1 to 11 in the next chapter. Only eleven of the 122 retained items had highest ratios in different syndromes as between boys and girls. Of these, six were variations between H/Q and Q/H, three between U/W and W/U, and in two the numbers of the girls were too small for reliability. In sum, the items as a whole are diagnostic of the same type of maladjustment in either sex. The sex differences were, as reported later, in the frequency of the manifestations.

Non-specific underreaction. Two major problems of classification remained. The first was that some items, while falling into one of the two broad divisions of underreacting and overreacting behaviour, were not unambiguous members of a particular syndrome. In the underreacting division the core groupings of U, D and W remained stable and satisfactory. But there was a group of six items which fitted equally well into U and W. Examples were 'Difficult to get a word out of him' and 'Shrinks from active play'. It would not be justifiable to say that they represented a mixture of U and W because these are, motivationally, two distinct and antipathetic types of behaviour. t was rather that each syndrome would, in certain situations, result in phenomenologically similar types of response. Such items have therefore to be interpreted as confirmatory of U or W according to the other indications of either syndrome. The same applied to four items which had similar ratios for W and D. Rather than try to squeeze any of these items into one of the basic syndromes, with the risk of blurring the emergent syndromic picture, they were allocated to a 'General underreacting' group.

Provisional new overreacting groupings. The second problem was the disposal of the large number of 'overreacting' items with good S-S ratios in both H and Q. Examination of these showed that the great majority were descriptive of what teachers and the adult world in general would regard as 'bad' behaviour. Three new groupings were therefore established (marked with an asterisk below) according to the general type of unacceptable or anti-social behaviour. This was done without any pretence about their finality or their fundamental significance, but rather to see to what extent they formed statistical clusters. Syndrome-specificity ratios were then calculated for each sex separately for the following ten groupings:

Core		_Non-core_	
Unforthcomingness	14	General underreacting	8
Withdrawal	9	*Norm violation	13
Depression	10	*Bad peer relations	11
Hostility	18	*Peer-group deviance	8
Inconsequence	9	Attention-seeking	7
		(The neurological and seven unclassified items being excluded)	

The rationale of _Norm Violation_ was that it consisted of behaviour which the child himself must know is 'wrong'—stealing, lying, truanting, destructiveness, hurting other children, 'laziness'.
Bad Peer Relations included squabbling and fighting with other children, misusing companionship to dominate, inability to keep friends, bad sportsmanship.
Peer-Group Deviance included showing off, pranks and mischief in order to 'Play to the gallery' and mixing with other unsettled children.
Of the above, Bad Peer Relations emerged as an entirely satisfactory grouping. Among the boys it gained the highest S-S ratio for ten of the postulated items, and came second in the eleventh; among the girls it gained the highest in eight, was a very close second in two, and fourth—but still not far below the top—in one.
Peer-Group Deviance came out equally well, being highest in all eight ratios among the girls and in seven of the eight among the boys.
The thirteen items grouped under Norm Violation failed to form a syndrome, nor was there any consistency as between the ratios for boys and girls. Deviant behaviour did not hold together as a taxonomic category even when peer-group deviance is extracted from it. This finding runs contrary to that of Jenkins and his school, but is not surprising to anyone who has had practical experience of delinquents. In his study of 102 delinquent youths Stott (1950) analysed the motivation of their lawbreaking by relating it to other objective indications. The five main motives—more than one of which was usually present in each youth—were (1) avoidance-excitement: the resort to substitutive emotions, such as could be aroused by the excitements of delinquency, as a means of blocking thoughts and

memories of a distressing family situation; (2) spite, retaliation and resentment against the parents: Hostility as defined in this monograph; (3) delinquent-attention: testing the breaking point of rejecting parents as a relief from the pains of anxiety; (4) an urge to secure physical removal from an anxiety-creating home situation; (5) inferiority—compensation: the counterpart of Inconsequence. Whether or not these motivations are confirmed in another group of delinquents, it is indisputable, first, that there is no one characteristic pattern of behaviour which includes delinquent acts, and, second, that delinquency or norm-violation has to be explained in terms of more fundamental behavioural processes.

It must even be asked how much further in our understanding of motivation we get by accepting the categories of Bad Peer Relations or Peer-Group Deviance, even though they form statistical clusters. They represent patterns or styles of deviant behaviour which show a reasonable consistency, but like the norm-violating behaviours they themselves need to be related to fundamental motivation.

The emergent model: primary dysfunctions and secondary complications

These reflections suggested a structuring for the classification which was that finally adopted. It has been seen that five syndromes, of a unitary type of behaviour, emerged at an early stage of the classification and maintained themselves with little alteration throughout. They consisted of three types of Underreaction—Unforthcomingness, Withdrawal and Depression; and two types of Overreaction—Hostility and Inconsequence. These may be regarded as basic forms of dysfunction of the behavioural system which are probably the nearest we can get to 'disease-entities'. This is not, however, to say that they are congenital or neurological in origin, although a case might be made out for this being so of Unforthcomingness and Inconsequence, and for a constitutional predisposition in the case of the others. Under the influence of varied environments each can give rise to secondary complications and pseudo-adjustments. Many Unforthcoming children find a retreat from the challenges and stresses of life in a 'dullness' which is all too readily accepted by teachers and psychologists as 'low intelligence'. The Inconsequent child may achieve a pseudo-adjustment in the role of a clown; but more often his thoughtless and uninhibited behaviour renders him unpopular and the object of rejection and retaliation. To this he retorts by hostile, anti-social attitudes. Hostility thus tends to become a secondary complication of a primary Inconsequence. But since it is an elemental form of response, being evidently compounded of the primitive reactions of attack and avoidance, it has something of the nature of a 'disease-entity', which is reflected in a homogeneous syndrome.

The upshot is that no simple classification by equal-ranking syndromes would be in accordance with reality or helpful diagnostically. What is needed is a two-tier structure of, on the one hand, a group of 'core' syndromes, which reveal the primary source or sources of the behavioural dysfunction; and a complex of *associated groupings* which reveal the compensatory life-style or pseudo-adjustment which the individual is able to make in his particular circumstances. These may form homogeneous and consistent groupings as do those of Bad Peer Relations or Peer-Group Deviance in the present study; or they may take the form of heterogeneous manifestations of anti-social behaviour without syndromic quality. In neither case do they have a primary explanatory value but are themselves understood developmentally by reference to the strength of the primary syndromes in the individual case. They are the outcome of the interaction of primary dysfunction (or predisposition) and environmental stresses or opportunities.

Since at this stage of the treatment of the data the establishment of a number of syndromes with adequate item-representation seemed assured, and the shorter the instrument by which an effective characterization of behaviour disturbance can be made the greater its general utility, a review was made of a number of items. There were some to which methodological objections might be raised on grounds of subjectivity, and others which remained ambiguous or which were conceptually not wholly consistent with the syndrome into which they fell statistically. This resulted in the elimination of ten additional items. These included five which were not sufficiently descriptive of specific behaviours, and lent themselves to too much interpretation or colouring by the attitude of the teacher to the child. If, for example, the teacher regarded the child as a 'baddy', this could produce a halo-effect.

The remaining 113 items were subjected, after the transfer of a few to other syndromes, to a sixth computer treatment. In furtherance of the two-tier structure described above, their syndrome-specificity ratios were calculated in two separate series. The first gave the syndromic placing of the item within the five core syndromes, the second that in the three secondary 'patterns'. As a reminder that the items grouped under Norm Violation did not hold together as a syndrome they were re-named *Non-syndromic Overreaction*. These secondary patterns or, in the case of the last, discrete instances of socially disapproved behaviour are nonetheless important diagnostically as being revealing of the style of life which the young person is developing.

41

5

The groupings and their rationale

The procedure essentially inductive—Unforthcomingness—Withdrawal — Depression — Undifferentiated Underreacting—Hostility — Inconsequence — Undifferentiated Overreacting (anti-social and delinquent)—'delinquent' items strongly associated with maladjustment—Neurological indications.

The procedure of classification used in this study amounted to an exercise in induction. It was not a matter of classification for its own sake—although in the broadest sense classification, as a means of registering consistent regularities, is the essence of the empirical method. It was rather a methodology for trying to gain further insight into the nature of the various forms of behaviour disturbance, their motivation, the dynamics of their interrelationships and, by implication, their origin. The statistical methods used might be described as an extension of the mental processes by which we in our ordinary thinking try to bring order in our observations. The computer became a counterpart to human thought, carrying out the same processes but immeasurably more rapidly and comprehensively.

A description of the classification which emerged and a discussion of its rationale form the subject matter of the present chapter. The tables list the items within each syndrome as they appeared in the final analysis. Beside each item is given:

1 The numbers of boys and girls scoring each (summarized in a sex ratio of boy/girl in the last column).
2 The scorer/non-scorer ratios for each sex and for both sexes (the degree of the association of the item with other members of the syndrome).
3 The syndrome-specificity ratios (the extent to which an item occurs more frequently in association with items within its own syndrome than with those of any other syndrome).

Table V.1 gives the thirteen items of the syndrome of Unforthcomingness. The capital letters separated by a diagonal stroke indicate the syndromes from whose scorer/non-scorer ratios each specificity ratio was obtained. For example, in the first row, U/W 2.09 means that the item in question has the highest S/N-S ratio in Unforthcomingness, and the next highest in Withdrawal. When that for the first is divided by the second, it is seen that the item is over twice as characteristic of Unforthcomingness as it is of Withdrawal.

The mean S-S ratios for boys and girls for all thirteen items were 1.59 and 1.45 respectively. Thus, on average, the items are one-and-a-half times better indicators of their own syndrome than of the second best, whether it be Withdrawal or Depression. For boys it is 1.74 times better than Withdrawal alone and 2.09 times

TABLE V.1 Scorer/non-scorer, syndrome-specificity and sex ratios   UNFORTHCOMINGNESS (U)

ITEMS	BOYS			GIRLS			Syndrome specificity ratio (both sexes)	Ratio of sex incidence
	N	Scorer/non-scorer ratio	Syndrome specificity ratio	N	Scorer/non-scorer ratio	Syndrome specificity ratio		
Seems afraid to begin (Manual tasks or free activity)	75	U 2.53 W 1.21	U/W 2.09	81	U 2.98 W 2.24	U/W 1.33	U/W 1.58	0.93
Chats only when alone with teacher (Talking with teacher)	128	U 2.25 D 1.65	U/D 1.36	109	U 2.55 D 1.41	U/D 1.81	U/D 1.55	1.18
Too shy to ask (Asking teacher's help)	69	U 3.58 W 2.61	U/W 1.37	102	W 4.32 U 4.21	W/U 1.03	W/U 1.09	0.68
Too timid to stand up for himself or ever to get involved in an argument (Physical courage)	170	U 2.92 W 1.90	U/W 1.54	232	U 3.96 W 3.87	U/W 1.02	U/W 1.52	0.74
Wants adult interest but can't put himself forward (Seeking attention or approval)	98	U 2.82 W 2.35	U/W 1.20	104	W 3.43 U 3.36	W/U 1.02	U/W 1.07	0.94
Has to be encouraged to take part (Team Games)	122	U 2.69 W 2.36	U/W 1.14	165	U 2.94 W 2.10	U/W 1.40	U/W 1.28	0.74

(table continues overleaf)

43

TABLE V.1 cont./

ITEMS	BOYS			GIRLS			Syndrome specificity ratio (both sexes)	Ratio of sex incidence
	N	Scorer/non-scorer ratio	Syndrome specificity ratio	N	Scorer/non-scorer ratio	Syndrome specificity ratio		
So quiet, you don't really know if he is following or not (Paying attention in class)	162	U 3.28 W 2.37	U/W 1.38	159	U 3.82 W 3.30	U/W 1.16	U/W 1.25	1.02
Associates with one other child only and ignores the rest (Companionship)	89	U 2.31 D 2.06	U/D 1.12	145	U 2.26 D 2.04	U/D 1.11	U/D 1.11	0.61
Shy but would like to be friendly (General manner with teacher)	206	U 3.42 W 1.41	U/W 2.43	206	U 3.88 W 1.74	U/W 2.33	U/W 2.32	1.00
Waits to be noticed (Greeting teacher)	171	U 2.77 D 1.17	U/D 2.37	161	U 3.13 W 1.81	U/W 1.73	U/D 2.39	1.06
Sits quietly and meekly (Sitting in desk)	147	U 3.15 W 1.73	U/W 1.82	215	U 3.26 W 2.49	U/W 1.34	U/W 1.47	0.68
Likes sympathy but reluctant to ask (Liking for sympathy)	55	D 1.83 U 1.81	D/U 1.01	56	U 2.77 W 1.63	U/W 1.70	U/W 1.47	0.98
Too timid to be any trouble (Classroom behaviour)	76	U 3.83 W 2.09	U/W 1.83	135	U 4.33 W 3.79	U/W 1.14	U/W 1.31	0.56

better than Depression alone. Unforthcomingness is thus confirmed as a distinct type of underreacting behaviour. As a concept it is analogous to Sontag's (1962) 'Social apprehensiveness', but includes apprehensiveness about coping with new tasks and activities. Unforthcomingness may be defined as a deficit of effectiveness-motivation (White 1959, Stott 1961) or of coping in the sense that Murphy (1962) used it. Coping involves encountering something new or not yet mastered: a novel situation, an obstacle, or a conflict. She recognized this as constituting an important individual difference, and could not find any child-rearing factor to account for it. Sontag (1962) and Stott (1959) found this deficit to be related to prenatal stress in the mother, and Thompson (1957) and Ader (1962) demonstrated that rats subjected to anxiety in pregnancy produced offspring that carried out less exploration of their environment and were apprehensive about emerging from their nest box in search of food. Unforthcomingness may, therefore, be regarded as a 'constitutional' impairment of temperament. Nevertheless, the child adjusts to his apprehensiveness by avoiding complex tasks or challenging activities, as well as being timid in his encounters with strangers. In the sense that he learns to avoid such anxiety-creating situations, his behaviour may be said to have a goal and to be motivated, even though negatively. This applies also to the skill which he develops in arousing the protective sympathies of adults and his unwillingness to forego his dependence. In extreme cases he learns that to become regarded as 'just dull' relieves him of challenges and pressures, a pseudo-adjustment which the adults around him reinforce. It can be said of the behavioural descriptions of Unforthcomingness that they represent a type of relationship which the child seeks to establish; its precise nature is determined by his temperamental coping-level.

The nine items in the Withdrawal syndrome (Table V.2) show a very satisfactory clustering, except for 'Never appeals to an adult even when hurt or wronged', which understandably has a certain representation in Hostility. The mean S-S ratios of 1.28 for boys and 1.65 for girls are not quite so good as those for Unforthcomingness, but it will be noted that in sixteen of the eighteen ratios the runner-up syndrome is Depression. The mean S-S ratios for Withdrawal/Unforthcomingness only are 2.60 for the boys and 3.68 for girls, which confirms the distinctiveness of Unforthcomingness from Withdrawal despite the difficulty, with observers without specialized training, in differentiating between these types of inhibited bahaviour.

The items of the Withdrawal syndrome describe, not a fearfulness about social encounters such as is characteristic of Unforthcomingness, but an indifference about human attachments or a set defensiveness against them. Within the limitations of the teacher's observation in the school situation, it is not possible to break down the motivation or the temperamental impairment more finely. Withdrawal as revealed by this schedule could be autism, conceptualized as a dysfunction of the mechanism for appraising the situation by the criterion of satisfactory social attachments; or it could be a defensiveness conditioned by repeated affectional disappointments, as in an institutionalized child or one who has had a number of foster-parents.

The ten items representing *Depression* (Table V.3) describe a lack of motivation. As explained above, the very uniformity of the lack of response makes it difficult to identify *varied* behaviours that could be meaningfully grouped in a syndrome, and the synomynity of the wordings naturally makes for clustering. Their relatively good and consistent specificity, however, points to a distinct mode of behaviour. The existence of a number of descriptive items, even though very similar to each

TABLE V.2 Scorer/non-scorer, syndrome-specificity and sex ratios WITHDRAWAL (W)

ITEMS	BOYS			GIRLS			Syndrome specificity ratio (both sexes)	Ratio of sex incidence
	N	Scorer/ non-scorer ratio	Syndrome specificity ratio	N	Scorer/ non-scorer ratio	Syndrome specificity ratio		
Never appeals to adult even when hurt or wronged (Liking for sympathy)	101	W 2.65 H 2.25	W/H 1.18	45	W 7.00 D 3.16	W/D 2.22	W/D 1.62	2.22
Never thinks of greeting (Greeting teacher)	216	W 4.68 D 2.91	W/D 1.61	83	W 5.44 D 4.19	W/D 1.30	W/D 1.50	2.63
Cannot bring himself to be that sociable (Helping teacher with jobs)	37	W 5.24	W/D 1.29	22	W 7.24 D 5.66	W/D 1.22	W/D 1.29	1.69
Never makes any sort of social relationship, good or bad (Helping teacher with jobs)	52	W 4.04 D 3.53	W/D 1.14	24	W 11.25 D 7.21	W/D 1.56	W/D 1.35	2.17
Remains aloof in a world of his own (Team games)	30	W 4.33 D 2.96	W/D 1.46	33	W 5.94 D 4.77	W/D 1.25	W/D 1.32	0.91

Avoids contacts with teacher and other children (Contacts with teacher)	21	W 6.36 D 4.99	W/D 1.27	9	W 9.97 U 4.02	W/U 2.42	W/U 2.79	2.33
Quite cut off from people, you can't get near him as a person (General manner with teacher)	77	W 6.13 D 5.24	W/D 1.17	50	W 12.33 D 7.72	W/D 1.60	W/D 1.38	1.54
Distant, never wants to talk (Talking with teacher)	68	W 4.26 D 3.21	W/D 1.33	45	W 9.33 D 5.88	W/D 1.59	W/D 1.47	1.52
Distant, ignores others (Companionship)	61	W 3.52 D 3.24	W/D 1.09	46	W 7.77 D 4.89	W/D 1.59	W/D 1.35	1.33
Has his own solitary activity to which he reverts (Informal play)	54	W 2.53 U 2.21	W/U 1.14	50	W 3.85 U 2.42	W/U 1.59	W/U 1.38	0.96

TABLE V.3 Scorer/non-scorer, syndrome-specificity and sex ratios
DEPRESSION (D)

ITEMS	BOYS			GIRLS			Syndrome specificity ratio (both sexes)	Ratio of sex incidence
	N	Scorer/ non-scorer ratio	Syndrome specificity ratio	N	Scorer/ non-scorer ratio	Syndrome specificity ratio		
Couldn't care whether teacher sees his work or not (Contacts with teacher)	153	D 3.53 W 3.23	D/W 1.09	58	D 6.83 Q 4.10	D/Q 1.67	D/Q 1.53	2.63
Shows complete indifference (Facing new learning tasks)	81	D 3.81 W 3.61	D/W 1.06	40	D 9.20 W 5.24	D/W 1.76	D/W 1.35	2.04
Always sluggish, lethargic (Team games)	25	D 5.79 W 3.02	D/W 1.92	14	D 9.29 W 6.22	D/W 1.49	D/W 1.69	1.79
Difficult to stimulate, lacks physical energy (Manual tasks or free activity)	144	D 5.97 W 3.36	D/W 1.78	90	D 8.15 W 4.19	D/W 1.95	D/W 1.85	1.59
Too lacking in energy to bother (Asking teacher's help)	76	D 6.14 W 3.18	D/W 1.93	32	D 12.07 W 7.01	D/W 1.72	D/W 1.83	2.38
Too lethargic to be troublesome (Classroom behaviour)	51	D 6.34 U 3.22	D/W 1.97	36	D 13.79 W 8.32	D/W 0.46	D/W 1.77	1.41

Unmotivated, has no energy (Working by himself)	81	D 6.48 W 3.91	D/W 1.66	37	D 10.29 W 5.09	D/W 2.02	D/W 1.79	2.17
You can't get his attention (Paying attention in class)	45	D 4.50 W 3.06	D/W 1.47	20	D 7.11 W 6.05	D/W 1.18	D/W 1.33	2.27
Apathetic (Paying attention in class)	84	D 5.45 W 3.25	D/W 1.67	48	D 8.61 W 5.28	D/W 1.63	D/W 1.65	1.75
Sits lifelessly most of the time (Sitting in desk)	121	D 5.82 W 3.31	D/W 1.76	61	D 7.70 W 5.47	D/W 1.41	D/W 1.60	2.00

TABLE V.4 Scorer/non-scorer, syndrome specificity and sex ratios
NON-SYNDROMIC UNDERREACTION (UR)

ITEMS	N	BOYS Cores	BOYS Allied groupings	Best specificity ratio	N	GIRLS Cores	GIRLS Allied groupings	Best specificity ratio	Ratio of sex incidence
		S/N-S				S/N-S			
Is too unaware of people to greet (Greeting teacher)	22	D 5.32 / W 4.10	UR 3.64 / NV 1.36	D/W 1.30	12	W 10.80 / D 5.62	UR 3.24 / PM 0.66	W/D 1.92	1.82
Difficult to get a word out of him (Talking with teacher)	122	W 3.21 / U 3.14	UR 2.88 / NV 0.96	W/U 1.02	92	W 5.78 / D 3.99	UR 3.06 / NV 1.37	W/D 1.45	1.33
Keeps a suspicious distance (Contacts with teacher)	37	W 3.66 / D 3.27	NV 2.38 / UR 2.24	W/D 1.12	15	D 7.02 / W 6.32	NV 4.25 / UR 3.65	D/W 1.11	2.44
Timid, poor spirited can't let himself go (Team games)	120	W 2.83 / D 2.74	UR 4.25 / NV 1.27	W/D 1.03	144	W 4.67 / D 3.85	UR 3.72 / NV 1.27	W/D 1.21	0.83
Shrinks from active play (Informal play)	96	W 3.04 / U 2.92	UR 4.30 / NV 1.11	W/U 1.04	107	W 5.60 / D 4.28	UR 4.27 / NV 0.96	W/D 1.31	0.90
Sometimes wanders off alone (Companionship)	135	U 2.18 / 1.95	UR 3.46 / PM 1.02	U/D 1.12	92	W 3.21 / U 2.90	UR 3.59 / NV 1.02	W/U 1.11	1.47
Lets the more forward push ahead of him (Standing in line)	136	U 3.08 / W 2.11	UR 3.73 / NV 0.70	U/W 1.46	120	W 3.81 / U 3.17	UR 3.33 / NV 1.05	W/U 1.20	1.14

other, makes it possible to gauge the degree of Depression by its generality over the range of the child's functioning. That W is the runner-up syndrome in all the S-S ratios except one confirms the greater similarity of these indicators of depression to W than to U.

The *Non-syndromic Underreaction* grouping (Table V.4) consists of those items which were not specific to Withdrawal, Unforthcomingness or Depression. It is seen from this Table that the best specificity ratios obtainable were near to unity. This means that the behaviour, or lack thereof, is common to two or all three as far as can be judged by teachers' observations. It must not be interpreted as partly one and partly another. For diagnosis the items marked would be allocated to whichever of the Underreacting core syndromes come out strongest. It will be noted that some of the items were of rare occurrence and their ratios may come out differently in another sample.

Hostility (Table V.5) is represented by eighteen items of very high specificity: 2.45 for the boys and 2.28 for the girls. It is conceptualized as being motivated towards maintaining or provoking a breach in an affectional relationship, and as such exploits the primitive executive-reactions of both attack and avoidance. The first is seen in such behaviours as 'Seems to go out of his way to earn disapproval', 'May spoil his work purposely', 'Uses bad language that he knows will be disapproved of', and rejecting the teacher's help by arguing (presumably in an antagonistic way). There is a further group suggesting a lack of any fear about worsening a relationship, which enables the child to give free rein to his attack-responses. Examples of these are aggressive defiance when corrected, and showing that he bears a grudge. In both these groups the runner-up syndrome is Q: the child who temperamentally is predisposed to impulsive attack-reactions against frustration is more likely to build this component into his hostility. On the other hand, the child who is temperamentally prone to avoidance is more likely to use the surly, moody type of response. By his refusal to smile, communicate verbally, to meet people's eyes or to cooperate in a joint activity, he signals his rejection of a social relationship. The group of items which describe this facet of hostility have Depression as the runner-up syndrome. As with the similar relationship of Withdrawal to Unforthcomingness, this does not mean that the behaviours in question are a compound of Hostility and Depression, but rather that—within the limits which the class-teacher can be expected to discriminate—there is a certain amount of confusion between the external manifestations of moody-surly Hostility and moody-lethargic Depression. Bronfenbrenner and Ricciuti (1960) point out that, 'A motive cannot be inferred from a single piece of behaviour, since both response tendencies and motives may lead to the same specific act ... to establish the existence of one or the other type of disposition requires additional evidence ... ' Hence the importance of an array of indications which give cumulative weight to an interpretation. The moody-surly aspect of Hostility is differentiated from Depression by indications of the provocative aspect except when the child is temperamentally an extreme 'avoider'. In such cases the defensive Hostility could border on Withdrawal.

The above interpretation of Hostility raises the question of why it should be directed against the teacher. At its normal level of operation Hostility can be best understood as a reaction of the jilted lover to being 'let down'. The aggrieved party summons up an unreasoning fury against the faithless one as a means of destroying an emotional involvement which, not being reciprocated, has proved too painful to

TABLE V.5 Scorer/non-scorer, syndrome-specificity and sex ratios
HOSTILITY (H)

ITEMS	N	BOYS Scorer/ non-scorer ratio	Syndrome specificity ratio	N	GIRLS Scorer/ non-scorer ratio	Syndrome specificity ratio	Syndrome specificity ratio (both sexes)	Ratio of sex incidence
Can be surly (Greeting teacher)	49	H 5.79 D 2.23	H/D 2.60	39	H 9.13 D 3.75	H/D 2.43	H/D 2.50	1.25
Will help unless he is in a bad mood (Helping teacher with jobs)	99	H 6.06 Q 1.89	H/Q 3.21	57	H 8.51 Q 3.43	H/Q 2.48	H/Q 2.84	1.72
Will answer, except when in one of his bad moods (Answering questions)	90	H 5.65 Q 2.00	H/Q 2.83	83	H 8.25 Q 3.48	H/Q 2.37	H/Q 2.54	1.09
Sometimes in a bad mood (General manner with teacher)	92	H 7.62 Q 2.13	H/Q 3.58	81	H 11.14 Q 3.31	H/Q 3.37	H/Q 3.45	1.14
Inclined to be moody (Talking with teacher)	102	H 5.68 D 1.98	H/D 2.87	76	H 9.03 D 3.55	H/D 2.54	H/D 2.68	1.33
Resentful muttering or expression for a moment or two (Attitude to correction)	187	D 6.57 Q 2.47	H/Q 2.66	128	H 9.92 Q 3.74	H/Q 2.65	H/Q 2.66	1.47

Bears a grudge, regards punishment as unfair (Effect of correction)	63	H 6.64 D 2.24	H/D 2.96	46	H 8.70 D 4.16	H/D 2.09	H/D 2.46	1.37
Has uncooperative moods (Working by himself)	119	H 6.18 Q 2.39	H/Q 2.59	67	H 9.25 Q 3.46	H/Q 2.67	H/O 2.62	1.79
Seems to go out of his way to earn disapproval (Seeking attention of approval)	39	H 5.90 Q 3.36	H/Q 1.76	10	H.10.67 Q 8.04	H/Q 1.33	H/Q 1.59	3.85
Openly does things he knows are wrong in front of teacher (Classroom behaviour)	89	H 4.68 Q 2.93	H/Q 1.60	31	H 7.18 Q 5.33	H/Q 1.35	H/Q 1.50	2.87
May spoil his work purposely (Manual tasks or free activity)	47	H 4.94 Q 2.69	H/Q 1.84	21	H 6.84 Q 3.46	H/Q 1.98	H/Q 1.89	2.22
Has stolen in a way that he would be bound to be found out (Other people's belongings)	10	H 6.51 Q 2.80	H/Q 2.33	5	H 2.70 W 2.65	H/W 1.02		2.00
Uses bad language which he knows will be disapproved of (Other deviant behaviour)	30	H 5.79 Q 3.09	H/Q 1.87	14	H 7.89 Q 3.37	H/Q 2.34	H/Q 2.03	2.13

(table continues overleaf)

53

TABLE V.5 cont./
ITEMS

ITEMS	BOYS			GIRLS			Syndrome specificity ratio (both sexes)	Ratio of sex incidence
	N	Scorer/non-scorer ratio	Syndrome specificity ratio	N	Syndrome specificity ratio	Scorer/non-scorer ratio		
Tries to argue against teacher (*Asking teacher's help*)	28	H 5.52 Q 2.65	H/Q 2.08	22	H 7.93 Q 4.43	H/Q 1.79	H/Q 1.92	1.27
Aggressive defiance (screams, threats, violence (*Attitude to correction*)	15	H 5.46 Q 2.35	H/Q 2.32	9	H 8.04 Q 4.14	H/Q 1.94.	H/Q 2.13	1.67
Becomes antagonistic (*Effect of correction*)	21	H 7.81 W 3.03	H/W 2.58	10	H 9.79 Q 2.57	H/Q 3.81	H/W 3.27	2.08
Squabbles, make insulting remarks (*Ways with other children*)	116	H 5.24 Q 2.57	H/Q 2.04	86	H 7.24 Q 4.34	H/Q 1.67	H/Q 1.83	0.74
Flies into a temper if provoked (*Physical courage*)	115	H 5.67 Q 2.30	H/Q 2.46	72	H 8.26 Q 3.79	H/Q 2.18	H/Q 2.32	1.60

be borne. Its temporary virulence stems from its motivation as an affection-killing mechanism. An original affectional relationship is a prerequisite for Hostility, and distinguishes it from the enmity or antagonism aroused when one has suffered injury from an enemy. One must therefore ask why the hostile child goes out of his way to destroy a good relationship with his teacher. It cannot originate from inconsiderate treatment or other reason for disliking a person, because these do not arouse the highly emotional and maladaptive hostility characteristic of the present syndrome; they are more likely to result in a shunning of the disliked person, the victim obeying the Law of Least Cost in his own best interests. Nor can we suppose that, in the great majority of instances, it is a reaction of disappointment against a spurned love-relationship vis-à-vis the teacher. The answer would seem to be that the mood of hostility, evoked when the child feels he is rejected by his parents, can be transferred to other human beings in the same way that, in everyday life, the attack-response to frustration can be vented upon an innocent object. If it is against the sensed disloyalty of his mother that the child is reacting, a woman teacher may 'get it in the neck'; if it is against the father's threats of disownment, it may be a man teacher, the police or the agents of authority in general.

Inconsequence (Table V.6) comes out with reasonably good S-S ratios considering the secondary complication of Hostility. Indeed the regularity with which this latter syndrome provides the runner-up S/N-S ratios confirms the Q/H interaction as the chief dynamic of overreacting maladjustment. Perusal of the eleven core-items in Q shows that none of them contains any trace of a hostile or even an aggressive reaction as such. The behaviour described is that of thoughtless, but not ill-intentioned nuisance. However, the implied distractibility, hyperactivity, impulsive seizing of opportunities for self-assertion and hit-and-miss approach to learning are exceedingly frustrating to the teacher, and must be equally so in the home. The hostility is thus a response of the child to the characteristic reaction which such behaviour stimulates in those who have dealings with him. It is consistent with this explanation of the Q/H interaction that the mean S-S ratio for Q is much better for girls (1.96) than for boys (1.30). The more aggressive and active nuisance of boys evokes sharper rejecting reactions from adults, and so boys show more concomitant hostility.

It may seem contradictory that in boys two Q items should have D as a runner-up, but this affords a further example of the difficulty of interpreting specific behaviours. They describe an inability to concentrate, the one upon manual tasks or in free-activity, the other in academic work. The depressed child evidently has a similar lack of concentration but for a different reason.

The nine items descriptive of *Attention-seeking* (Table V.7) present an interesting problem of classification. They cluster well, and statistically form a good 'syndrome', but since the common factor is an interpretation at the phenomenological level of seeking attention, this does not give us much insight into their motivation. For this we have to refer to the core syndromes. Q comes highest in fifteen of the eighteen S-S ratios for attention-seeking and second in the remaining three, and the mean ratios for boys and girls are 1.25 and 1.50 in favour of Q. In all except one, however, H is the runner-up. Nevertheless, none of the behaviours described in the wording of the items contains any suggestion of Hostility. One has to conclude that the association of the latter with attention-seeking is further evidence of the dynamic structuring of the modes of behaviour disturbance which is apt to blur and complicate any purely statistical classification.

TABLE V.6 Scorer/non-scorer, syndrome-specificity and sex ratios
INCONSEQUENCE

ITEMS	BOYS			GIRLS			Syndrome specificity ratio (both sexes)	Ratio of sex incidence
	N	Scorer/ non-scorer ratio	Syndrome specificity ratio	N	Scorer/ non-scorer ratio	Syndrome specificity ratio		
Attends to anything but his work (Paying attention in class)	179	Q 4.24 H 3.28	Q/H 1.29	80	Q 8.59 H 4.99	Q/H 1.72	Q/H 1.47	2.22
Never gets down to any solid work (Working by himself)	132	Q 3.40 D 3.11	Q/D 1.09	50	Q 6.73 H 3.75	Q/H 1.79	Q/H 1.33	2.63
Never really gets down to a job and soon switches to something else (Manual tasks or free activity)	197	Q 3.56 2.56	Q/D 1.39	92	Q 7.37 H 3.54	Q/H 2.08	Q/D 1.68	2.13
Misbehaves when teacher is engaged with others (Classroom behaviour)	293	Q 3.57 H 3.16	Q/H 1.13	104	Q 7.29 H 5.13	Q/H 1.42	Q/H 1.24	2.86
Has a hit and miss approach to every problem (Facing new learning tasks)	150	Q 3.19 H 2.54	Q/H 1.26	70	Q 6.20 H 3.30	Q/H 1.88	Q/H 1.49	2.13

Item							
Doesn't seem to understand that he should keep in his seat (Sitting in desk)	65	Q 3.08 H 2.67	Q/H 1.15	30	Q 6.84 H 2.89	Q/H 2.37	Q/H 1.56	2.17
Borrows books from desk without permission (Other people's belongings)	70	Q 3.08 H 2.85	Q/H 1.08	39	Q 5.92 H 4.42	Q/H 1.34	Q/H 1.20	1.79
Responds momentarily, but it doesn't last for long (Effect of correction)	355	Q 4.29 H 2.49	Q/H 1.72	157	Q 7.96 H 2.98	Q/H 2.67	Q/H 2.05	2.27
Twists about in his seat, slips onto floor, climbs about on desk (Sitting in desk)	191	Q 3.23 H 2.17	Q/H 1.49	88	Q 7.28 H 3.54	Q/H 2.06	Q/H 1.73	2.17
Constantly restless (Nervous habits)	281	Q 4.33 H 2.85	Q/H 1.52	101	Q 7.47 H 3.98	Q/H 1.88	Q/H 1.64	2.78
Presses for jobs but doesn't do them properly (Helping teacher with jobs)	93	Q 2.97 H 2.44	Q/H 1.22	43	Q 6.34 D 2.69	Q/D 2.36	Q/H 1.61	2.17

TABLE V.7 Scorer/non-scorer, syndrome-specificity and sex ratios
ATTENTION SEEKING

ITEMS	BOYS				GIRLS				Ratio of sex incidence
	N	Cores	Allied groupings	Syndrome specificity ratio	N	Cores	Allied groupings	Syndrome specificity ratio	
		S/N-S				S/N-S			
Hails teacher loudly (Greeting teacher)	113	Q 2.47 H 2.34	AT 5.17 PM 2.94	Q/H 1.06	71	Q 3.59 H 3.00	AT 5.32 GD 5.13	Q/H 1.20	1.59
Constantly seeks help when he could manage alone (Asking teacher's help)	115	Q 2.44 H 2.26	AT 4.82 PM 2.77	Q/H 1.08	117	Q 3.72 H 2.43	AT 5.91 PM 4.42	Q/H 1.53	0.98
Overfriendly (General manner with teacher)	58	Q 1.74 H 0.84	AT 5.93 NV 1.75	Q/H 2.07	71	Q 3.10 H 1.93	AT 6.63 PM 4.55	Q/H 1.61	0.82
Overtalkative (tires with constant chatter) (Talking with teacher)	112	Q 2.34 H 1.67	AT 5.72 GD 2.31	Q/H 1.40	90	Q 5.47 H 3.73	AT 7.84 PM 6.13	Q/H 1.47	1.25
Talks excessively to teacher about own doings, family or possessions (Talking with teacher)	59	H 2.26 Q 1.85	AT 5.50 PM 2.79	H/Q 1.22	65	Q 3.05 H 2.31	AT 6.24 PM 4.20	Q/H 1.32	0.91

Brings objects he has found even though not really lost. (Desire for approval or attention)	19	Q 2.12 / H 1.30	AT 4.42 / PR 3.10	Q/H 1.63	16	Q 4.23 / H 3.24	PR 6.00 / NV 5.32	QH 1.31	1.19
Gets up to all kinds of tricks to gain attention (Seeking attention or approval)	125	H 4.16 / Q 3.50	PR 5.04 / AT 4.99	H/Q 1.19	46	Q 5.27 / H 3.44	AT 7.01 / PM 6.64	Q/H 1.53	2.70
Tells fantastic tales (Truthfulness)	22	D 2.40 / Q 2.30	AT 3.36 / PM 3.36	D/Q 1.04	15	Q 6.17 / H 3.99	AT 6.40 / GD 6.09	Q/H 1.55	1.47
Shouts out or waves arms before he has had time to think (Answering questions)	169	Q 3.06 / H 2.25	AT 5.48 / PM 3.14	Q/H 1.36	67	Q 4.26 / H 2.19	AT 6.27 / PM 4.36	Q/H 1.94	2.50

TABLE V.8 Scorer/non-scorer, syndrome-specificity and sex ratios PEER MALADAPTIVENESS

ITEMS	N	Cores (S/N-S)	BOYS Allied groupings	Syndrome specificity ratio	N	Cores (S/N-S)	GIRLS Allied groupings	Syndrome specificity ratio	Ratio of sex incidence
Starts off others in scrapping and rough play, disturbs others, games (Informal play)	116	H 4.28 Q 3.18	PM 5.60 NV 4.41	H/Q 1.35	16	H 7.86 Q 6.24	NV 8.65 GD 8.62 PM 7.86	H/Q 1.26	7.14
Spiteful to weaker children when he thinks he is unobserved (Ways with other children)	45	H 3.86 D 2.21	PM 5.00 NV 3.31	H/D 1.75	22	H 5.77 D 3.18	PM 5.76 NV 4.46	H/D 1.81	2.04
Attacks other children viciously (Physical courage)	30	H 6.63 Q 2.29	PM 6.66 NV 4.32	H/Q 2.90	9	H 8.13 Q 3.95	PM 8.23 NV 7.11	H/Q 2.06	3.33
Tries to dominate and won't cooperate when he can't get his own way (Informal play)	75	H 4.63 Q 2.31	PM 5.82 AT 3.73	H/Q 2.00	71	H 4.73 Q 3.51	PM 7.68 AT 4.67	H/Q 1.35	1.05
Misuses companionship to show off or dominate (Companionship)	48	H 4.17 Q 2.84	PM 6.78 NV 4.80	H/Q 1.47	35	H 5.10 Q 4.25	PM 7.84 AT 5.35	H/Q 1.20	1.37

Statement	n			H/Q	n			H/Q	
Tries to push in front of smaller children (*Standing in line*)	94	H 2.86 Q 2.44	PM 4.27 NV 3.12	H/Q 1.17	59	H 4.23 Q 4.18	PM 5.85 AT 4.95	H/Q 1.01	1.59
Snatches things from other children (*Other people's belongings*)	74	H 5.25 Q 3.31	PM 5.87 NV 4.78	H/Q 1.59	37	H 5.93 Q 5.21	PM 7.45 GD 7.12	H/Q 1.14	2.00
Bad loser (*Team games*)	128	H 4.82 Q 2.46	PM 5.35 AT 3.16	H/Q 1.96	61	H 6.53 Q 3.13	PM 6.09 GD 5.00	H/Q 2.09	2.08
Bad sportsman (*Team games*)	40	H 5.11 Q 3.03	PM 5.46 NV 4.48	H/Q 1.69	27	H 6.24 Q 4.41	PM 7.80 NV 5.52	H/Q 1.41	1.47
Tells on others to try to gain teacher's favour (*Ways with other children*)	91	H 3.26 Q 2.36	PM 4.22 AT 3.04	H/Q 1.38	86	Q 3.65 H 3.50	PM 6.29 AT 4.77	H/Q 1.04	1.05
Can never keep a friend for long, tries to pal up with newcomers (*Companionship*)	38	H 3.73 Q 2.32	PM 4.14 NV 3.03	H/Q 1.61	35	H 4.30 Q 4.03	PM 5.13 NV 4.57	H/Q 1.07	1.09

61

TABLE V.9 Scorer/non-scorer, syndrome-specificity and sex ratios PEER GROUP DEVIANCE[1]

ITEMS	N	BOYS			N	GIRLS			Ratio of sex incidence
		Cores S/N-S	Allied groupings	Best specificity ratio		Cores S/N-S	Allied groupings	Best specificity ratio	
Invents silly ways of doing things (Manual tasks or free activity)[2]	72	Q 2.92 H 2.23	GD 3.48 AT 3.26	Q/H 1.31	12	D 3.35 H 3.28	GD 6.18 AT 4.45	D/H 1.02	6.00
Shows off (Ways with other children)[2]	195	Q 3.47 H 2.44	GD 4.08 AT 3.50	Q/H 1.42	37	H 5.55 Q 4.55	GD 9.76 NV 6.63	H/Q 1.22	5.27
Follower in mischief (Other deviant behaviour)[3]	185	H 2.51 Q 2.46	GD 3.07 NV 2.94	H/Q 1.02	46	Q 3.98 H 3.89	GD 8.25 NV 5.39	Q/H 1.02	4.02
Mixes mostly with unsettled types (Companionship)[3]	131	H 3.18 Q 2.77	GD 3.26 PR 3.07	H/Q 1.15	55	Q 4.70 D 4.06	GD 7.82 NV 5.59	Q/D 1.16	2.38
Foolish or dangerous pranks with a gang (Physical courage)[3]	71	Q 2.81 H 2.66	GD 4.21 PR 4.11	Q/H 1.06	10	Q 5.76 H 5.20	GD 11.20 NV 7.83	Q/H 1.11	7.10
Is often the centre of a disturbance. (Standing in line)[4]	309	H 4.78 Q 4.18	GD 5.32 PR 5.03	H/Q 1.07	106	Q 6.51 H 5.88	GD 9.11 NV 6.52	Q/H 1.11	2.91

| Inclined to fool around (Team games)[2] | 232 | Q 3.38 H 2.39 | GD 4.57 PR 3.75 | Q/H 1.41 | 72 | Q 5.97 H 5.20 | GD 8.30 NV 5.21 | Q/H 1.15 | 3.22 |

[1] This grouping was dispersed as indicated in the subsequent footnotes.
[2] Transferred to Inconsequence.
[3] Transferred to a 'Peer-group deviance' section of Non-syndromic overreaction.
[4] Transferred to a 'Defiance of social norms' section of Non-syndromic overreaction.

63

The place of attention-seeking in this structure of interactions is very similar to that of Q. We have thus to ask whether it can be regarded as a variety of Inconsequence. To answer this question we have to elaborate upon our theoretical model of the behavioural system. From about the age of fifteen months the normal child is regularly seeking approval and praise from adults for his achievements. He has also discovered that his control of the responses of adults can afford him a valuable means of personal effectiveness; it is possible to transfer power to himself by commanding the attentions and monopolizing the time of the physically more powerful adults. Attention-seeking is thus a means of 'pushing the world around', of being the prime mover and manipulator rather than being moved and controlled. If unchecked, such behaviour becomes irksome to adults, because they suffer a corresponding diminution in their effectiveness and freedom of action. Consequently, it becomes normally part of the social training of the young child to desist from excessive demands upon adults' time and attention. In short, the child has to learn to inhibit this all-too-easy form of gratification. It follows that if he suffers from an impairment of the ability to inhibit his impulses he will both remain an attention-seeker and, by exceeding the tolerance-limits of the adults around him, will excite rejecting responses in them. Attention-seeking may therefore be classed as an aspect of Inconsequence, with Hostility as its habitual bedfellow.

Three associated groupings remain to be examined. They consist of behavioural items which did not fit unambiguously—for either statistical or conceptual reasons—into any of the core syndromes, yet fall under the rubric of overreacting behaviour. Their association with H or Q, as the case may be, is usually a fairly close one, but not specific enough to enable them to rank as primary indications of these types of behaviour disturbance. The best we can do with them is to classify them phenomenologically, that is to say, by some self-evident similarity which carries no implications as to their motivation. For the latter we have to refer, in the individual case, to concomitant indications of the core syndromes.

The first is Peer-Maladaptiveness, containing eleven items as in Table V.8. Of these, seven depict aggressive attempts at dominance over other children or resort to aggression—without necessarily any suggestion of hostility—as a means of achieving goals. As such they suggest the temperamental impairment of Inconsequence, because behaviour of this sort brings bad consequences in terms of worsened peer-relations. One of the indicators, 'Can never keep a friend long, tries to pal up with newcomers' (implying a failure to gain friends by normal methods) is a typical 'stimulus-characteristic' (social feedback) in the categorization of Bronfenbrenner and Riccuiti. The remaining three could derive from various temperamental tendencies or motivations. 'Attacks other children viciously' could be an indication of a gross failure to inhibit physical attack responses to frustration or teasing such as is found in postencephalic and other brain-damaged children. It has an excellent syndrome-specificity ratio of 2.61 for Hostility, and but for the above consideration would be placed there. In many cases it may indicate a transfer of a general attitude of hostility from the parents on to other children in the same way as hostility can be transferred on to other adults. 'Tells on others to try to gain teacher's favour' has evidently a mixed motivation, that of hostility to other children and an anxiety to gain adult approval. 'Spiteful to other children when he thinks he is not observed' could again be actuated by hostility; or it could betray a fundamental impairment of social feeling. In terms of our behavioural model this latter means that the mechanism for appraising situations in order to ensure secure social attachments is in a state of dysfunction. A child who is not concerned about his social relationships or his acceptance by his peers, and hence has no feelings of guilt about ill-treating them, is free to exploit means of effectiveness— by bullying and delight in causing pain and distress— which are rejected by normal children. If it were possible to establish a satisfactory syndrome for the juvenile psychopath from the observation of school behaviour, this would doubtless be one of the items.

As a whole the items of the Peer-Maladaptiveness grouping have good S-S ratios for Hostility, even though, as has been seen, seven of them are conceptually more consistent with Inconsequence. For this and the other reasons stated, the motivation of any of their manifestations has to be inferred from the general pattern of disturbed behaviour in the individual child.

Peer-Group Deviance, the second of the associated groupings (Table V.9), consists of seven items, with low to moderate S-S ratios in Q or H, whose common denominator is a readiness to 'break the rules' in an attempt to gain favour with age-peers. The behaviour ranges from showing-off to disruptiveness and gang-deviance. The three items representing the last ('Follower in mischief', 'Mixes mostly with unsettled types', and 'Foolish or dangerous pranks with a gang') are of interest as being cognate with the indications of Jenkins's socialized delinquency and the 'Group Delinquent Reaction' in his most recent suggested classification (Jenkins 1969). This he regards as a phenomenon of 'social pathology rather than psychiatric pathology' (Jenkins 1966), representing 'not a failure of socialization but a limitation of loyalty to a more or less predatory peer group'. The implication is that boys or girls who adopt this pattern of deviance are not intrinsically maladjusted, but limit their adjustment to their peer culture. The theories which have given rise to this view are discussed in Chapter Twelve. At this stage it can be noted, first, that the above three items descriptive of group-delinquency form a fairly tight grouping with behaviour which may be popularly described as 'playing to the gallery'. In so far as these afford immediate gratification at the expense of unfavourable consequences, they are maladaptive. The same is likely to apply to the delinquent behaviour which is associated therewith. In the second place, the above three items are relatively good indicators of maladjustment, being respectively sixteen, twelve and six times more frequent among the worst than among the best adjusted.

The three 'showing-off' items have highest S-S ratios for Q, and could have been placed in that syndrome but for their inconsistency as between the sexes. They fit into the concept of Inconsequent behaviour in the sense of preferring immediate gratification without thought for the consequences. In a diagnostic procedure they could be scored as Q. With the removal for diagnostic purposes of the three 'showing-off' items from Peer-Group Deviance, this grouping is left with the three gang-deviance items mentioned above, together with a fourth, 'Inclined to fool around' (in team games). It will be seen from Table V.9 that all four have highest S/N-S ratios in Q for girls, but among the boys the highest ratios for two of them are in H. Diagnostically it would be convenient and appropriate to group them among the non-syndromic overreacting items.

The nine items of *Non-syndromic Overreaction* (anti-social and deviant behaviour) (Table V. 10) fail, as the title given to this group implies, to form a statistical syndrome. At an earlier stage most of them were grouped. under the heading 'Norm Violation', but to forestall misunderstanding they are better not given a name that would imply a syndrome. It will be seen that the low frequency

TABLE V.10 Scorer/non-scorer, syndrome-specificity and sex ratios
NON-SYNDROMIC OVERREACTION

ITEMS	N	BOYS Cores S/N-S	BOYS Allied groupings	Best specificity ratio	N	GIRLS Cores S/N-S	GIRLS Allied groupings	Best specificity ratio	Ratio of sex incidence
Destructive, defaces with scribbling (*Belongings*)	90	H 4.07 Q 2.96	NV 3.83 GD 3.52	H/Q 1.37	22	H 6.01 Q 5.10	NV 5.74 PR 5.32	H/Q 1.18	4.09
Has stolen within school in a cunning underhand way (*Other people's belongings*)	23	H 3.85 Q 2.76	PR 4.56 NV 4.06	H/Q 1.39	8	Q 5.29 D 2.83	NV 5.51 GD 4.48	Q/D 1.87	2.87
Slumps, lolls about (*Sitting in desk*)	188	H 3.30 D 2.99	PR 3.56 NV 3.07	H/D 1.10	70	H 4.78 D 4.16	NV 5.56 GD 4.48	H/D 1.15	2.69
Damage to public property (*Other deviant behaviour*)	15	D 2.78 H 2.24 Q 1.76	NV 3.89 GD 2.52	D/H 1.24	3	Q 3.72 H 3.47	GD 7.34 NV 4.33	Q/H 1.07	5.00
Tries to buy favour with others (*Companionship*)	23	Q 2.43 D 2.29	PR 3.49 AT 3.30	Q/D 1.06	21	H 3.22 Q 3.04	PR 5.10 NV 4.39	H/Q 1.06	1.09

Has truanted once or twice, often suspected of truancy (Attendance)	17	H 3.16 D 3.17	PR 2.82 NV 2.55	H/D 1.46	5	D 7.48 W 6.72	NV 5.32 GD 2.89	D/W 1.11	3.40
Damage to personal property (Cars, gardens teacher's belongings, etc.) (Other deviant behaviour)	11	H 3.67 Q 2.08	NV 4.57 PR 3.87	H/Q 1.76	1	H 1.48 U 0.62	GD 3.59	H/U 2.39	11.00
Not restless but works only when watched (Working by himself)	134	Q 2.32 D 2.28	PR 2.89 NV 2.61	Q/D 1.02	63	Q 4.22 D 3.34	NV 5.23 GD 5.19	Q/D 1.26	2.13
Sometimes a fluent liar (Truthfulness)	65	H 4.21 Q 2.40	PR 3.37 NV 3.14	H/Q 1.72	37	H 4.36 Q 3.91	PR 5.83 GD 5.12	H/Q 1.11	1.76
Habitual slick liar, has no compunction about lying (Truthfulness)	31	H 3.66 Q 3.28	PR 5.93 NV 4.41	H/Q 1.12	23	H 6.14 D 5.27	NV 6.60 PR 4.95	H/D 1.16	1.35

TABLE V.11 Scorer/non-scorer, syndrome-specificity and sex ratios NEUROLOGICAL

ITEMS	N	BOYS			N	GIRLS			Ratio of sex incidence
		Cores	Allied groupings	Best specificity ratio		Cores	Allied groupings	Best specificity ratio	
		S/N-S				S/N-S			
Makes aimless movements with his hands (Nervous habits, fidgets, etc.)	45	N 7.07 H 2.25 Q 2.02	AT 2.37 NV 2.35	N/H 3.14 H/Q 1.11	18	N 5.77 Q 2.52 D 1.89	AT 2.56 NV 2.19	N/Q 2.29 Q/D 1.33	2.50
Too restless and overactive to heed even for a moment (Effect of correction)	19	N 5.01 Q 3.31 D 1.94	AT 4.50 NV 3.74	N/Q 1.51 Q/D 1.71	8	Q 4.66 N 4.27 H 2.43	AT 4.90 PM 4.40	Q/N 1.09 Q/H 1.92	2.38
Very jumpy and easily scared (Physical courage)	53	N 5.51 D 2.06 U 1.73	UR 2.27 AT 1.64	N/D 2.67 D/U 1.08	27	N 2.60 U 1.85 W 1.73	UR 2.63 AT 2.32	N/U 1.40 U/W 1.07	1.96
Has unwilled twitches, jerks, (Nervous habits, fidgets, etc.)	23	N 9.21 Q 1.52 W 1.47	NV 1.70 UR 1.59	N/Q 6.06 Q/W 1.03	8	N 4.27 H 2.81 Q 2.40	GD 4.58 AT 3.72	N/H 1.52 H/Q 1.17	2.86
Bites nails badly (Nervous habits)	24	N 5.46 H 1.95 Q 1.92	NV 2.75 PM 2.60	N/H 2.80 H/Q 1.02	20	N 2.04 D 1.99 W 1.66	PM 2.44 AT 2.18	N/D 1.02 D/W 1.20	1.20
Gets confused and tongue tied (Answering questions)	128	N 3.27 U 2.28 D 1.69	UR 1.93 NV 1.17	U/D 1.35	100	N 2.76 U 2.40 W 2.38	UR 2.99 AT 1.39 GD 1.28	U/W 1.01	1.28

of some makes it difficult to place them. Very little truancy, for example, was reported, but as in the original classification published in 1956 it is related to the variety of basic types of disturbance. It is evident that behaviours involving breach of the law or violation of norms have to be interpreted diagnostically by the general pattern of maladjustment of the individual case.

Three of the Non-syndromic Overreacting items describe formally delinquent, that is illegal, behaviour (vandalism, theft and damage to the personal possessions of others). They were eleven, thirty-three and seventeen times more frequent among the worst compared with among the best adjusted—in other words they were characteristic of very maladjusted boys and girls. This is at variance with the tendency in recent years to explain delinquency mainly along cultural lines and to deny or minimize the personal factor of intrinsic behaviour disturbance. This issue is further discussed in relation to the findings on the delinquents within the sample in Chapter Twelve.

There remained a *Neurological* grouping of six items, as in Table V. 11, which showed good syndromic clustering and specificity. They are not motivated behaviours, but maladaptive at the mechanical level of dysfunction. The most characteristic, with very high S-S ratios for N, had overreacting core syndromes of Q or H as runners-up, which suggests some neurological impairment in the predisposition to such behaviour. They are reminiscent of the cowardice of supposedly tough delinquent youths when faced with dental treatment.

6
Unract-Ovract

Under- and over-arousal—Unforthcomingness as an under-estimation by the individual of his power to change his environment (effectiveness-deficit)—pervasive inhibitory impairment in Inconsequence—its aggressive aspects link with the predisposition to overreaction in Hostility—negative correlation of Unract and Ovract scores—Extraversion and Introversion statistical artifacts—the quantification of maladjustment—the Unract/Ovract compromise—validation of the items in terms of their discriminatory power in Unract or Ovract.

If, in the processing of sensory information, a situation has been appraised as significant (in terms of opportunity or danger) the next stages are, first, arousal, and second, the choice of the appropriate executive response. We should therefore be able to discern types of maladaptive behaviour which arise from dysfunction of these stages of the behavioural system. To what extent under- or over-arousal may be due to abnormal function of the limbic system is beyond the scope of this monograph.

Under-arousal is seen at its purest in the syndrome of Depression. Whether it be from constitutional deficiency or exhaustion—or a combination of both—the affected individual fails to respond to opportunities for fulfilment and in extreme cases does not react to danger. He does not bring into play the first among the hierarchy of executive reactions—that of applying greater mental and/or physical resources when faced with frustration.

At the other pole we find individuals in whom the arousal mechanisms are set on too fine a spring. Local neural damage excepted, the six Neurological items may indicate this form of dysfunction: the over-readiness to behave, at the physiological level, is seen in spontaneous activation of the skeletal muscles, just as normal individuals will tremble in moments of extreme fear or excitement. The association between this neurological hypersensitivity and the overreacting behavioural syndromes of Q and H has already been noted.

For the choice of the appropriate executive response the individual has to carry out a further monitoring of the stimulus-situation. He has to assess the task of effecting a change as within, or beyond his powers. If the threat or challenge is viewed as 'weaker than me', the executive response is that of attack or coping; if it is 'stronger than me' the response is that of avoiding. This fundamental dichotomy of the decision-process is reflected in the overreacting and underreacting poles of abnormal behaviour.

Unforthcomingness may be conceptualized as a tendency to assess the stimulus as 'stronger then me'. It was suggested that this might be due to an impairment of effectiveness-motivation. The affected individual is content to tolerate relationships

70

with his environment which afford him only a minimal, static range of effectiveness. He lacks the determination with which to overcome difficulties, and prefers to function within a familiar, well-practised sphere. It may be that the Unforthcoming child is constitutionally not abnormally anxious or apprehensive, but that he lacks the urge to overcome normal anxiety or apprehensiveness. Essential aspects of effectiveness-motivation are the demand for independence—to be allowed to cope with challenges oneself—and the conquering of one's own inhibiting fears. Of the latter Murphy (1962, pp. 168—90) quotes several good examples in a girl of four years, who is able to verbalize about her determination to overcome her fear of a jumping board, of thunder and a jet plane, and of visits to the dentist. By mastering problems the balance of assessment swings towards the 'weaker than me' side of the scale: the child progressively gains the confidence to cope with problems of greater complexity. Conversely, the child who has not a sufficiently strong effectiveness-urge allows his apprehensiveness to dominate him: he becomes conditioned to rely upon others for help, and perhaps to assume a consistent role of incompetence which is diagnosed as 'dullness'. This restriction of effectiveness to a narrow, familiar sphere of function, with the concomitant apprehensiveness and dependence, affords us a complete definition of Unforthcomingness.

Dysfunction in the direction of being over-sanguine—having too much confidence and courage—can equally be maladaptive, and under primitive conditions could have had lethal results. For the choice of the appropriate executive response there has to be a balance between the urge to meet challenges and the cautionary inhibition which gives enough time for a rehearsal of the probable consequences of the proposed act. This balance can be upset either because of an excessive urge to establish progressively more effective relationships à la Napoleon, which exceeds the person's resources of inhibition; or by an impairment of the inhibitory mechanisms as in Inconsequence. In our contemporary Western culture the first—that of overconfidence—would be rated as a good personality-trait, even though it occasionally results in serious mistakes or injury. Some superficially hyperactive pre-school children fall into this category; they can be distinguished from those whose hyperactivity is due to inhibitional failure by the constructive, goal-directed style of their behaviour. For the study of maladjustment we can limit ourselves to overreacting due to inhibitional failure, which may be associated with only very moderate effectiveness-needs. Indeed, one remarks how easily some Inconsequent children can accept a style of coping which includes the avoidance of all complex—and especially intellectual—tasks and is limited to primitive physical forms of domination. Typical of Inconsequence, then, is any exploitation of opportunities for effectiveness which does not demand reflection or forethought. It is often accompanied by a failure to inhibit attack-responses to frustration. His inhibitional failure thus makes the Inconsequent child a consistent overreactor on two counts—his indiscriminate, hit-and-miss bids for effectiveness, and his aggressive lack of control.

Faced with a given degree of family-insecurity and parental rejection one child will remain phlegmatic while another will react by hostility. A mother threatens to run away. Some of her sons shrug it off, saying, 'She won't'; another gets upset, runs away, steals at home and in school. Uncontrolled, life-dominating hostility would seem to rest upon a predisposition to an over-arousal of the elemental attack and avoidance reactions from which the hostility-response seems to have evolved.

The same predisposition to overreaction which makes the Inconsequent child respond aggressively to frustration underlies the reversion to Hostility.

In sum, it is not hard to hypothesize a number of different dysfunctions of the behavioural system which will cause some children to overreact and some to under-react. At an early stage of our classification a marked tendency to react consistently in one direction or another became apparent, and in our across-the-table research-group talks we used the terms 'Unract' and 'Ovract'. In the scorer/non-scorer ratios the runner-up syndrome was nearly always on the same side of this dichotomy.

A product-moment correlation between Unract and Ovract scores gave a near-zero result of −.0154, indicating virtually no relationship. The large number of zero scores rendered the use of this statistical measure of dubious value in that it would have prevented the emergence of a significant correlation. There are, in addition, reasons for suspecting random factors in the low scores (1-2 in Unract and 1-3 in Ovract) associated with good general adjustment. It has been earlier pointed out that a single behaviour is unreliable as an indication of maladjustment. Theoretically this would be even more true of behaviours which—even though they are good indicators of maladjustment in general—occur in isolation within an over-all picture of good adjustment. Special situational factors—the pattern of family upbringing, the peer-group sub-culture, ill-health, accommodation to physical defect, etc.—may stimulate behaviours which meet descriptions of 'maladjusted' items but which in their context are adaptive. Allowances must also be made for differences in teachers' ideas as to what constitutes, say, over-talkativeness; it would be too great a feat of description to guarantee that the teachers' judgments of the border line between an adaptive and a maladaptive re-sponse were always drawn at exactly the same place. Finally, in choosing among over one hundred items, some teachers are going to misconstrue an item now and then.

These sources of error among the low scorers are likely to blur the general relationship between Unract and Ovract. Consequently a further correlation was carried out excluding all children having 'well-adjusted' scores both in Unract (0-2) and in Ovract (0-3). This gave coefficients of −.3168 for the boys, −.4196 for the girls and −.3625 for both sexes. The marked dichotomous tendency in the Unract and Ovract scores revealed by these inverse correlations show that there is no common factor of 'maladjustment' corresponding to the postulated g of 'intel-ligence'. It is tempting to conceptualize Unract and Ovract as two fundamental behavioural dimensions. But—following the principle in the classification of biological phenomena put forward at the beginning of this monograph—this would be justified only if the dichotomy rested upon a single or common set of antecedents in the form of evolved structures. But the broad division into Unract and Ovract may be the phenotypic end-result of disparate dysfunctions of different origin, each of which affect the response style of the individual in a somewhat similar manner. Unless each wing of the dichotomy can be shown to arise from some 'disease-entity' within the behavioural system, we are not justified in erecting either of them into fundamental principles of taxonomy. Extraversion and Introversion are statistical artifacts each embracing discrete modes of behaviour, both adaptive and maladaptive. One person may be classed as an extravert because he is a resolute 'coper' with abnormally high effectiveness-needs; another may be a stimulus-dominated Inconsequent who sets himself low standards of effectiveness. The affectionate but apprehensive introvert bears only a superficial resemblance to one who is placid from lack of motivation, or to another whose withdrawal from human relationships arises from a deep distrust of human affiliations.

Nevertheless, there are factors making for a certain cohesiveness between the indications of Unract on the one hand and Ovract on the other. With Unract it may be nothing more than the previously noted difficulty of discriminating, by a teacher within the classroom, between varieties of not-behaving. With Ovract there is the chain of social interactions by which Inconsequence tends to generate Hostility, and the possibility of a common factor of inhibitional failure which pervades several aspects of the control of behaviour and emotion.

In Unract and Ovract we have, in sum, conglomerations of behaviour which phenotypically have a certain similarity in that the one consists of underreacting and one of overreacting types of maladjusted response. Each, however, contains discrete components which render them of little theoretical or diagnostic value in themselves. Nevertheless they serve some purpose in providing a basis of comparability within each broad type of response, and hence may be useful in assessing, equally broadly, the validity of behavioural items as indicators of maladjustment of one type or the other.

The quantification of maladjustment

To what extent we are justified in summating syndrome frequencies to give a total score for maladjustment depends upon the use to which the latter is put. For the diagnosis of the individual case it is obviously better to retain the scores for the separate syndromes and their associated groupings. The same would apply in experimental studies where the behavioural variables need to be defined precisely. Examples are research into the relationships between behaviour disturbance and reading disability, stressful family situation and delinquency, illness and genetic constitution. When it comes to surveys of the prevalence of maladjustment within a juvenile population, there is an obvious convenience in, and excuse for, an over-all parameter. This would correspond to a statistic of the incidence of disease within a community. Nevertheless, the adding together of symptoms to form a score poses a conceptual and philosophical dilemma. How can we say that one sympton, or one type of disturbance is, ultimately, more serious than another? We do not know enough about prognosis to say that a Withdrawn child will present greater or less problems to himself and to society than an Inconsequent one. And whether a demonstrably hostile delinquent is to be preferred to an unmotivated Depressive is a matter of personal or cultural predilection.

The compromise that we accepted in the following analysis of the incidence of behaviour disturbance as between the sexes, age-groupings and social class was that of the Unract-Overact dichotomy. Theoretically this is open to the same objections as those against an over-all maladjustment score; but the external similarity of each type of behaviour and the contrasts they offer to each other do something to absolve us from the elementary arithmetical fault of adding quantities of unlike objects. The offence, in short, is reminiscent of the plea of the servant girl who had an illegitimate baby, that it was a little one.

Item-validation in terms of Unract/Ovract

When it comes to the validation of the items of a behavioural schedule it is obviously more meaningful to do so by examining their association with an array of items which intercorrelate than with an array consisting of two negatively correlating groupings such as Unract and Ovract. The latter finding demonstrates that there is no 'general factor' in maladjustment. The discriminatory value of the items is therefore better judged in terms of the broad dichotomy of underreacting and overreacting behaviour.

Separate item-validations were carried out according to whether the items were members of the syndromes or groupings forming Unract or Ovract. The results are expressed in indices registering, for the Unract items, how much more frequently each item was marked among children scoring highly in Unract (9 or over) compared with among the low Unract scorers (0-2); and, correspondingly for the Ovract items, how much more frequently each item was marked for high Ovract scorers (13 or more) than among the low Ovract scorers (0-3). They were calculated by age-groups for both sexes together, and for all ages for boys and girls separately. The tabulated results are too lengthy to reproduce in this monograph, but are given in the Manual to the Bristol Social Adjustment Guides (Stott 1974).

TABLE VI.1 Discriminatory power of items as indicators of underreacting or overreacting maladjustment

| | Means of indices of item-validity (ratios of high/low scorer frequencies) | |
	Unweighted	*Weighted*
UNRACT items:		
boys	38.27	28.91
girls	35.00	31.56
OVRACT items:		
boys	33.78	31.64
girls	42.31	39.73

In the second column the means are weighted according
to the number of cases scoring the items

The means of these indices for all items in Unract and Ovract are given in Table VI.1. They show that, on average, the Unract items discriminate between strongly underreacting and not-underreacting children by a factor of between twenty-eight and thirty; and between strongly overreacting and not-overreacting children by one of between thirty-two and forty. It is claimed that this represents a satisfactory degree of validity of the items, and—unless the conception of maladjustment embodied in the items chosen is quite out of accord with reality—of the instrument as a whole. Naturally the items show considerable variation in their discriminatory value. The distribution is summarized in Table VI.2.

TABLE VI.2 Distribution of ratios of high/low scorer frequencies

	Less than 10	≥10 <20	≥20 <30	≥30 <50	≥50 <100	≥100	Total
UNRACT, boys	10	9	8	5	5	4	41
girls	8	9	10	4	7	3	41
OVRACT, boys	6	21	13	14	7	3	64
girls	8	9	12	13	19	3	64

Inspection of the mean high/low scorer ratios as given in Table VI.1 shows that for both forms of maladjustment they are higher for girls; in other words, the items chosen are on the whole somewhat more definitive indicators of maladjustment for girls than for boys. Not much significance can be attached to the sex difference in the Unract means, but for Ovract it is considerable. One explanation may be that, although girls are less prone to overreacting forms of maladjustment, those who are so react in a more definitive and extreme manner.

7

Incidence by sex and age

Previous studies of sex-incidence—attempts to estimate total incidence—distribution of Unract and Ovract scores for both sexes—the same for the sexes separately—sex-ratios by type of maladjustment—Unforthcomingness more prevalent among girls— Boys have twice the incidence in W, D and Q—doubts about attribution to learned sex roles—consistent sex differences point to genetic determination—greater biological vulnerability of males.

Virtually no age-differences in Unract scores—increase in Ovract scores with age in boys, and in pubertal girls—trend of the main types of maladjustment by year of age.

Sex differences

Almost universally a greater incidence of behaviour disturbance has been reported for boys than for girls. From a review of twenty-three studies Glidewell and Swallow (1968) found that about three times as many boys are maladjusted. One suspects, however, that some of these surveys had an anti-male bias because they were of cases referred for anti-social or 'problem' behaviour; parents and teachers are more likely to seek outside help in respect of children who are difficult to manage than in respect of the withdrawn and inhibited. In only two of the studies summarized was there a greater incidence of any type of disturbance among girls, and these were in respect of 'nervous habits' and 'withdrawn' behaviour. Estimating on the basis of a 3:1 ratio the above authors suggest as the best approximations that 45 per cent of boys and 15 per cent of girls show some school maladjustment, and 15 and 5 per cent respectively need some professional attention. The former figures seem unrealistically high until it is appreciated that we are dealing with a continuum rather than a discrete condition. Findings from surveys using the BSAG demonstrate this continuum clearly, but the criteria used for maladjustment (score of 20 or more) and for 'unsettledness' (score of 10-19) give a rather lower incidence. To give a realistic picture of what the criterion score of 20 meant, the items marked for three borderline cases with this score were listed to form descriptions (Stott 1966a). These showed that the children in question must have been seriously handicapped in their social relations, happiness and academic progress on account of their behaviour disturbance.

The most representative findings based on the BSAG are summarized in Table VII.1. In broad summary, the above data show that between 11 and 15 per cent of boys and 8 per cent of girls could be rated as maladjusted in Britain in the 1960s. In addition some 23 per cent of the boys and 18 per cent of the girls qualified as

TABLE VII.1 Summary of three surveys of maladjustment in Britain (percentages in each adjustment category)

Sample	Age-range in years	N	Stable and Quasi-stable (0 - 9)	Unsettled (10 - 19)	Maladjusted (20 +)
			%	%	%
BOYS					
Controls of truants (Britain)	6 - 15	429	69.7	19.1	11.2
Random sample (Crawford, Liverpool)	7 - 8	387	62.4	23.1	14.8
Classes in secondary schools (Chazan[1], Swansea)	13 - 14+	211	61.6	27.5	10.9
GIRLS					
Controls of truants (Britain)	16 - 15	169	75.7	16.0	8.3
Random sample (Crawford, Liverpool)	7 - 8	386	72.6	19.7	7.8
Classes in secondary schools (Chazan[1], Swansea)	13 - 14+	211	73.5	19.0	7.6

[1] Chazan 1963.

'Unsettled', or as showing some degree of disturbance. It will be noted that the bigger sex difference is in the more severe category.

The point at which a child is adjudged maladjusted depends upon the administrative or clinical purpose of the assessment. In a survey in the Isle of Wight, in southern England, Rutter and Graham (1966) attempted an estimate of the number of children suffering from 'psychiatric disorders', defined presumably as those needing the help of a psychiatrist. They arrived at the figure of 6.3 per cent, of which 2.2 per cent suffered from severe disorders. As in every estimate the criterion used is influenced by contemporary concepts of pathology and normality. All that can be said with confidence is that the numbers requiring treatment exceed by many times the resources available.

Of greater scientific interest than over-all estimates using necessarily arbitrary criteria is the relative incidence of behaviour disturbance by sex, age and social class. In the present study adjustment categories were established by scores on Unract and Ovract items which gave comparable over-all percentages for each of these two dimensions. These are given in Table VII.2. The score-groupings for Ovract are larger because there is a larger number of such items in the schedule. The mean scores and standard deviations for each of the two broad divisions over the whole sample were:

	Mean Score	*S.D.*
Unract	2.91	3.71
Ovract	3.96	5.95

TABLE VII.2 Score-groupings in Unract and Ovract

Unract score group	*Number of cases*	*Per cent*	*Ovract score group*	*Number of cases*	*Per cent*
0 - 2	1547	61.22	0 - 3	1686	66.92
3 - 5	506	20.02	4 - 7	346	13.69
6 - 8	233	9.22	8 - 12	203	8.03
9+	241	9.54	13+	292	11.56
Total	2527	100.00	Total	2527	100.00

Table VII.3 shows that in Unract the girls had only a slight advantage, marginally more of them being in the best-adjusted (0-2) score-group, and marginally fewer in the next-to-worst-adjusted group (6-8).

The higher incidence of disturbance among boys is almost entirely accounted for by their higher Ovract scores, as seen in Table VII.4, and Figures VII.1 and 2 overleaf. There are over 2½ times as many boys in the worst-adjusted category, and over twice as many in the two worst combined. This is offset by 33 per cent more girls in the best-adjusted category. The percentages of maladjustment for each sex are given in Chapter Ten (Table X.8 and Figure X.4) in relation to proneness to multiple impairment.

A finer analysis was made of the differences of type of maladjustment in boys and girls by calculating sex-ratios for all items. These represented the incidence among boys divided by that among girls. Thus an exactly equal incidence in each sex would give a ratio of one, a preponderance among boys a ratio of greater than

TABLE VII.3 Incidence of Unract by sexes

Score group	BOYS Number	Per cent	GIRLS Number	Per cent
0 - 2	777	59.54	770	63.01
3 - 5	269	20.61	237	19.39
6 - 8	133	10.19	100	8.18
9+	126	9.66	115	9.41
Total	1305	100.00	1222	100.00

Mean 3.05   Mean 2.84

$t = 1.4103$ not significant

TABLE VII.4 Incidence of Ovract by sexes

Score group	BOYS Number	Per cent	GIRLS Number	Per cent
0 - 3	751	57.55	935	76.51
4 - 7	209	16.02	137	11.21
8- 12	165	12.64	84	6.87
13+	180	13.79	66	5.40
Total	1305	100.00	1222	100.00

Mean 5.15   Mean 2.76

$t = 8.7165$ $p < .001$

one, and a preponderance among girls a ratio of less than one. The sex-ratios for each item within a syndrome or grouping were then averaged to give a measure of the relative incidence of each type of maladjustment for each sex. The results are given in Table VII.5 with notes on intra-syndromic variability. They may be compared with the percentages of boys and girls rated as maladjusted which are given in Table X.8.

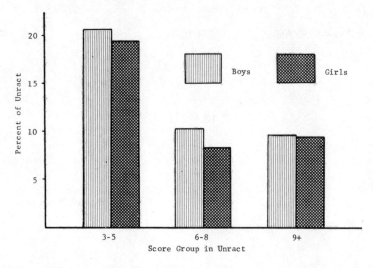

Figure VII.1   Incidence of Underreacting Maladjustment among boys and girls

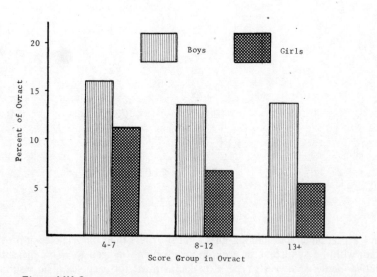

Figure VII.2   Incidence of Overreacting Maladjustment among boys and girls

TABLE VII.5 Sex-ratios of relative incidence of types of maladjustment

Type	Mean ratio M/F	Intra-syndromic variability
Unforthcomingness	0.85	Fairly consistent by item
Withdrawal	1.82	Fairly consistent by item
Depression	2.00	Fairly consistent by item
Hostility	1.75	Provocative, norm-violating, aggressive manifestations have the higher ratios (3.85 - 1.67); the moody have the lower (1.79 - 1.14)
Inconsequence (Q)	2.30	Very consistent (all items except one greater than 2.0)
Attention-seeking	1.49	Great variability: very high for attention-seeking by boisterous or disruptive behaviour, less than unity for excessive 'socializing'
Peer-aggression	2.20	Great variability: physical aggression very high (7.14 - 2.00)
Peer-deviance	4.41	Variable but always high (7.14 - 2.38)
Undifferentiated anti-social	3.56	Very high except for lying (but still greater than unity)
Neurological	2.03	High for involuntary movements

Unforthcomingness, with a ratio of less than unity, was the only basic type of behaviour disturbance more prevalent among the girls. Depression was twice as prevalent among boys, and Withdrawal nearly so. This further confirms U as a mode of disturbance distinct from other types of underreacting, overly inhibited or 'introverted' behaviour. The only other place where the markings for girls exceeded those for the boys was for the items in the attention-seeking group which described attempts at excessive social interaction (talking, seeking help, overfriendly general manner). Boisterous and disruptive forms of attention-seeking were more characteristic of the boys.

It will be noted that while deviant and other anti-social behaviour is, as expected, very much more prevalent among males, they are also on average about twice as prone to the basic patterns of disturbance of W, D and Q. It is fashionable at the present time to attribute behavioural differences in boys and girls to learned sex roles. Aggressive and anti-social types of behaviour may be conceivably explained in this way. But it is hard to see how this explanation can be applied to the greater amount of withdrawn, depressed or thoughtless-impulsive behaviour among males; in Western culture these are no more condoned or encouraged among boys than among girls. In their review of possible reasons for sex differences in

81

TABLE VII.6 Percentage distribution of Unract scores by age-groups

Age-groups (to birthdays)	Score Groups 0 - 2	3 - 5	6 - 8	9+	N in age-group	Mean score for age-group
			BOYS			
5 - 8	56.4	23.0	9.4	11.2	374	3.20
8 - 11	64.5	16.2	10.6	8.7	425	2.75
11 - 14	57.3	23.5	10.1	9.1	417	3.16
14+	59.6	18.0	12.4	10.1	89	3.35
					1305	
			GIRLS			
5 - 8	67.0	14.5	7.1	11.4	351	2.86
8 - 11	63.7	21.7	6.6	8.1	410	2.63
11 - 14	58.8	22.1	10.2	8.9	381	2.98
14+	62.5	16.3	11.3	10.0	80	3.18
					1222	

No difference between the means for the age-groups reach the .05 level of significance.

behaviour disturbance Glidewell and Swallow (1968) point out that boys have higher mortality and morbidity rates, and show a greater biological vulnerability in many ways. Among 450 mentally normal controls used by Stott (1957) in a study of the aetiology of mental retardation, nearly twice as many boys as girls were recorded as suffering from serious non-epidemic illness in the first three years of life (22.8 per cent of the boys, 12.2 of the girls). The proportion is very similar to the greater incidence of primary maladjustment among boys as shown by the mean sex-ratios for the core syndromes in Table VII.5. A genetic determinant of common childhood illnesses has been demonstrated by concordance in twins (Marshall et al. 1962). If there is a foundation of neurological dysfunction for the main types of behaviour disturbance, it would be reasonable to hypothesize that in these also sex differences can be accounted for, at least in part, along the same lines.

Age differences

In Tables VII.6 and 7 the distributions of the Unract and Ovract scores are analysed by sex and age-groups.

The breakdown by age-groups reveals surprisingly small variations: there was thus apparently little or no age bias in the choice of the behavioural items. The figures for the over-fourteens must be accepted with reserve since the subjects in

TABLE VII.7 Percentage distribution of Ovract scores by age-groups

Age-group (to birthdays)	Score Groups				N in age-group	Mean score for age-group
	0 - 3	4 - 7	8 - 12	13+		
BOYS						
5 - 8	63.6	14.2	12.6	9.6	374	4.24
8 - 11	55.5	16.5	12.2	15.8	425	5.73
11 - 14	55.2	17.0	11.5	16.3	417	5.44
14+	52.8	16.9	20.2	10.1	89	4.84
					1305	
GIRLS						
5 - 8	75.8	12.8	6.8	4.6	351	2.72
8 - 11	77.3	11.7	6.6	4.4	410	2.60
11 - 14	76.1	9.2	7.1	7.6	381	3.03
14+	77.5	11.3	7.5	3.8	80	2.50
					1222	

The only significant differences between the means for the age-groups are those for boys between the youngest and the next youngest ($p. < .01$) and between the youngest and the 11–14-year-olds ($p. < .05$).

question were atypical in having stayed behind a year longer than usual in elementary school.

In the Unract types of maladjustment hardly any trend for age is discernible either for boys or girls. There is a regular improvement for both sexes between the youngest and next-youngest age-groups, which could be due to a gain in confidence or familiarization with the school situation. More definite conclusions about this must await the analysis by type of disturbance at each age-group reported below. The same applies to the apparent deterioration in the eleven to fourteen age-group, where there is a suggestive fall in the percentage in the best-adjusted (0-2) category and corresponding rises in those scoring six or more. This could be related to pubertal changes. The slightly higher means for the over-fourteens could be due to an excess of Unforthcomingness, a form of behaviour disturbance associated with learning disability.

In the Ovract types of maladjustment the boys show a distinct deterioration after their eighth birthday, both by the reduction in the percentage of the best adjusted and the rise of that for the worst adjusted. Partly this could be due to a growing confidence in being aggressive or to the growth in Hostility as an

TABLE VII.8 Trends of mean scores for syndromes by year-groups

BOYS

Age (No.)	U	W	D	Q	H	Ovract	Unract	BSAG
5- 6 (88)	1.83	0.56	0.32	1.43	0.49	3.20	3.47	6.76
6- 7 (146)	1.52	0.47	0.49	1.74	0.51	3.71	3.01	6.80
7- 8 (140)	1.37	0.54	0.61	2.40	0.86	5.32	3.15	8.55
8- 9 (160)	1.14	0.46	0.55	2.77	0.83	6.30	2.56	9.11
9-10 (139)	1.09	0.62	0.55	1.80	0.93	5.01	2.75	7.86
10-11 (126)	1.32	0.44	0.64	2.11	1.10	5.70	2.97	8.77
11-12 (140)	1.49	0.58	0.99	2.27	1.30	6.22	3.54	9.94
12.13 (160)	1.26	0.48	0.74	1.72	1.02	4.58	3.02	7.72
13-14 (117)	0.95	0.65	0.74	1.67	1.39	5.59	2.75	8.48

GIRLS

Age (No.)	U	W	D	Q	H	Ovract	Unract	BSAG
5- 6 (71)	2.17	0.49	0.35	1.05	0.59	2.32	3.71	6.08
6- 7 (122)	1.57	0.34	0.23	1.12	0.52	2.43	2.71	5.21
7- 8 (158)	1.44	0.29	0.37	1.42	0.52	3.02	2.58	5.68
8- 9 (137)	1.56	0.18	0.30	0.99	0.54	2.47	2.65	5.17
9-10 (136)	1.28	0.17	0.23	0.94	0.47	2.35	2.09	4.54
10-11 (137)	1.75	0.27	0.35	1.04	0.83	2.85	2.93	5.89
11-12 (134)	1.70	0.26	0.26	1.28	0.77	3.07	2.61	5.72
12.13 (146)	1.61	0.30	0.43	1.02	0.89	2.88	2.77	5.69
13-14 (101)	1.88	0.56	0.59	0.99	0.95	3.06	3.58	6.71

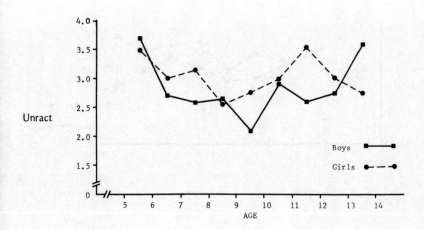

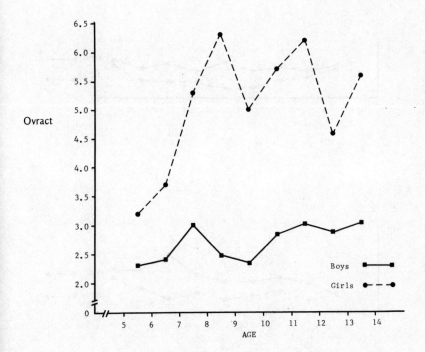

Figure VII.3   Mean scores in Unract and Ovract by age

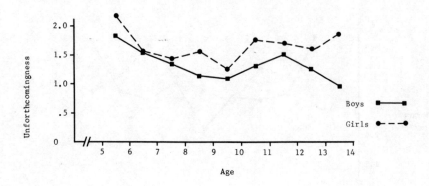

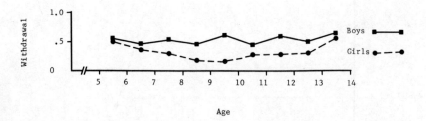

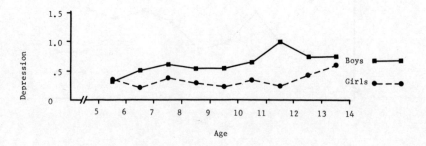

Figure VII.4   Mean scores in Underreacting core syndromes by age

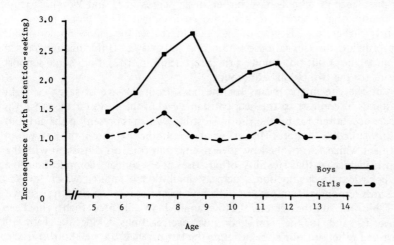

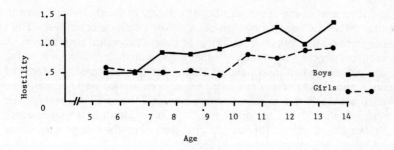

Figure VII.5 Mean scores in Overreacting core syndromes by age

environmental complication. Once more, analysis by type of maladjustment is needed before definite conclusions can be drawn. The Ovract distribution for girls shows an interesting picture. Their representation in the worst-adjusted category over all age-groups is only 39 per cent of that for the boys, but they show a significant jump in the eleven to fourteen age-group, which is confirmed by the rise in the mean score. This is reminiscent of the popular impression of pubertal unsettledness of a certain number of girls of that age, evidenced in the hysterical adulation of pop singers and in religious emotionality. At all age-levels, over three-quarters of the girls fall into the best-adjusted Ovract score-group.

The incidence of the main types of maladjustment at each year of age, from birthday to birthday, is shown in Table VII.8 and the graphs in Figures VII.3, 4 and 5. It will be noted, first, that the relative constancy of the Unract scores found in the analysis by age-groups is confirmed. Children between the ages of five and six—their first year in school—have higher mean scores in U and W, which is no doubt a quasinormal response to a strange environment. The Unract means are consequently higher for this year of age, but thereafter they show no consistent trend. Nevertheless the clinical observation of a fall-away of Unforthcomingness at puberty among boys but not among girls (Stott 1966, p. 182), finds some support in the means for the two oldest year-groups.

In Ovract the rise in the means for the boys from the age of seven or eight onwards stands in contrast to the near-constant level of the curve for the girls. It is in large part accounted for by the rise in Hostility, which is present in the girls but not to so marked a degree. This is what would be expected of a type of maladjustment which is provoked by adverse environment. It is consistent with the suggestion made earlier that Hostility often arises as a secondary complication to a primary behavioural dysfunction, such as inhibitional failure, which evokes rejecting stress-responses from parents. There were corresponding rises, not shown in the Table or in the graphs but examined in Chapter Eight, in Peer Maladaptiveness and in the non-syndromic overreactions taking the form of delinquent and other anti-social behaviour. The last parallels the well-known rise in delinquency rates up to the age of thirteen or fourteen years, and can be explained—with differing emphasis according to predilection—as the result of growing confidence in making pseudo-adjustments or of the learning of patterns of deviant behaviour.

While an increase in a type of maladjustment with age can fairly be attributed to environmental influences, constancy cannot be held to indicate basic dysfunction due to impairment of the neural structures or of their biochemical environment. A child can recover naturally from such dysfunctions, and their incidence may fall with age, as has been noted in asthma. The trend for the combined syndrome of Inconsequence and Attention-seeking, which has been attributed to inhibitional dysfunction, produces bi-modal curves with peaks at 7-9 and 11-13 years in the boys, and at 7-8 and 11-12 for girls. It is as if one pattern of Inconsequence becomes displaced by another. This will be discussed when the changing incidence of individual items is examined in the next chapter.

8
Phenotypic and genotypic continuity

Kagan's concepts of genotypic continuity and phenotypic discontinuity—application to the core syndromes—shift in prominence of the behavioural symptoms with age—absolute frequency of items within each age-group—strong phenotypic continuity in Unract items—increase of Depression and Hostility with age—genotypic continuity observed in inhibitional failure— the general picture otherwise of phenotypic continuity.

Wright, it was earlier noted, questioned the value of classifying behaviour by phenotypic similarity, and Bronfenbrenner accepted as a valid principle of classification a similarity of goal or end-state, even though the actual behaviour may be different. Kagan (1969) has postulated an underlying, or genotypic continuity despite phenotypic discontinuity: 'A core set of basic dimensions ties one epoch of development to the next ... Some processes remain stable but find expression in different actions at different times.'

The ideal test for Kagan's thesis would be to follow a number of individuals from near birth to adulthood. He and Moss (1962) were able to do this with seventy-one adults by comparing data from the case-records of the Fels Behavior Institute with contemporary assessments. As an example of genotypic continuity he quotes a failure to meet traditional standards of masculinity. In boys between six and ten years this was seen in their passivity in times of stress; as adults they did not show such passivity in most stress situations, but did not get involved in heterosexual relationships, avoided competitive activities and vocations and had non-masculine interests. Kagan quotes in addition two short-term follow-up studies in support of his thesis. In that by Emmerich (1964) children who were just over three years of age at the beginning of the study were observed during four consecutive semesters at nursery school. Complete (i.e. phenotypic and genotypic) continuity was observed for introversion-extroversion, but children who had been extroversive and mildly hostile (aggressive?) became socially poised and non-aggressive. The underlying genotypic continuity, Kagan suggests, may have been 'a high expectancy of adult acceptance' which enabled the three-year-old to be a little undisciplined but amenable to social learning by the age of five. Similarly, children who had been introversive and socially cooperative became socially insecure and awkward, the underlying genotypic continuity in this case being—Kagan suggests—anxiety over adult acceptance. In the second study (Bryam 1966) peer-aggression among three-year-old boys predicted masculine-role play and assertiveness at five years. Social isolation at three had no phenotypic counterpart at five, but rather a genotypic continuity in the form of feminine-role behaviour. Kagan postulated 'the occurrence of transformations in the external form of responses while underlying dimensions remain stable over time'.

The experimental verification of this concept requires, first, that the same sequence of phenotypic discontinuity appears regularly in successive investigations. If it does not there is no point in attempting *post hoc* interpretations. Second, there must be some measure of agreement as to the basic dimension responsible for any observed regularity. There is obviously some advantage in accepting as the integrating factor dimensions which already have some experimental foundation such as would be provided by syndromic clustering. The core syndromes which emerged from the present study meet these requirements to some degree. For each the integrating factor was defined in terms of a type of relationship which the agent tends to establish with his environment. In Unforthcomingness it was one of retreat from complexities and other tests of competence, in other words a low level of effectiveness-motivation. In Withdrawal it was a retreat from affectional relationships, in Depression an unwillingness to respond to stimuli which are ordinarily motivating, in Inconsequence a failure to inhibit first impulses, in Hostility the destruction of an unreliable affectional relationship. These criteria may be used as touchstones of motivation or of underlying dysfunction, as the case may be, with a reasonable measure of agreement. If, consequently, behaviour observed at different ages can be placed in the same category, even though they are phenotypically dissimilar, we can proceed to the experimental verification of the hypothesis of genotypic continuity.

Two procedures were used as a means of ascertaining the degree to which phenotypic or genotypic continuity existed in the present sample. The first set out to answer the question: If a child suffers from a given type of maladjustment, will this be evidenced by similar behaviours at each age, or will some be more characteristic of younger and some of older children? The ratios described in Chapter Six—showing how much more frequently each item was marked for the maladjusted compared with the well-adjusted children—were used as a basis. A high ratio indicated that the behaviour described by the item is typical of children of a given age. If an item shifts from the position of having a high ratio within its syndrome among young children to that of having a low one for older children, we may say that it is a typical manifestation of maladjustment for the young age-group but not of the older. Within each syndrome all the items (marked for a minimum of ten cases) were accordingly ranked by their ratios in each of the age categories up to fourteen years, and shifts in position noted. The criterion of a significant shift was a change in rank from the top to the bottom third, or the reverse. Consistent with the final classification, the Inconsequent and Attention-seeking syndromes were amalgamated, and Peer-Group Deviance was added to Non-syndromic Overreaction.

Of the 108 items nineteen showed a significant shift, but five did so inconsistently or cancelled each other out. Among the remaining fourteen, certain trends could be discerned. Four Unract items descriptive of extreme timidity, passivity or social isolation moved from a high rank in the under-eights to a low rank in the 11-14 and 14+ year groups. This could be due to the school environment being more familiar and less threatening to an older child, or a natural recovery from Unforthcomingness and Withdrawal at puberty. Of the Ovract items those listed below moved from the top to the bottom third, and so were more characteristic of younger children. The ranks in the four age-groups (from birthday to birthday: under 8, 8-11, 11-14, over 14) are given in brackets, a dash indicating insufficient cases.

Flies into a temper if provoked (6, 7, 12, 14)
Bad loser (4, 4, 9, 8)
Snatches things from other children (2, 2, 10, -)
Habitual slick liar, has no compunction about lying (4, 1, 12, -)
Mixes mostly with unsettled types (1, 9, 13, 7)

The first three of these items are suggestive of an impulsivity calculated to make for bad relations with age-peers. Either it becomes modified by social learning or there is a natural recovery. It is interesting that slick lying is most characteristic of the younger maladjusted child, and especially so of those in the 8-11-year group. Certainly the child of this age who can lie 'without turning a hair' is well known clinically; possibly the adeptness is lost with the self-consciousness of adolescence. The alternative is that they became such accomplished liars as to go undetected, but few liars even of ripe years achieve such virtuosity. It is, on the other hand, a real surprise that the youngest maladjust most characteristically 'mixes with unsettled types'. It will be seen later that the older actually do so more in absolute terms, but other types of deviance in them gain even greater prominence.

The following five Ovract items shifted from the bottom to the top third as between any two age-groups, indicating that they were more characteristic of older children:

Bad sportsman (11, 1, 6, 4)
Tries to push in front of other children (5, 11, 1, -)
Seems to go out of his way to earn disapproval (13, 11, 2, 2)
Uses bad language which he knows will be disapproved (15, 11, 15, 3)
Slumps, lolls about (8, 6, 3, 1)

Apart from the first, which meets the criterion only because of an understandable low rank in the youngest age-group, the four others describe a greater confidence among the older in overt norm-violation as an expression of hostility or indifference to social approval.

It must be borne in mind that the above shifts represent changes in the relative importance of items as indicators of maladjustment at different ages. They tell us nothing about the absolute frequency of each manifestation (which is examined below). Even so, the over-all impression is a remarkable consistency in order of importance. By this form of analysis, in short, the verdict would be that the manifestations of behaviour disturbance covered by the BSAG show high phenotypic continuity between the age-groups of 5-8 and 14 years and over. This finding was confirmed by a test of the congruence of rank within each core syndrome using Kendall's coefficient of concordance, which is a non-parametric method of multiple correlation. The following coefficients relate to the three age-groups up to the fourteenth birthday for all items having ten or more cases in each. Unity indicates perfect concordance and zero perfect discordance.

Unforthcomingness	.7857	$<.01$
Withdrawal	.7119	$<.05$
Depression	.6196	$<.05$
Hostility	.6067	$<.05$
Inconsequence + Attention-seeking	.8291	$<.001$

The second method of testing the type of continuity was by an examination of the number of children scoring each item within each of the four age-groups. Since the total numbers within each age-group varied they were converted into percentages. The comparison was limited to those items with a minimum of ten cases in each age-group, and a change of incidence of 25 per cent as between any two age-groups was regarded as significant. Phenotypic discontinuity would be shown by items within a syndrome changing in opposite directions.

In the Unforthcoming syndrome twelve of the thirteen showed no significant change as between the four age-groups, and indeed their incidence was remarkably constant. The same applied to the thirteenth, 'Wants adult interest but can't put himself forward' except for its low representation among the 8-11-year-olds. In Withdrawal four showed no change and four with minimal changes showed no consistent trend. In Depression seven items showed marked rises in incidence, with no trend in the other three. In the grouping of Non-syndromic Underreaction, solitary play is about twice as frequent in the under-eights compared with the 8-14's, and four times so compared with the over-fourteens. 'Wandering off alone' drops steadily from a percentage incidence of 11.5 per cent to one of 5.3 per cent. These trends no doubt reflect the gregariousness of adolescence. Twice as many under-eights let the more forward push ahead of them as do the over-elevens.

In Hostility thirteen of the eighteen items show a steady rise with age. How marked this is up to fourteen years is shown by the rise in the mean incidence (unweighted) for those items with fifty or more cases over all age-groups:

5th to 8th birthday	4.27
8th to 11th birthday	5.83
11th to 14th birthday	7.92
Over 14	6.69*

This once more demonstrates the important experiential element in Hostility; but at every age Hostility tends to be manifested, in differing proportions, by the same behavioural phenotypes.

The changing incidence of several items in the combined syndrome of Inconsequence and Attention-seeking confirms Kagan's suggestion that inhibitional failure will be associated with a different set of pseudo-adjustments at the various ages. The young Inconsequent child is unable to inhibit gross physical activity, attention-seeking or excessive verbalizing. The older has more sophisticated means of gaining attention, but has also learnt to avoid learning and problem solving situations. The trends for the items in question are given in Table VIII.1.

In Non-syndromic Overreaction the steady rise in 'Not restless but works only when watched' from 5.52 to 11.24 per cent underlines the development of avoidance in the face of failure. The rise in two items indicative of group-deviance 'Mixes mostly with unsettled types' (4.55 to 14.20) and 'Foolish or dangerous pranks when with a gang' (1.93 to 5.92) is what would be expected. The unstable, overreacting youth tends to join with others of his sort.

By the second method of analysis, nonetheless, the general picture is once again that of a surprising phenotypic continuity in the range of maladjusted behaviour covered by the present study. Such phenotypic discontinuity as could be detected

* The atypical over-fourteens tended to be high Unract scorers.

92

TABLE VIII.1 Differing manifestations of Inconsequence at various ages

Percentage incidence

	Under 8 (725)	8 - 11 (835)	11 - 14 (798)	over 14 yrs (169)
Falls with age				
Twists about in his seat, slips onto floor, climbs about on desk	14.48	12.69	7.02	7.10
Doesn't seem to understand he should keep his seat	4.28	3.83	3.38	2.37
Constantly seeks help when he could manage alone	9.79	11.14	7.64	4.14
Talks excessively (to teacher)	5.79	5.51	4.26	1.18
Shouts out or waves arms before he has had time to think	9.38	11.50	8.14	4.14
Rises with age				
Presses for jobs but doesn't do them properly	4.55	5.51	6.39	3.55*
Never gets down to any solid work	6.62	5.87	8.40	10.65
Borrows books from desk without permission	2.48	4.43	5.39	6.51

* Six cases only

consisted in the progressive control over the years of elemental impulsivity, and the growth of anti-social pseudo-adjustments in compensation for academic failure and personal rejection. The explanation may be that the core syndromes do indeed represent basic response-patterns arising from dysfunction and/or stressing of the behavioural system. Because they are maladaptive they show comparatively little flexibility or variety. The normal child has a greater freedom in adjusting his motivations to the age, sex and social roles that he is expected to play.

9

Social-class and cultural differences

Classification of schools by socio-economic neighbourhood—near-constant Unract scores for each social class—higher Ovract scores in the Lower class accounted for by a greater number of more seriously maladjusted—comparison with British National Child Development Study—age of manifestation of disturbance as pointer to aetiology.

Rural children better adjusted than city children—similar differences found in the 'Dutch' schools—the Dutch sample: differences with father's income and occupation—comparison of Dutch with main sample taking account of rural/urban differences.

Social-class differences

For the main sample it was not possible to obtain data on social class for the cases

TABLE IX.1 Percentage distribution of Unract scores by neighbourhood socio-economic groups

Socio-economic group	Score Groups				N in s-e group	Mean Unract score
	0 - 2	3 - 5	6 - 8	9 +		
			BOYS			
Upper	58.3	19.4	10.1	12.2	139	3.36
Middle	62.7	18.0	8.9	10.4	383	2.95
Lower-Middle	53.6	24.0	11.6	10.9	267	3.31
Lower	56.1	22.6	12.8	8.5	164	3.29
			GIRLS			
Upper	71.2	10.4	8.8	9.6	125	2.69
Middle	66.7	15.2	6.9	11.2	376	2.89
Lower-Middle	60.0	22.7	10.4	6.9	260	2.82
Lower	58.1	19.6	10.8	11.5	148	3.00

No significant differences between means

individually. Since, however, the City had fairly well demarcated social-class neighbourhoods, and pupils were enrolled in neighbourhood schools, the schools were taken as socio-economic units. Officials of the Board of Education placed each elementary school in one of five groups, rated as Upper, Upper-Middle, Middle, Lower-Middle and Lower, according to the neighbourhood from which its pupils were drawn. But so few schools were placed in the Upper that it was amalgamated with the Upper-Middle, making four socio-economic neighbourhood groups. The Unract and Ovract scores are analysed, in the same way as for age, in Table IX.1 and 2, and Figures IX.1 and 2 overleaf.

The Unract distribution shows some interesting variations but no consistent trends. There are more high-scoring underreactors (9+) among the Upper than among the Lower-class boys, but this may be due to the chances of the sampling, for the position is reversed in the next highest score-class (6-8). The mean Unract scores both for boys and girls are reasonably constant for all socio-economic neighbourhood groups. There are no consistent trends and such differences as there are do not reach statistical significance.

In Ovract there is a consistent rise in the mean scores from the highest to the lowest social class among the boys, and this reaches a moderate level of significance. The same trend is discernible among the girls, but to a lesser degree.

TABLE IX.2 Percentage distribution of Ovract scores by neighbourhood socio-economic groups

Socio-economic group	0 - 3	Score Groups 4 - 7	8 - 12	13+	N in s-e group	Mean Ovract score
		BOYS				
Upper	64.8	15.1	9.4	10.8	139	4.09
Middle	55.9	17.5	12.0	14.6	383	5.26
Lower-Middle	51.7	16.5	14.6	17.2	267	5.89
Lower	58.5	11.0	14.6	15.9	164	6.04
		GIRLS				
Upper	76.0	11.2	8.8	4.0	125	2.65
Middle	81.7	10.1	3.7	4.5	376	2.31
Lower-Middle	75.0	11.9	7.3	5.8	260	2.81
Lower	69.6	12.2	12.2	6.1	148	3.00

The only significant differences between means for boys are between the Upper and Lower ($t = 2.1125$) and between the Upper and Lower Middle ($t = 2.5774$) $p < .02$. For girls the only significant difference is between the Middle and Lower ($t = 2.3541$) $p < .02$

95

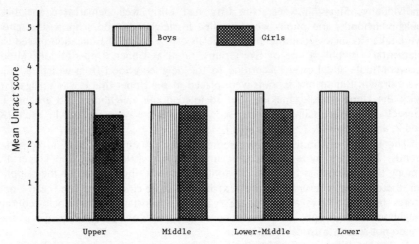

Figure IX.1   Mean scores for Underreacting Maladjustment by four neighbourhood socio-economic groups

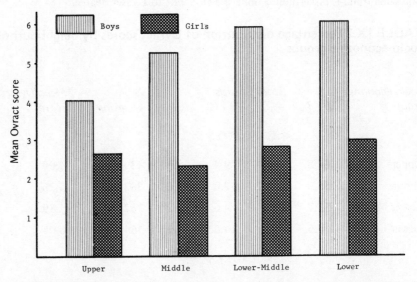

Figure IX.2   Mean scores for Overreacting Maladjustment by four neighbourhood socio-economic groups

There is a higher incidence of more serious overreacting behaviour (scores of 8 and over), amounting to approximately 50 per cent for both boys and girls, in the Lower compared with the Upper class. On the other hand, the Lower class has only 10 per cent fewer boys and 8½ per cent fewer girls in the best-adjusted Ovract score-group compared with the Upper class, and the latter actually has more in the mildly disturbed group (4–7). Among the Middle-class boys the distribution is hardly more favourable than for the Lower class, but the Middle-class girls resemble those of the Upper.

TABLE IX.3 Percentage of children showing significant behaviour disturbance (BSAG score of 10 or more) among British 7-year-olds (NCDS) and 5–14-year-olds in the City sample by comparable socio-economic groups

Occupation group of father (NCDS)	Boys	Socio-economic neighbourhood (City)	
1 Professional, managerial	31.5	Upper	34.5
2 Minor professional, small business	32.5	Middle	38.9
3 Skilled manual	41.3	Lower-Middle	45.4
4 Semi-skilled manual	48.6 }	Lower	43.3
5 Unskilled	57.5 }		
	Girls		
1 Professional, managerial	20.6	Upper	26.4
2 Minor professional, small business	17.3	Middle	22.3
3 Skilled manual	28.7	Lower-Middle	26.0
4 Semi-skilled manual	28.6 }	Lower	33.1
5 Unskilled	38.2 }		

A fair summary of the social-class differences in this study would be to say that while they are in the expected direction they are small, and limited to a slight but significant excess of more serious overreacting behaviour in the lower socio-economic neighbourhoods.

Social-class differences are also less than those found in the British National Child Development Study (Pringle, Butler and Davie 1966) for seven-year-old children using the 1956 edition of the BSAG. Their results are reproduced in Table IX.3, and for the sake of comparability between the two studies, in the form of percentages of Unsettled and Maladjusted children (total BSAG score of 10+) in the five paternal occupation groups. Alongside them, for broad comparison, are the percentages of City children scoring the approximate equivalent (9+) in the experimental revised edition used in the present study.

It is unlikely that there was a much greater social-class bias in the 1956 edition of the BSAG, so that the smaller class differences among the City children could be due either to their wider and older age-range, or to objectively smaller social-class differences in the City compared with in Britain.

97

The reasons for these class differences in social adjustment, as for those in test-intelligence, are likely to be a continuing subject of controversy. In a limited way the ages at which they appear and are most prominent may throw some light on the issue. If the differences are already apparent among young children, say those between five and eight years, it could be argued that they are either congenital or due to early postnatal influences. If they appear only in the teens, when children begin to be susceptible to the peer-group acceptance and approval, they can be attributed to cultural 'infection'.

The results from the present study present a complex picture, but they are quoted if only because they should act as a deterrent to hasty conclusions. We need deal only with the Ovract means since, as has been seen, there are no consistent or appreciable class differences in the Unract means. Since the trends are different for each sex they must be studied separately. The most striking difference in the mean Ovract scores is found among the 5-8-year-old girls. The numbers in each class are given in brackets.

Upper (37)	1.16
Middle (115)	2.14
Lower-Middle (77)	3.29
Lower (49)	4.04

Not only do the means decrease with improvement in socio-economic neighbourhood, but that for the Lower is 3½ times higher than that for the Upper. The differences between the Upper and Lower-Middle, and the Upper and the Lower are significant at the .01 level. In the 8-11-year group the same trend is discernible but it is marginal and not significant as between any of the socio-economic groups. In the 11-14-year group the Upper girls have actually the highest mean, but again none of the differences are significant. These results could be interpreted as pointing to congenital or early-life determinants.

Among the 5-8-year boys the Upper group is the best adjusted, but there is no clear trend. None of the differences are significant:

Upper (33)	3.00
Middle (121)	4.43
Lower-Middle (93)	4.26
Lower (54)	3.91

Among the 8-11-year boys, however, the means for all classes rise, in comparison with the younger age-group, but more steeply in the lower socio-economic neighbourhoods:

Upper (47)	4.21
Middle (117)	6.42
Lower-Middle (73)	7.14
Lower (61)	6.28

The difference between the Upper and the Lower-Middle is significant at the .05 level.

Among the 11-14-year boys the position is very similar except that the Middle group come out as rather better adjusted:

Upper (50)	4.08
Middle (122)	4.70
Lower-Middle (85)	6.83
Lower (45)	7.91

The difference between the Upper and the Lower is significant at the 0.5 level, that between the Middle and the Lower at the .01, and that between the Middle and Lower-Middle at the .05.

The results from these two age-groups indicate the presence of a considerable cultural determinant in boys. In sum, the factors contributing to maladjustment may be rather differently weighted for each sex, being more those of early development in younger girls, and more those of the peer-group environment in older boys.

Rural and city children

There is a tradition that country children are more stable and mature than city children. Since the populations of the Rural County and the industrial City were

TABLE IX.4 Comparative scores for City and Rural children

	BOYS		GIRLS	
	City (989)	Rural (160)	City (951)	Rural (131)
UNRACT				
Best adjusted (0-2) per cent	58.8	63.1	64.0	67.2
Worst adjusted (6+) per cent	20.5	19.4	18.4	11.5
Mean Unract score	3.13	2.82	2.92	2.28
t	0.98 not sig.		1.74 not sig.	
OVRACT				
Best adjusted (0-3) per cent	56.6	65.0	77.0	80.9
Worst adjusted (8+) per cent	28.0	18.1	11.9	12.2
Mean Ovract score	5.36	3.86	2.71	2.62
t	2.57 $p<.01$		0.19 not sig.	

fairly large, this traditional view could be tested by comparing the relative social adjustment of the children from each of these areas. Table IX.4 shows the percentages in the best and worst adjustment classes for Underreacting and Over-reacting behaviour, and the mean scores for each type. By both methods of analysis the rural show themselves better adjusted than the city boys and girls. This is most evident in the small percentage (11.5) of rural girls in the highest Unract score-group, and the smaller amount of Overreacting behaviour among the rural boys (18.1 compared with 28.0 per cent). These differences are reflected in the consistently lower mean Unract and Ovract scores of the rural children, although only that for the Ovract boys is statistically significant.

Comparison with the mean scores given in Tables IX.1 and 2 shows that the rural children are consistently better adjusted even than those of the highest social-class neighbourhoods within the city. These differences do not reach significance, but are consistent for all comparisons. It is clear that the superiority of the rural children is not due to a social-class factor. Indeed, the average income in the country would almost certainly be less than that of skilled workers within the city.

The explanation of this better rural adjustment is a matter of choice. That which first comes to mind is the existence of a culturally disadvantaged stratum in the city and urban areas. But it was seen that the Rural sample were consistently, even though only slightly, better adjusted than the upper-class City. It can be nevertheless that urban boys, irrespective of social class or religious affiliation, are influenced somewhat by the norm-violating models of overreacting behaviour to which they are exposed. In addition, rural boys would have their energies directed to outdoor occupations, which are more acceptable to the unsettled youth by the activity and change of scene they afford than is an indoor occupation. The deviant boy motivated by avoidance-excitement craves for an active, open-air life, even though it involves physical hardship (Stott 1950).

TABLE IX.5 Social adjustment of children of Dutch origin compared with that of the City and Rural samples

Mean scores for:	City		Dutch		Rural
BOYS	(989)		(156)		(160)
Unract	3.13		2.79		2.82
		$t = 1.0750$		$t = 0.0794$	
Ovract	5.36		5.19		3.86
		$t = 0.2796$		$t = 1.7481$	
GIRLS	(951)		(140)		(131)
Unract	2.92		2.82		2.28
		$t = 0.2790$		$t = 1.4594$	
Ovract	2.71		3.26		2.62
		$t = 1.2190$		$t = 1.0405$	

The children of Dutch origin

Nearly all the parents of these children emigrated to Canada from Holland during the decade following the Second World War. Of the 245 for whom a definite immigration date was supplied for both parents, the date of entry of the one arriving later (if they came separately) fell between 1950 and 1954 for 74 per cent of them. Only five came in 1960 or later. Two mothers and one father were Canadian-born, but the latter was of Dutch parents; one father came over as a boy; there was one Canadian-born child living with Dutch foster-parents. Thus, as regards ethnic origin and length of stay in Canada, the parents were a very homogeneous group, and nearly all their children were born and reared in Canada.

Of the 290 children for whom family data were obtained, all had both parents living except for four who had a mother only and one who had a father only. No data were obtained on the incidence of parental separation. The average number of children was 3.8.

In Table IX.5 the incidence of behaviour disturbance among the children from Dutch-immigrant families—given as mean scores in Unract and Ovract—is compared with that among the City and Rural samples. In effect about two-thirds of the Dutch sample could be classified as 'urban', defined as living in a population-centre of over 10,000; but there was no significant difference or consistent trend as regards social adjustment between them and the remaining third who lived in smaller population units and might be classified as 'rural'.

The mean Unract scores for the 'Dutch' children differ very little from those of the City or Rural, this parameter showing itself once again remarkably impervious to social or cultural influences. The Dutch Ovract scores, on the other hand, resemble those of the City children. For girls they are indeed marginally higher, although the difference is not significant.

The general picture is that of cross-cultural similarity, with urban or rural location being more important in this instance than ethnic origin or religious affiliation. One gets the impression that these Dutch immigrant families had become assimilated to a Canadian way of life, or that such distinctiveness as remained was not reflected in the social adjustment of their children. Out of the 272 from whom the data were obtainable only nine lived in families in which the Dutch language only was still spoken. It is curious that both the boys and the girls in question had much higher mean scores in both Unract and Ovract than the other Dutch children. There was little difference in the scores of the 143 children in whose homes a mixture of Dutch and English was spoken, compared with the 120 where the language of the home was English only.

The findings for the Dutch children offer one incidental point of interest, in showing that the presumably stricter upbringing in families which follow the Dutch Reformed religion does not have the effect of repressing the overreacting forms of maladjustment.

There was no consistent relationship within the Dutch sub-sample between family size and social adjustment, the mean scores being given in Table IX.6. The only significant difference, in eighteen comparisons, was that between sizes 3-5 and 6 or more for girls in Ovract ($t = 2.347, p < .05$).

The typical occupations of the Dutch fathers were market gardening, horticulture, and garden landscaping and maintenance. In economic terms they were a fairly homogenous group. According to broad estimates of income-category made

101

TABLE IX.6 Family-size and social adjustment (Dutch sample)

Size of family	Unract means	N	Ovract means
		BOYS	
1 or 2	2.27	44	4.41
3, 4 or 5	2.90	83	5.70
6 or more	3.24	29	4.90
		GIRLS	
1 or 2	3.31	29	3.24
3, 4 or 5	2.83	87	2.74
6 or more	2.21	24	5.21

by the teachers, only five had incomes below the 'poverty line' of $3,000 and eighteen came in the upper-middle-class income bracket. For the testing of the relationship between father's income and social adjustment of the child a figure of $7,000 was chosen since it divided the families into two groups of nearly equal size. The percentages of children falling in the standard Unract and Ovract score-groups are given in Table IX.7. The usual social-class difference—in overreacting behaviour—is not apparent, but there is an excess of the underreacting type of maladjustment in the lower-income group which just reaches significance at the .05 level by a chi^2 test of the numbers in each score-group. Their mean Unract scores are higher for boys and girls separately, and for both together reach significance over that for the upper-income group also at the .05 level (t = 2.3707). These results are hard to interpret, if they call for interpretation, since the Unract scores

TABLE IX.7 Social adjustment and father's income level among children of Dutch origin

Father's income* $	No.	best (0 - 2)	middle (3 - 5)	worst (6+)	chi^2 df = 2
		UNRACT			
Below 7000	128	46.9	32.0	21.1	
7000 or above	139	61.9	23.7	14.4	6.09 $p<.05$
		OVRACT			
		(0 - 3)	(4 - 7)	(8+)	
Below 7000	128	62.5	17.2	20.3	
7000 or above	139	58.3	20.1	21.6	0.56 not sig.

% in each adjustment category

* Not provided for 29 subjects

bore little relationship to socio-economic neighbourhood in the City sample (where indeed the Unract means for the boys in neighbourhoods of lower socio-economic status were marginally lower than those of the upper-status group). The Ovract score for the Dutch lower-income group was slightly lower than that of the higher income, which again contradicts the usual trend.

TABLE IX.8 Unract and Ovract scores for children of Dutch origin by father's occupation*

	N	Unract means	Ovract means
1. Professional and other non-manual	87	2.03	4.32
2. Foremen and fully skilled manual	48	2.10	5.35
3. Semi-skilled manual and specialized manual	115	3.75	4.58
4. Unskilled and casual	19	2.84	3.11

The only significant differences are those in Unract between categories 1 and 3, and 2 and 3.

* Not provided for 27 subjects

In further exploration of the social-class differences among the Dutch children, they were placed in three categories by their fathers' occupations, as shown in Table IX.8. Once again no consistent trends are discernible. It would appear that the Dutch families were culturally homogeneous irrespective of income-level and parental occupation. Possibly the crucial factor is not the social-class difference as such, but cultural integrity. Only when low socio-economic status is accompanied by cultural disintegration or a failure to adapt a traditional pattern of culture to modern urban conditions may one find a deterioration in social behaviour.

10
Maladjustment, ill-health and physical handicap

Teachers' observations of chronic health conditions—relationship between such and maladjustment in earlier studies—this relationship found to be closer among girls—chronic ailments associated with higher Unract and Ovract scores—the morbidity/maladjustment relationship valid for the core behavioural syndromes—close association of 'Neurological' grouping with common ailments—depressive effect of ill-health not the only explanation—the morbidity/maladjustment relationship holds for purely somatic conditions—confirmation of the hypothesis of multiple impairment—closer relationship again found in girls—multiple impairment as a yardstick of congenitality—increase in all types of maladjustment with larger number of morbid conditions—inference of a congenital factor in all types—the morbid conditions which contribute most to a hypothetical multiple-impairment syndrome—relationship of these to maladjustment—speculations about the origin of multiple impairment.

On the back page of the BSAG are a number of items relating to general health, physical defects, speech, size and physical appearance. These are not categories of illness such as a doctor might use, but signs and symptoms that a class teacher might be expected to be able to observe. For example, the teacher is not asked to say specifically if a child has asthma, but only to note whether he had some kind of breathing difficulty. Such information is obviously no substitute for that provided by an individual medical examination; on the other hand the teacher, by daily contact with the child, is in a position to observe chronic or intermittent indications of ill-health over a period of time. The ability of teachers to note such signs doubtless varies, but such as are noticed are likely to be fairly marked and reliable, and hence serve collectively as an index of chronic ill-health within a population of children of school age.

The correlation of indications of behaviour disturbance with the above morbidity indications yielded a number of positive findings in earlier studies (Stott 1962, 1966b). In a combined sample of 818 boys placed on probation and their non-delinquent controls, 31 per cent of the maladjusted (scores 20+) had some respiratory ailment, compared with 9 per cent of the best-adjusted group (BSAG scores 0-4). The corresponding percentages for other ailments were 25 and 6, for physical defects 19 and 4, for growth abnormality (diminutive in stature, very fat or very thin) 15 and 4, all these differences being significant as well beyond the

.001 level. This relationship between maladjustment and ill-health could not be attributed to a common factor of adverse physical environment since the differences between the means remained at the same level of significance among the delinquents whose homes were rated of adequate standard from the point of view of furnishings and cleanliness.

It was further found that boys with two or more distinct morbid conditions tended to be much more maladjusted than those with only one such condition. These findings are summarized below in terms of mean BSAG scores:

	Probationers	Controls
Healthy	16.4	6.5
One morbid condition	19.7	8.1
Two or more distinct morbid conditions	26.9	11.0

The differences in the means were more significant between the one- and two-condition subjects than between the one-condition and the healthy.

The cumulative nature of the statistically related but presumably somatically independent conditions suggested a law of multiple congenital impairment: the presence of one morbid condition, whether of physical health or of behaviour, confers a greater likelihood of another, two such conditions make a third more likely, and so on in geometrical progression.

The relationship between maladjustment and poor health was found to be closer among girls in an all-British study of truants and matched controls. The mean BSAG scores for the controls of the truants are given below with the number of cases in brackets:

	BSAG means	
	Boys	Girls
Respiratory Condition	12.2 (59)	15.7 (14)
No such	7.3 (371)	6.0 (155)
Other ailment	14.0 (37)	15.2 (18)
No such	7.4 (393)	5.6 (151)
Ratio of means (presence/absence of condition)	1.67	2.63
Other ailments	1.91	2.58

Whereas the girls were much less prone to chronic ill-health (as shown by the bracketed numbers), those who were unhealthy tended to be more maladjusted, and those who were healthy were less maladjusted, than the corresponding groups of boys. For this complex picture, of a greater over-all health vulnerability of boys, but with a stronger tendency to multiple impairment in girls, it is hard to think of other than a congenital explanation. If this is correct it would be reasonable to explain the general relationship between maladjustment and ill-health along similar lines.

TABLE X.1 Preponderance of maladjustment in children with chronic morbid conditions

	Scorer/non-scorer ratios (no. of cases in brackets)			
	Unract		Ovract	
	Boys (1305)	Girls (1222)	Boys (1305)	Girls (1222)
Poor breathing, wheezy, asthmatic, easily winded	1.22 (46)	1.24 (26)	1.20 (46)	1.43 (26)
Frequent colds, tonsillitis, coughs	1.30 (122)	1.95 (120)	1.32 (122)	1.47 (120)
Skin troubles, sores	1.42 (24)	2.01 (17)	1.27 (24)	0.93 (17)
Complains of tummy aches, feeling ill or sick; is sometimes sick	1.43 (76)	1.48 (95)	1.94 (76)	1.49 (95)
Headaches; bad turns, goes very pale; fits	1.41 (18)	1.56 (29)	1.67 (18)	1.34 (29)
Stutters, stammers, can't get the words out	1.36 (136)	1.76 (61)	1.10 (136)	2.16 (61)
Thick, mumbling, inaudible speech	2.38 (101)	2.78 (48)	1.32 (101)	1.50 (48)
Jumbled speech	1.89 (42)	1.71 (21)	1.62 (42)	3.41 (21)
Incoherent rambling chatter	1.68 (26)	1.67 (27)	1.94 (26)	2.83 (27)
Babyish (mispronounces simple words)	1.15 (64)	2.44 (42)	1.56 (64)	2.09 (42)
Bad eyesight	1.22 (68)	1.18 (74)	1.43 (68)	1.42 (74)
Squint	1.55 (25)	1.16 (24)	1.46 (25)	1.82 (24)
Poor hearing	1.79 (21)	1.75 (12)	1.10 (21)	1.51 (12)
Gawky (bad coordination)	2.25 (60)	2.13 (25)	1.52 (60)	3.48 (25)
Very fat	1.38 (29)	1.61 (34)	1.47 (29)	1.81 (34)

In the present study Unract and Ovract scorer/non-scorer ratios were first calculated by sexes for each of the fifteen morbid items which were present in at least ten cases of either sex. The procedure was to divide the mean Unract and Ovract scores of those children having the morbid condition by the corresponding mean scores of those not having it. The results are given in Table X.1. To take as an example the S/N-S ratio of 1.22 in the Unract column in respect of the first condition, 'Poor breathing, etc.', this means that the boys suffering therefrom had on average a 22 per cent higher score for the underreacting sorts of maladjustment than the boys who did not suffer in this way (but who nevertheless may not have been healthy in other respects).

It is seen that the ratio is greater than unity for all fifteen morbid conditions except for 'Skin troubles, sores' in relation to the Ovract scores of girls, the number of those affected being in any case low. Not all the ratios are statistically significant owing to the small numbers. However, the finding that fifty-nine of the sixty reveal at least some preponderance of maladjustment among those affected by the various conditions is highly significant. It is, however, important only in highlighting the regularity of the maladjustment/sickness relationship as a whole.

The highest ratios are found among the speech impairments (jumbled speech 3.41) and bad coordination (3.48). Of the nine ratios over 2 but less than 3, eight are in the same areas. These happen to be the sorts of physical defect which can most directly be attributed to neurological dysfunction. With them, at least, it would appear that the maladjustment/sickness relationship is due to a neurological common factor. The other morbid conditions lend themselves to this explanation in varying degrees. Alternatively they may reflect more generally pervasive impairments. In any case the somatic basis for the behavioural system lies in the nervous structures which govern behaviour. In short, the consistent maladjustment/sickness relationship points to the existence of a neurological basis for a significant number of cases of behaviour disturbance.

A common factor in social disadvantage?

First to be checked of possible explanations for this surprisingly consistent relationship between maladjustment and chronic ill-health is that of a common factor of social disadvantage. The neighbourhood groupings of the schools as described in Chapter Nine were taken as a basis. Within each, separate scorer/non-scorer ratios were calculated for the fifteen chronic health conditions in terms of Unract and Ovract, and these were then averaged, taking account of the frequency of each condition. The resulting over-all mean S/N-S ratios by social class of neighbourhood are given in Table X.2 for boys and girls separately.

We should first examine the mean behavioural scores for those pupils who were healthy for the various conditions (the h columns). Their Unract means vary little as between the socio-economic groups, this being consistent with the findings reported in the previous chapter. Their Ovract means show a steady rise—more pronounced among boys than girls—with lower socio-economic group, this also being consistent with the earlier analysis.

Examining next the mean scores for those pupils who suffered the adverse health conditions, they are without exception higher than the means for the healthy within each social group. The m/h (morbid/healthy) ratios serve as a measure of the

107

TABLE X.2 Socio-economic influence on maladjustment/morbidity relationship

Social-class rating of school neighbourhood

	Upper		Middle		Lower-Middle		Lower	
	m	h	m	h	m	h	m	h
UNRACT								
Boys, means	5.97	3.24	4.54	2.88	4.17	3.25	4.56	3.01
ratio *m/h*		1.84		1.58		1.28		1.51
Girls, means	5.28	2.63	4.89	2.81	4.40	2.76	4.42	3.08
ratio *m/h*		2.01		1.74		1.59		1.44
OVRACT								
Boys, means	5.32	4.01	6.54	5.13	8.36	5.75	7.87	5.63
ratio *m/h*		1.33		1.27		1.45		1.40
Girls, means	4.33	2.38	3.80	2.21	4.78	2.73	5.12	3.32
ratio *m/h*		1.82		1.72		1.75		1.54

m = weighted mean behavioural score (Unract or Ovract) of cases showing each morbid condition

h = ditto for cases healthy for the condition

excess of each type of maladjustment among the unhealthy within each socio-economic category.

These findings leave no doubt that the relationship between maladjustment and ill-health holds good irrespective of any common factor of social disadvantage. It is rather a question of asking whether this factor has any such influence at all. With the underreacting types of maladjustment it certainly does not have, because—as has been seen—there is no discernible social-class factor operating either among the healthy or the unhealthy. For overreacting maladjustment the rise in mean score with lower social class is approximately paralleled for both. As between the Upper and Lower-class boys it is 41 per cent for the healthy compared with 48 per cent for the unhealthy; for the corresponding girls, 18 per cent compared with 14 per cent. The slightly steeper rise for the unhealthy is not statistically significant and does not disturb the general findings of a true relationship between maladjustment and morbidity.

The above maladjustment/sickness relationship could conceivably be one of direct cause and effect. Notably, the child who has a chronic respiratory or other infective condition may feel below par and lack physical energy in a way that would produce a score for Depression. We have therefore to ask whether the relationship was due to the depressive effect of illness rather than any more fundamental linkage between behaviour disturbance and physical disorders.

This explanation could be tested by discovering whether it held good for behaviour disturbance apart from Depression. The mean S/N-S ratios of the fifteen morbid conditions were therefore calculated for each of the five core syndromes and the Neurological grouping. To take Unforthcomingness as an example of the

TABLE X.3 Relationship between type of maladjustment and ill-health

Type of behaviour disturbance	Mean S/N-S ratios of 15 morbid conditions		Mean S/N-S ratios of 4 somatic conditions	
	Unweighted	Weighted	Unweighted	Weighted
Unforthcomingness	1.45	1.43	1.27	1.36
Withdrawal	1.71	1.44	1.63	1.51
Depression	2.22	2.00	2.04	1.93
Inconsequence	1.56	1.45	1.12	1.33
Hostility	1.59	1.67	1.48	1.53
Neurological	2.61	3.32	2.04	2.16

procedure, the mean U-score of children having a particular morbid condition was divided by that of children not having it. The next stage was to average the S/N-S ratios in Unforthcomingness obtained by all the fifteen morbid items. It was difficult to decide, in doing so, whether this should be a simple averaging of all their ratios, or an average weighted by the frequency of the conditions. The first could be justified on the grounds that theoretically it was the relationship that matters irrespective of the prevalence of the phenomena; on the other hand a weighting in favour of the more frequent items would heighten reliability. Mean S/N-S ratios were therefore calculated by both methods.

Table X.3 shows that each type of average produced essentially similar results. To remind the reader of what these ratios tell us, that of 1.43 for Unforthcomingness at the head of the second column means, strictly, that the morbid conditions were associated with this syndrome by 43 per cent in excess of expectation (a nil association giving a ratio of unity). By and large, it may be said that the children suffering from chronic health conditions or physical defects had this percentage of greater incidence of Unforthcomingness than the healthy children.

The ratios in Table X.3 are informative on three counts. The first is that the Neurological grouping shows the closest association with the fifteen morbid conditions, as would be expected considering that they included speech and motor impairments, and squint. Nevertheless the ratio for the Neurological grouping is as high as 2.04 unweighted, (2.16 weighted) for the first four morbid conditions only, which are phenomenologically purely somatic. Either there is a common factor of neural dysfunction underlying these common minor ailments or they are related by some other common aetiology of a genetic or at least congenital nature. The comparatively rare cases of postnatal brain damage could not have produced statistical relationships such as those found. It is suggestive for the aetiology of behaviour disturbance that its relationship to morbid conditions holds good for organic defects such as bad eyesight and poor hearing.

Second, the relationship with morbid conditions holds for each main type of maladjustment. No doubt a number of special explanations could be adduced in respect of each of them on an ascending hierarchy of empirical unverifiability. But the explanation which applies to them all is that the impairments of behaviour on

109

the one hand, and of health and physique on the other, have a common source. In the case of the physical defects the overwhelming likelihood is that this is prenatal, and the probability is that the same applies, as far as concerns the predisposition, to the other morbid conditions. Since, moreover, a pervasive source of impairment acting at an early stage of development could affect the behavioural system only by damaging or retarding the development of its underlying neurological structure or by providing this structure with a noxious metabolic environment, we may postulate a neurological factor in this broad sense in all the main types of behaviour disturbance. It is noteworthy that the relationship holds for Hostility despite the environmental component in this type of maladjustment, suggesting that it also rests on a congenital predisposition.

Third, it will be observed that, except for the Neurological grouping in boys, Depression has the highest ratio by both the weighted and unweighted computations. It could be that the most clearly observable form of damage to the behavioural system on the part of the postulated early developmental influences consists in an impairment of motivation. On the other hand this close relationship between Depression and the morbid conditions lends support to the hypothesis of their having a direct depressive effect. The extent of this can be assessed if we make the assumption that the depressed type of behaviour disturbance has a congenital component comparable with that of the other four core syndromes and the Neurological grouping. If then Depression is found to have a closer relationship with the morbid conditions than they, this would, by so much, be attributable to the direct depressive effect of ill-health. Conversely, if the relationship is not significantly closer as far as Depression is concerned, there is no reason for assuming it to be exceptional among the types of behaviour disturbance in being directly caused by the ill-health rather than having a common cause therewith. The mean for both sexes of the S/N-S ratios of the morbid conditions apart from Depression in the five (Unforthcomingness, Withdrawal, Inconsequence, Hostility and the Neurological) is 1.74 by the unweighted method of computation, giving Depression an excess of 0.48 or 26.7 per cent, and 1.86 for the weighted, giving D an excess of 0.14 or 5.9 per cent. Even if the higher of these estimates be accepted, the relationship of Depression to morbidity is very much of the same order as that of the other forms of behaviour disturbance, and the main part of the relationship between maladjustment and ill-health in Depression cannot be attributed to a direct depressive effect of illness.

The consistent relationship—seen in the two righthand columns of Table X.3—between the behaviour-disorder syndromes and the first four conditions as listed in Table X.1, which are commonly regarded as physical, prompts the same aetiological speculations. Can it be that these illnesses and maladjustment have a common basis in neural dysfunction? Or do both types of impairment originate in noxious influences which act prenatally? It is suggestive in this regard that the relationship holds also for organic defects such as bad eyesight and poor hearing. For most of the other fifteen morbid conditions—headaches, bad turns, seizures, varied speech defects, squint, motor impairment—a neurological basis is *prima facie* plausible. Their relationship to behaviour disturbance thus points to a pervasive neural involvement that has the appearance of being congenital, except for the comparatively rare cases of known brain damage, which would not produce statistical relationships such as those found.

In view of the earlier finding that the relationship between behaviour

TABLE X.4 Mean scorer/non-scorer ratios of ill-health by sex and type of maladjustment (15 morbid conditions)

	BOYS		GIRLS	
	Unweighted	Weighted	Unweighted	Weighted
Unforthcomingness	1.17	1.26	1.36	1.47
Withdrawal	1.15	1.02	2.10	2.03
Depression	1.47	1.58	2.61	2.30
Inconsequence	1.27	1.40	0.97	1.26
Hostility	1.31	1.42	1.64	1.65
Neurological	2.38	2.78	1.70	1.46

disturbance and ill-health was closer for girls, the mean S/N-S ratios were calculated for healthy and unhealthy children of each sex separately. It is seen from Table X.4 that except for Inconsequence and the Neurological grouping this finding is confirmed within all the main syndromes.

Multiple impairment

The hypothesis of multiple impairment arose from the observation, referred to above, that children suffering from two morbid conditions tended to be more maladjusted than those suffering from one, and those from one more so than the healthy. The number of cases in the present study made possible a more extended test of this hypothesis than heretofore.

Among the fifteen morbid conditions listed in Table X.1 were nine distinct types of illness or defect, as shown below:

Respiratory (Poor breathing, etc. Frequent colds, etc.)
Skin troubles
Digestive (complains of tummy aches, etc.)
Headaches, bad turns, etc.
Speech defect (5 items as in Table X.1)
Optical defects (Bad eyesight, Squint)
Hearing defect
Coordination defect
· Very fat

The mean Unract and Ovract scores for the boys and girls who were recorded as healthy, and for those suffering from one up to four or five such morbid conditions, are given in the first two columns of Table X.5 and in Figures X.1 and 2 (none suffered from more than five). The earlier findings are confirmed in both respects. Mean Unract and Ovract scores rise consistently with the number of distinct morbid conditions from which the children suffer. The ratios in the two right-hand columns of Table X.4 show the degree to which children suffering from each number of distinct morbid conditions are more maladjusted than the healthy children of the same sex. For example, the ratio of 1.58 in the third column means

TABLE X.5 Maladjustment in relation to number of distinct morbid conditions

No. of morbid conditions	N	Mean UNRACT	Mean OVRACT	Ratio of disturbance morbid/healthy*	
				UNRACT	OVRACT
Boys					
0 (healthy)	755	2.31	4.34	—	—
1	377	3.64	5.46	1.58	1.26
2	118	4.65	7.03	2.01	1.62
3	46	5.39	10.17	2.33	2.35
4 - 5	9	7.33	10.22	3.17	2.35
Girls					
0 (healthy)	812	2.10	2.05	—	—
1	281	3.93	3.66	1.87	1.79
2	90	4.89	4.43	2.33	2.16
3	29	5.24	6.79	2.49	3.32
4 - 5	10	6.80	8.70	3.24	4.24

* Mean Unract or Ovract score for children
with each number of distinct morbid conditions
divided by the corresponding mean score for
the healthy.

that boys suffering from one such are on average 58 per cent more prone to under-reacting types of maladjustment than the healthy boys.

It is seen that in Ovract the rise is much steeper for the girls than the boys, but in Unract only marginally so. In Unract the higher ratios of the girls are due to the lower baseline score for the healthy. In Ovract the means for the girls are somewhat lower for each number of morbid conditions, but again the rise in the ratio is in the main due to the good adjustment of the healthy. The ten girls suffering from four or five health conditions showed over three times more maladjustment of the under-reacting and over four times more of the overreacting type than did the healthy girls.

The above findings are as would be predicted by the hypothesis of multiple congenital impairment. They are also consistent with the general picture of a lower incidence of impairment among girls. At the same time, such girls as are subject to whatever noxious influences produce multiple impairment tended to be affected more severely. An unhealthy girl is likely to suffer more from behaviour disturbance, especially of an overreacting type, than an unhealthy boy. This finding parallels that reported above of higher mean scorer/non-scorer ratios in respect of unhealthy girls.

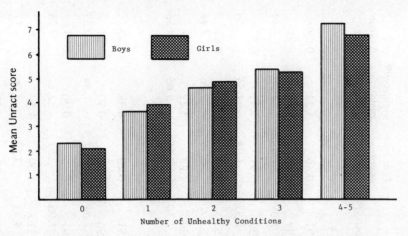

Figure X.1 Relationship of Underreacting Maladjustment to ill-health

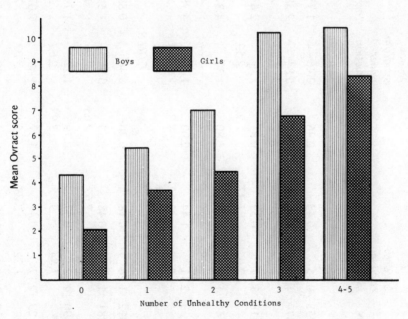

Figure X.2 Relationship of Overreacting Maladjustment to ill-health

TABLE X.6 Types of maladjustment in relation to number of morbid conditions

Mean scores for syndromes or groupings (morbid-healthy ratios in italics)

No. of morbid conditions	N	Unforth-coming-ness	Withdrawal	Depression	Non-syndromic under-reaction	Inconsequence	Hostility	Peer-mal-adaptive-ness	Non-syndromic over-reaction	Neurol-ogical
BOYS										
0 (healthy)	755	0.95	0.43	0.46	0.46	1.75	0.91	0.46	1.21	0.09
1	377	1.44 *1.52*	0.55 *1.28*	0.81 *1.76*	0.84 *1.83*	2.38 *1.36*	0.97 *1.07*	0.66 *1.43*	1.45 *1.20*	0.31 *3.44*
2	118	1.97 *2.07*	0.59 *1.37*	0.91 *1.98*	1.19 *2.59*	2.83 *1.62*	1.39 *1.53*	0.91 *1.98*	1.91 *1.58*	0.50 *5.56*
3	46	1.20 *1.26*	1.00 *2.33*	1.80 *3.91*	1.39 *3.02*	4.37 *2.50*	1.83 *2.01*	1.24 *2.70*	2.74 *2.26*	0.67 *7.44*
4 - 5	9	2.11 *2.22*	1.44 *3.35*	2.00 *4.35*	1.78 *3.87*	4.78 *2.73*	1.00 *1.10*	1.22 *2.65*	3.22 *2.66*	1.67 *18.56*
GIRLS										
0 (healthy)	812	1.26	0.18	0.20	0.46	0.88	0.51	0.28	0.38	0.09
1	281	1.97 *1.56*	0.48 *2.67*	0.53 *2.65*	0.95 *2.06*	1.54 *1.75*	0.96 *1.88*	0.45 *1.61*	0.70 *1.84*	0.21 *2.33*
2	90	2.32 *1.84*	0.57 *3.17*	0.79 *3.95*	1.21 *2.63*	1.79 *2.03*	1.01 *1.98*	0.73 *2.61*	0.90 *2.37*	0.34 *3.78*
3	29	2.17 *1.72*	0.41 *2.28*	1.17 *5.85*	1.48 *3.22*	2.07 *2.35*	2.21 *4.33*	1.00 *3.57*	1.52 *4.00*	0.28 *3.11*
4 - 5	10	1.80 *1.43*	1.10 *6.11*	2.10 *10.50*	1.80 *3.91*	4.50 *5.11*	1.60 *3.14*	1.10 *3.93*	1.50 *3.95*	0.70 *7.78*

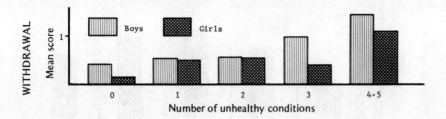

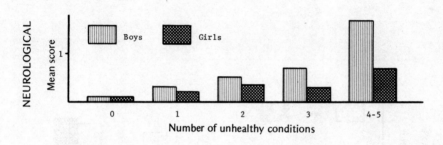

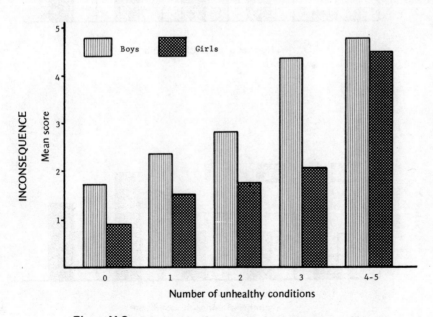

Figure X.3 Relationship of each type of maladjustment to ill-health

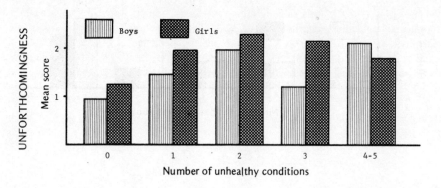

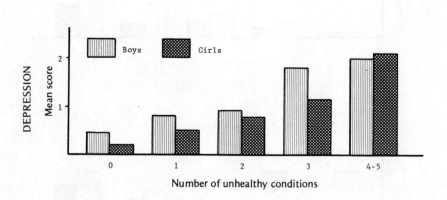

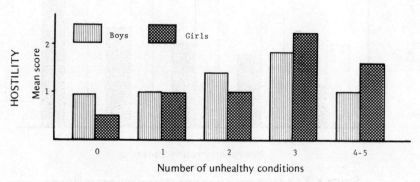

Figure X.3 cont./

The consistency of this relationship between maladjustment and multiple health handicaps, and the overwhelming probability of its having a congenital origin, permit us to use the latter as a yardstick for the presence of a congenital factor in each type of maladjustment. Accordingly, similar means and ratios were calculated for the syndromes and associated groupings of disturbed behaviour. Since the trends for Inconsequence and Attention-seeking were similar in this and other respects, they were amalgamated, and the same was done with the non-syndromic group of Overreacting items (Delinquency, Peer-group deviance, Defiance of social norms). In Table X.6 the mean scores for the syndromes and groupings are arranged in the same way as those for the Unract-Ovract means in Table X.5. They are shown graphically in Figure X.3. The ratios indicating by how much the mean scores of children having the morbid conditions exceeded those of the healthy children are given below each in italics.

Both for boys and girls there is, with few exceptions, a consistent rise in mean score for all types of maladjustment with increasing number of morbid conditions. The exceptions have the appearance of being due to the chances of sampling, except possibly the drop in the Hostility scores for both boys and girls between the 3 and 4-5 morbid-condition categories, but even here we are dealing with only nine boys and ten girls. A non-parametric method of demonstrating the consistency of the trend is to note that only two of the fifty-four means in the 1, 2 and 3 morbidity categories are lower than those in the lesser morbidity category. There are six such among the eighteen means of the 4-5 morbidity category, but they are not in the same types of maladjustment for boys and girls except for Hostility, and probably reflect the unreliability of small numbers.

It may be concluded that all the types of maladjustment dealt with in the present study obey what we may begin with confidence to call a law of multiple impairment. If the inference of a congenital origin for the two main divisions of behaviour disturbance is well-founded, the same would apply to each type of disturbance separately—despite an apparent additional direct effect of illness in Depression, and the unquestionable situational and cultural factors in Hostility and the non-syndromic deviant forms of overreaction.

In order to show what are the chances of maladjusted children being unhealthy, and unhealthy children being maladjusted, the relationship is expressed in Tables X.7 and 8 as a series of percentages and ratios, as follows:

a Percentage of the maladjusted who were unhealthy
b Percentage of the well-adjusted who were unhealthy
 a/b Ratio showing the greater risk of ill-health among the maladjusted
c Percentage of the unhealthy who were maladjusted
d Percentage of the healthy who were maladjusted
 c/d Ratio showing the greater risk of maladjustment among the unhealthy

For the Unract and Ovract scales the above ratios are calculated for those children who met the criterion scores for 'maladjustment' in the BSAG norms for severity. For the core syndromes, however, this criterion gives too small numbers, so that the cut-off points for 'moderate maladjustment' were used. 'Unhealthy' was defined as suffering from three or more distinct morbid conditions.

It is seen from Table X.7 that the Underreacting children were 4½ times, and the Overreacting 5½ times, more likely to suffer from multiple health conditions

TABLE X.7 Risks of ill-health among the maladjusted and of maladjustment among the unhealthy

		boys	girls	both sexes
	UNRACT			
a	Per cent of underreactors who are unhealthy	10.0	7.0	8.6
b	Per cent of not underreactors who are unhealthy	2.6	1.3	1.9
a/b	Greater risk of ill-health among underreactors	_3.92_	_5.35_	_4.43_
c	Per cent of unhealthy who are underreactors	23.6	20.5	22.3
d	Per cent of not unhealthy who are underreactors	6.1	4.7	5.4
c/d	Greater risk of underreaction among the unhealthy	3.88	4.39	4.17
	OVRACT			
a	Per cent of overreactors who are unhealthy	9.1	12.3	10.0
b	Per cent of not overreactors who are unhealthy	2.0	1.6	1.8
a/b	Greater risk of ill-health among overreactors	_4.55_	_7.76_	_5.62_
c	Per cent of unhealthy who are overreactors	34.5	25.6	30.8
d	Per cent of not unhealthy who are overreactors	13.8	3.8	8.6
c/d	Greater risk of overreaction among the unhealthy	2.51	6.73	3.58

than the not-underreacting and the not-overreacting respectively. Conversely, the multiple-unhealthy were 3½ and 4 times more likely to be maladjusted.

This form of analysis enables us to see to what extent each type of maladjustment fits into the concept of multiple impairment. Since, in behaviour, we are dealing with the final manifestation of a sequence of processes, with the possibility of dysfunction at any stage of the system, we cannot expect to find a simple molar relationship between behaviour disturbance and physical morbid conditions. If we assume, barring a direct cause-and-effect relationship, that any correlation between a behavioural and a physical condition has an origin in the same genes or traumata, or a combination of both, the most likely finding would be, not a homogeneous multiple impairment, but groups of correlated impairments.

We have consequently to break the data down by types of maladjustment in order to see which of them fit most clearly into a pattern of multiple impairment. In Table X.8 the method of presentation used for Unract and Ovract in Table X.7 is used for each of the core syndromes.

Among them Depression stands out as having the highest ratios, indicating the closest relationship with the multiple health conditions. In this case we have to make allowances for direct cause and effect, and environmental common causes such as malnutrition and incorrect sleeping habits. Nevertheless the marked sex difference in ratios—showing that the relationship is much closer for girls than for

TABLE X.8 Risks of ill-health associated with each core syndrome of maladjustment, and of the latter with ill-health

	a	b	a/b	c	d	c/d
			Unforthcomingness			
Boys	4.7	3.9	*1.20*	7.3	4.6	*1.57*
Girls	4.76	2.5	*1.90*	15.4	7.9	*1.95*
Both	4.7	3.3	*1.46*	10.6	6.3	*1.68*
			Withdrawal			
Boys	8.7	3.1	*2.78*	25.5	9.9	*2.56*
Girls	3.9	2.6	*1.47*	7.7	3.7	*2.08*
Both	7.1	2.9	*2.49*	18.1	6.7	*2.70*
			Depression			
Boys	14.3	2.5	*5.64*	30.9	5.7	*5.43*
Girls	17.3	1.9	*9.20*	23.1	2.0	*11.71*
Both	15.2	2.2	*6.94*	27.7	3.8	*7.35*
			Inconsequence			
Boys	9.9	2.8	*3.59*	30.9	10.7	*2.88*
Girls	10.9	2.5	*4.34*	17.9	3.2	*5.61*
Both	10.2	2.6	*3.86*	25.5	6.8	*3.74*
			Hostility			
Boys	5.1	3.1	*1.63*	10.9	8.2	*1.33*
Girls	8.2	2.1	*3.92*	17.9	4.7	*3.84*
Both	6.4	2.8	*2.34*	13.8	6.4	*2.17*

a   Per cent of those suffering from each type of maladjustment who are unhealthy

b   Per cent of those not suffering from each type of maladjustment who are unhealthy

a/b   Greater risk of ill-health among those suffering from each type of maladjustment

c   Per cent of unhealthy among those suffering from each type of maladjustment

d   Per cent of healthy among those suffering from each type of maladjustment

c/d   Greater risk of each type of maladjustment among the unhealthy

TABLE X.9 Differential sex patterns in multiple impairment

	boys	girls	relationships with ill-health closer for: *
	Percentage maladjusted		
Unract	10.0	9.3	girls
Ovract	16.0	6.6	girls
Unforthcomingness	6.5	10.3	girls
Withdrawal	12.3	6.3	boys
Depression	9.1	4.3	girls
Inconsequence	13.2	5.2	girls
Hostility	9.0	7.0	girls
	Percentage unhealthy		
	4.2	3.2	

* Summarizing a/b and c/d ratios as given in Tables X.6 and 7

boys—is evidence for a genetic factor. This phenomenon of a closer multiple-impairment pattern for girls is discussed below.

Unforthcomingness fits least well into the pattern, although all the ratios except that showing the excess of Unforthcomingness among unhealthy boys (a/b) are well above unity. Again we have to ask whether children suffering from mild chronic ailments are on that account more likely to be timid and apprehensive. Adler with his theory of organically derived inferiority-compensation would have predicted the opposite. The higher ratios for girls—indicating that nearly twice as many of those who are unhealthy were maladjusted, and nearly twice as many of the maladjusted were unhealthy—points to a congenital/genetic factor.

In Withdrawal the multiple-impairment pattern is more pronounced, except for only a moderate tendency to withdrawal in unhealthy girls (the a/b ratio). This is the only type of maladjustment in which the ratios are higher for boys. The inferences we can make about Withdrawal as a type of maladjustment are limited because, as explained earlier in this monograph, teachers cannot be expected to report fine enough discriminations for us to distinguish between the presumably congenital, autistic deficits in social-attachment behaviour and the conditioned defensiveness of children who have suffered traumatic deprivation. More sophisticated data are therefore needed before we can understand the nature of the relationship between the withdrawn types of behaviour and physical morbid conditions. All we can say at the present stage is that these withdrawn behaviours collectively show a degree of this relationship which is different from that of Unforthcomingness and Depression.

Inconsequence comes out with uniformly high ratios, especially for girls. It will be seen in the next chapter that the same applies to the relationship between Inconsequence and motor impairment. There is a further indication that this type

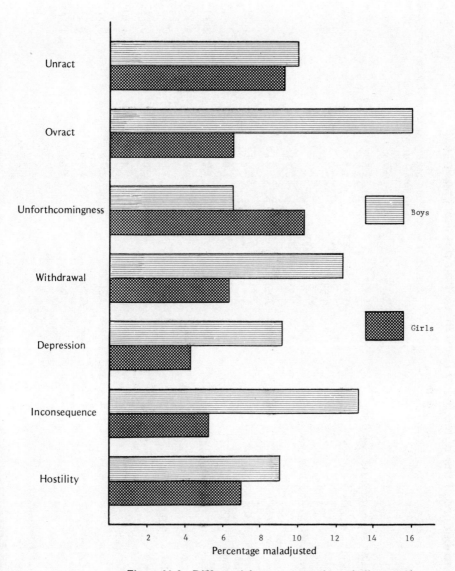

Figure X.4   Differential sex patterns in maladjustment

TABLE X.10 Contributions of the 15 morbidity items to multiple physical impairment

	Ratios of occurrence among multiple-disease compared with single-disease children		
	Boys	Girls	Both sexes
Poor breathing, wheezy, asthmatic, easily winded	1.43*	1.69*	1.52*
Frequent colds, tonsillitis, coughs	0.94	1.15*	1.04
Skin troubles, sores	0.58	0.62	0.60
Complains of tummy aches, feeling ill or sick; is sometimes sick	1.53*	0.54	0.87
Headaches; bad turns, goes very pale; fits	7.83*	1.63*	2.88*
Stutters, stammers, can't get the words out	1.13	0.99	1.09
Thick, mumbling, inaudible speech	3.67*	1.68*	2.59*
Jumbled speech	2.75*	1.24	2.00*
Incoherent rambling chatter	3.75*	4.35*	3.94*
Babyish (mispronounces simple words)	0.50	1.09	0.65
Bad eyesight	0.64	0.99	0.73
Squint	0.92	1.45*	1.30
Poor hearing	0.86	0.77	0.81
Gawky (bad coordination)	0.79	1.03	0.87
Very fat	1.25	1.09	1.16*

* Six highest in each sex-category

of maladjustment has a sex-linked genetic basis: it is found in some 11 per cent even of the healthy boys, but in only 3 per cent of healthy girls. Among the unhealthy boys it reaches 30.9 per cent, and among the unhealthy girls 17.9 per cent. (The rise in association with physical morbidity of less than three times for boys but over 5½ times for girls is characteristic.)

Hostility shows an inconsistent picture. Its relationship with ill-health is strong for girls but weak for boys. Applying our line of argument, this would suggest that there is a greater environmental element in male than in female Hostility. But there is little point in attempting to explain the *minutiae* of these relationships until their constancy is established by further studies.

The anomaly of a greater incidence of nearly all types of maladjustment in boys, but of closer relationships between them and ill-health among girls, is summarized for the present data in Table X.9. The differential sex patterns for maladjustment are illustrated in Figure X.4. The criteria for maladjustment and multiple ill-health are as used in Tables X.7 and 8. Only Unforthcomingness is more prevalent among girls (6.5 per cent compared with 10.3 per cent) and only in the 'conglomerate' Withdrawal is the relationship between maladjustment and ill-health closer among boys. Similar findings are reported with regard to motor impairment in the next chapter, where some speculations are hazarded as to its evolutionary significance.

Theoretically it is of interest to see whether all the types of childhood morbidity taken account of in the present study contribute to the picture of multiple impairment—in other words, whether the presence of every such condition confers a greater likelihood of others. On the hypothesis of an over-all morbidity 'syndrome', or tendency to ill-health and physical defect, what amounted to an item-validation was carried out. The items were the fifteen morbid conditions listed in Table X.1, and their relative frequency in multiple-disease children (those with positive ratings in three or more of the nine distinct conditions) was compared to that in single-disease children. To give a true picture of excess over statistical expectations, these relative frequencies were divided by 3.2, the average number of . distinct morbid conditions in the multiple-disease children.

The resulting ratios are given in Table X.10. They indicate the extent to which each condition is a contributor to the hypothetical multiple-disease syndrome. For example, the ratio of 1.43 for 'headaches; bad turns, goes very pale; fits' among boys means that this item occurs some 43 per cent more frequently along with two or more other morbid conditions than in isolation. Ratios of less than unity indicate that the items in question tend to occur more as single morbid conditions than in a multiple physical impairment combination.

It is seen that there is a close correspondence, as regards the chief contributors, among the boys and girls. Four of the items—poor coordination; headaches, etc.; squint; chronic respiratory conditions—occur among those with the six highest ratios both among boys and girls separately and for both sexes together.

This degree of consistency as between the sexes suggests fundamental linkages between the various types of chronic ill-health in children. In view of the close relationship between them and behaviour disturbance reported earlier in this chapter, the existence of an over-all multiple-impairment syndrome would imply that those health items tending to occur in a multiple form should also be those most closely associated with maladjustment. However, it was seen in Table X.1 that of the above four morbid conditions only poor coordination has high scorer/non-scorer ratios in Unract and Ovract. In contrast, the speech defects, which came out as the most highly associated with maladjustment, have a below-average association with the other morbid conditions. Perhaps the most reasonable hypothesis would be that this series of interrelationships is the result of various combinations of morbid (including behavioural) conditions. We could speculate that these go back to genetic linkages, and/or the stage of pregnancy or a noxious influence. In an earlier study, Stott (1959) found that whereas Unforthcomingness and non-epidemic infantile illnesses were both very significantly related to pregnancy stress, they were quite unrelated to each other. The answer could only be that each was related to different sorts of stress during the pregnancy, and it was in fact found that the illnesses were related to those occurring earlier and the Unforthcomingness to those occurring in the later stages of pregnancy. The same explanation could apply to the present findings. The morbid conditions most closely related to behaviour disturbance—speech defects, poor muscular coordination and poor hearing—suggest impairments of neurological origin. Any impairment of behaviour from prenatal influences must also represent an impairment of the neurological structures through which the behaviour system operates. That there is some relationship between respiratory conditions and maladjustment may mean that the nervous system is also involved, resulting in sluggishness of the ciliary hairs and of other reactions to respiratory congestion. At all events, the phenomena of multiple related impairments, although statistically demonstrable, are complex and call for further study.

11
Maladjustment and motor impairment

Difficulty of establishing a neurological factor in behaviour disturbance—use of motor function as the yardstick—the Test of Motor Impairment—the experimental sub-sample—sex-incidence of motor impairment—relation between motor impairment and each type of maladjustment: Underreaction; Overreaction; Unforthcomingness; Withdrawal; Depression; Inconsequence; Hostility; Over-all Maladjustment—the close relationship with Neurological grouping acts as a cross-validation—the closer relationship among girls (bearing out other multiple-impairment findings) and speculation as to the reasons.

Difficulty of establishing a neurological factor in behaviour disturbance

In the previous chapter a consistent relationship was observed between maladjustment and number of chronic morbid conditions. The hypothesis of a direct causal relationship has to be rejected, first, because only a minority of those suffering from multiple morbidity were maladjusted, and only a minority of the maladjusted were multiple-impaired in a physical sense. In the second place, the morbid conditions most closely associated with maladjustment—speech impairment and poor muscular coordination as observed by teachers—pointed to common neurological origins rather than a direct causal relationship.

The attempt to establish a neurological factor in an area of function such as that of social adjustment presents problems of methodology. Neural impairment can be inferred with confidence only if the nature of the observed dysfunction is such that it can hardly be attributed to any other cause. This applies to conditions such as aphasia or cerebral palsy; but, except for comparatively rare post-encephalitic or post-meningitic conditions, maladaptiveness in social behaviour is patently the result of many influences. We have therefore to seek independent evidence of concomitant neural lesion or dysfunction. However, as Birch (1964) points out, the classical neurological examination, relying upon gross failure of reflexes and the like, may miss fairly subtle derangements which are nonetheless sufficient to produce observable impairment of speech, motor control and adaptive behaviour. Moreover, because the behaviour of other people is of such primary importance to us, human beings have evolved very sensitive mechanisms for interpreting it, and this applies particularly to signs of maladaptive social behaviour. If we add to this the complexity of the processes of behavioural adaptation—the transmission of sensory information to the brain, its interpretation, storage, retrieval, the appraisal of the significance of each new situation, the decision-making process—it can be appreciated that even minor dysfunction at any point in the sequence may result in inappropriate responses. What we need, therefore, is a means of measuring minimal and subclinical inefficiency of neural function in a concomitant area where the neurological factor can be isolated more certainly than in social behaviour. Two such areas are motor function and speech.

Use of motor function as the yardstick. In the present study motor function was chosen as this concomitant. It offered the advantages that, first, small derangements produce observable effects; second, these effects are susceptible to objective measurement; and third, by the judicious choice of tasks the influence of learning can be minimized.

Several tests of motor-perceptual function were available, but these have been compiled on the assumption of a unitary motor-perceptual factor, which has not been established. Perceptual failure may be due to lack of sufficient attention. Just as the Inconsequent child does not give himself time to think, so he cannot inhibit physical responses for long enough to deal adequately with sensory information. Consequently a built-in perceptual variable is likely to contain a large element of impulsivity. To use such a test as a concomitant of behaviour disturbance would be circular.

What was needed was a test of motor function which excluded so far as practicable every variable except neural dysfunction. This meant reducing to a minimum the variances attributable to individual differences in perception, physique, muscular strength, mental ability, motivation, emotionality, sex and previous learning—as regards the latter, notably cultural variations in opportunities for developing skills in various activities and in judging space and distance. It is in effect impossible to find a motor task, except one requiring only reflex responses, which does not involve all the above factors. Perceptual monitoring is necessary in virtually all motor acts, a certain level of understanding is essential, and it must be assumed that even the most elementary activities are improved by practice. It is thus a matter of choosing those which—short of patent incompetence—are relatively undiscriminating in these areas because they do not approach the limit of ability of the vast majority of children. Especially in view of the above-quoted findings demonstrating a tendency to multiple impairment and the consequent greater risk of physical, mental and emotional handicaps in a child showing neuro-motor dysfunction, the demands made in these other areas must be kept at a modest level.

The Test of Motor Impairment

Some five years previous to the commencement of the present study, Stott (1965), seeking a means of estimating the part that neural dysfunction plays in other conditions, notably behaviour disturbance and reading disability, embarked upon a revision of the Oseretsky Test of Motor Ability. In the form that it then was, it was administratively unwieldy, many of its items relied upon subjective judgments by the tester, and the above-mentioned extraneous variables were by no means reduced to the necessary minimum. The unwieldiness was eliminated by adopting the scoring system proposed by Göllnitz (1961), which recorded failure only in performance at the child's own age-level and below. There resulted a test which, apart from this variation in method of scoring, followed the form of Oseretsky's, but in which nearly all the items were new or greatly modified (Stott, Moyes and

Henderson 1972). It was designed as a test of minor motor impairment which could reasonably be attributed to neural dysfunction. No assumption was made that the neurological factor amounted to 'minimal brain damage' in the sense of tissue-destruction; the neural incompetence could be due to immaturity, toxicity, hormonal disturbance, malnutrition, hypoxia, or causes as yet undiscovered.

Re-named a *Test of Motor Impairment* in order to emphasize that it measured subnormal functioning only, it was applied to various samples of children within school systems in order to validate and standardize its items. These were modified as necessary in successive editions. The fourth, which was used in the present study, had not reached the stage of final standardization by age-level, but this did not bias the results as given below because the same tasks were given to all the children of each age and sex. (In the original Oseretsky Test there are different tasks for each sex at some age-levels, but in the revised Test identical tasks with little sex bias were chosen so that the incidence of dysfunction as between boys and girls could be compared.)

The Test of Motor Impairment as used covers five areas of function: static balance, upper-limb control, mobile balance, manual dexterity and simultaneous movements. The subject loses two points for failure in any one at a single age-level. In the event of failure the item within the same category is tested at the age-level below. This procedure is continued until the subject reaches a level at which he passes in all five categories. The criteria for passing each task are fixed in such a way as to give a failure rate of between 10 and 15 per cent. Experience has shown that a score of between six and seven registers a degree of motor impairment that will be a definite disadvantage to a child in his everyday life. Six was accordingly chosen as a cut-off point in the treatment of the data. Any score can represent specific impairment, that is to say, in one of the five categories only, or impairment spread over two or more. In the present study only 14 per cent of the cases scoring six or over were 'specific' as thus defined, even when static and mobile balance were treated as one area.

The experimental sub-sample. To obtain a representative sub-sample of the 1940 City children for whom behavioural data had been obtained, the schools they were attending were arranged in four lists by socio-economic group in the order of the number of members of the original sample each contained. By testing from each category in turn in descending order, the socio-economic composition of the number tested at any one time reflected fairly accurately that of the City sample as a whole. This resulted in a sub-sample of 713 (366 boys and 347 girls).

Sex-incidence of motor impairment. Since the items were selected so as to give neither sex a *prima facie* advantage, the Test could be used as a measure of the relative incidence of motor disability as between boys and girls (see Table X1.1).

The greater incidence of motor impairment among boys follows the pattern for behaviour disturbance and ill-health but to a less marked degree. Whereas—using a global estimate—twice as many boys as girls are maladjusted, only some 50 per cent more are motor-impaired.

Social-class differences in motor disability likewise resembled those for behaviour disturbance. There was no trend within the first three socio-economic neighbourhood groups, but the lowest showed higher mean impairment scores, of which only that for boys reached significance at the .05 level. For some reason which

127

TABLE XI.1 Incidence of motor disability by sexes

	Score-category			
	0 - 1	*2 - 5*	*6 and over*	*Total*
Boys	169	143	54	366
	46.2	*39.1*	*14.8*	*100.0*
Girls	190	123	34	347
	54.8	*35.4*	*9.8*	*100.0*
Both sexes	359	266	88	713
	50.4	*37.3*	*12.3*	*100.0*

Percentages in each score-category are in italics

$chi^2 = 6.78$ $p < .05$

defies explanation, both the boys and girls of the next-to-lowest socio-economic group were the least impaired of their sex, but the only significant difference that this produced was in comparison with the lowest group for both sexes.

Relation between motor impairment and each type of maladjustment

The probability of a factor of neurological impairment in maladjustment can be gauged—provided the Motor Test is valid as an indicator of such impairment—by the degree of relationship between the scores for motor impairment and those for the various types of maladjustment. Since neither the distribution of the first nor the second set of scores was normal (about half of each parameter being 0) product-moment correlation could not be used. However, inspection of Table X1.2 shows a general tendency for the mean score for each type of maladjustment to be higher, the greater the motor impairment. For convenience of comparison this tendency is shown in the last column in the form of ratios obtained by dividing the mean maladjustment scores of the worst-coordinated (score of 6 and over) by those for the best-coordinated (0-1). It is seen that all these ratios are above unity, suggesting the possibility of some relationship between all types of maladjustment and motor impairment. The fairly consistent rise in the mean maladjustment scores with increase in motor impairment in the two main Unract/Ovract scales (which include all the scores for the core syndromes plus those of the non-syndromic groupings of underreaction and overreaction) makes a formal statistical test of significance hardly necessary. In fact, if the mean for each category of motor impairment is compared with those of all the less well-coordinated categories for the same type of maladjustment, this trend is reversed in only 36 of the 162 comparisons ($Chi^2 = 27.09, p < .001$).

The results are presented in Tables X1.3 and 4 as percentages and in terms of the risks of having one condition if the other is present, following the format of Tables X.7 and X.8. The score-criteria for each type of maladjustment are the same as used in these Tables.

We are now in a position to use the motor-impairment scores as a divining rod for a neurological factor in each type of maladjustment in two ways. First, from Table X1.2, we can note the rise in the maladjustment means with increase in

TABLE XI.2 Mean scores for types of maladjustment by degree of motor impairment

Motor Impairment score-category

	0 - 1	2 - 3	4 - 5	6+	RATIO:
BOYS AND GIRLS					mean for 6+ / mean for 0-1
	N = 359	N = 181	N = 85	N = 88	
Unract	2.37	3.02	3.55	3.31	1.40
Ovract	2.99	4.12	3.40	6.05	2.02
Unforthcomingness	1.20	1.48	1.73	1.39	1.16
Withdrawal	0.37	0.43	0.44	0.56	1.51
Depression	0.31	0.49	0.64	0.57	1.84
Inconsequence	1.49	1.77	1.66	3.26	2.19
Hostility	0.62	0.98	0.60	0.98	1.58
Neurological	0.12	0.17	0.26	0.25	2.08
Over-all maladjustment	5.36	7.14	6.95	9.35	1.74
BOYS					
	N = 169	N = 97	N = 46	N = 54	
Unract	2.60	3.27	3.09	3.46	1.33
Ovract	4.40	4.60	4.39	7.80	1.77
Unforthcomingness	1.12	1.36	1.22	1.26	1.13
Withdrawal	0.50	0.61	0.43	0.69	1.38
Depression	0.44	0.66	0.80	0.72	1.64
Inconsequence	2.24	1.99	2.00	4.11	1.83
Hostility	0.84	0.98	0.78	1.28	1.52
Neurological	0.16	0.20	0.24	0.30	1.88
Over-all maladjustment	7.00	7.87	7.48	11.26	1.61
GIRLS					
	N = 190	N = 84	N = 39	N = 34	
Unract	2.16	2.73	4.10	3.06	1.42
Ovract	1.74	3.57	2.23	3.26	1.87
Unforthcomingness	1.27	1.62	2.33	1.59	1.25

(table continues overleaf)

	Motor Impairment score-category				
	0 - 1	2 - 3	4 - 5	6+	RATIO:
GIRLS					mean for 6+ / mean for 0-1
Withdrawal	0.25	0.21	0.44	0.35	1.40
Depression	0.19	0.29	0.44	0.32	1.68
Inconsequence	0.83	1.52	1.26	1.91	2.30
Hostility	0.43	0.98	0.38	0.50	1.16
Neurological	0.08	0.14	0.28	0.18	2.25
Over-all maladjustment	3.91	6.30	6.33	6.32	1.62

motor impairment, summarized in ratios as between the worst and best coordinated; second, we can observe what proportion of the maladjusted, compared to the well-adjusted, are motor-impaired and vice-versa. To give the reader a quick over-view and to show in real terms what the relationships between maladjustment and motor impairment amount to, these comparisons are summarized in Tables X1.3 and 4 as percentages and ratios, as follows:

a Percentage of maladjusted who are motor-impaired
b Percentage of well-adjusted who are motor-impaired
   The ratio a/b shows by how much more the maladjusted are motor-impaired
c Percentage of motor-impaired who are maladjusted
d Percentage of well-coordinated who are maladjusted
   The ratio c/d shows by how much more the motor-impaired are maladjusted

The relationships shown by these ratios are illustrated in Figure X1.1 as contrasting proportions of motor impaired among the maladjusted and the well-adjusted, and in Figure X1.2 as contrasting proportions of maladjusted among the poorly and well coordinated.

Underreacting maladjustment. The mean scores on the Unract scale are some 40 per cent higher among the motor-impaired compared with the well-coordinated. Some 83 per cent more of the motor-impaired suffer from a significant degree of this type of maladjustment. Reversing the comparison, of the underreacting children some 73 per cent more are motor-impaired than of the not-underreacting. There is thus an over-all probability of a neurological factor in underreacting behaviour disturbance, assuming that motor impairment as measured by the test has a similar basis.

Overreacting maladjustment. The relationship here is even closer. For boys and girls combined, the mean score of the motor-impaired on the Ovract scale is over twice that of the well-coordinated, and about 24 per cent of the maladjusted—about 2½ times that of the stable—are motor-impaired.

TABLE XI.3 Risks of motor impairment among the maladjusted and of maladjustment among the motor-impaired

UNRACT

(both sexes)

a	Per cent of underreactors who are motor-impaired (13/69)	18.8
b	Per cent of not underreactors who are motor-impaired (50/459)	10.9
a/b	Greater risk of motor impairment among underreactors	1.73
c	Per cent of motor-impaired who are underreactors (13/88)	14.8
d	Per cent of not motor-impaired who are underreactors (29/359)	8.1
c/d	Greater risk of underreaction among the motor-impaired	1.83

chi^2 (df=4) 13.42 $p < .01$ (df=1) 5.16 $p < .05$

OVRACT

a	Per cent of overreactors motor-impaired (18/74)	24.3
b	Per cent of not overreactors motor-impaired (49/491)	10.0
a/b	Greater risk of motor impairment among overreactors	2.44
c	Per cent of motor-impaired who are overreactors (18/88)	20.5
d	Per cent of not motor-impaired who are overreactors (25/359)	7.0
c/d	Greater risk of overreaction among the motor-impaired	2.93

chi^2 (df=4) 16.44 $p < .01$ (df=1) 16.49 $p < .001$

OVER-ALL MALADJUSTMENT

a	Per cent of maladjusted who are motor-impaired (18/70)	25.7
b	Per cent of not maladjusted who are motor-impaired (32/372)	8.6
a/b	Greater risk of motor impairment among the maladjusted	2.99
c	Per cent of motor-impaired who are maladjusted (18/88)	20.5
d	Per cent of not motor-impaired who are maladjusted (21/359)	5.8
c/d	Greater risk of maladjustment among the motor-impaired	3.50

chi^2 (df=4) 23.52 $p < .001$ (df=1) 23.83 $p < .001$

The figures in brackets give the frequencies on which each percentage is based. They are for the highest and lowest categories of adjustment and motor ability respectively.

Chi^2's are calculated for these extreme categories, giving one degree of freedom, and for three degrees of adjustment and three degrees of motor impairment, giving four degrees of freedom.

131

TABLE XI.4 Risks of motor impairment associated with each core syndrome of maladjustment, and of the latter with motor impairment (both sexes)

a %	b %	a/b	c %	d %	c/d	chi² df=4	chi² df=1
			UNFORTHCOMINGNESS				
9.7	11.3		6.8	7.8		7.19	.0002
(6/62)	(55/487)		(6/88)	(28/359)		ns	ns
		0.86			0.87		
			WITHDRAWAL				
15.8	11.7		13.6	9.2		2.13	1.64
(12/76)	(65/555)		(12/88)	(33/359)		ns	ns
		1.35			1.48		
			DEPRESSION				
19.5	11.6		9.1	3.6		9.23	5.19
(8/41)	(65/559)		(8/88)	(13/359)		< .05	< .05
		1.68			2.51		
			INCONSEQUENCE				
31.3	10.2		23.9	5.8		27.29	26.84
(21/67)	(59/579)		(21/88)	(21/359)		< .001	< .001
		3.08			4.09		
			HOSTILITY				
18.6	11.6		9.1	5.0		4.13	2.44
(8/43)	(69/594)		(8/88)	(18/359)		ns	ns
		1.60			1.81		

a   Per cent of maladjusted of each type who are motor-impaired
b   Per cent of not maladjusted of each type who are motor-impaired
a/b   Greater risk of motor impairment among maladjusted of each type
c   Per cent of motor-impaired among maladjusted of each type
d   Per cent of well-coordinated among maladjusted of each type
c/d   Greater risk of each type of maladjustment among the motor-impaired

The figures in brackets give the frequencies on which each percentage is based. They are for the highest and lowest categories of adjustment and motor ability respectively.

Chi^2's are calculated for these extreme categories, giving one degree of freedom, and for three degrees of adjustment and three degrees of motor impairment, giving four degrees of freedom.

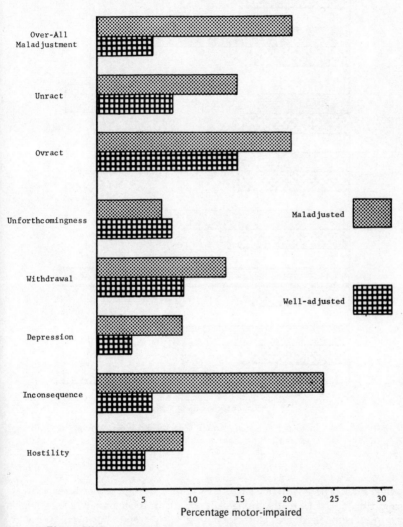

Figure XI.1   Incidence of motor impairment among the maladjusted (general and types)

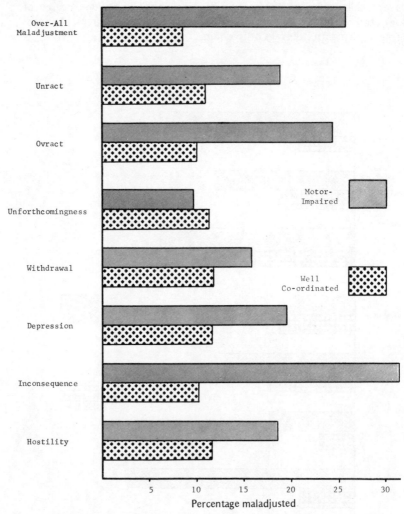

Figure XI.2   Incidence of maladjustment (general and types) among the motor-impaired

Unforthcomingness. There is here a slight inverse relationship: rather fewer than a chance proportion of the Unforthcoming children are motor-impaired, and rather fewer of the motor-impaired are Unforthcoming. This trend, however, is not significant, and the low ratios of the means as between the extreme motor categories bear out the lack of a relationship. If there is a neurological factor in Unforthcomingness it has no affinity with any such factor in motor impairment.

Withdrawal. The excess of Withdrawn behaviour among the motor-impaired, as shown by the means in Table XI.2, about equals the average for underreacting behaviour in general, and the comparison of the extreme categories by cases gives the same result.

Depression. The mean scores for Depression are 84 per cent higher among the motor-impaired, and the ratio of the percentage of the Depressed impaired to that of the Not-Depressed impaired points in the same direction. Over 2½ times as many motor-impaired are in the highest category for Depression. The numbers, however, were small.

Inconsequence. This type of behaviour disturbance stands out as having by far the closest relationship with motor impairment. Some 31 per cent of the Inconsequent children are also motor-impaired; of the motor-impaired, 24 per cent are Inconsequent. These percentages are three and four times respectively those for Not-Inconsequents. These findings are in accordance with general observation, but care has to be taken in making aetiological deductions therefrom. A direct causal relationship cannot be assumed because 31 per cent of the Inconsequents are well-coordinated, and 66 per cent of the motor-impaired are not Inconsequents. Nor does this degree of relationship support the thesis that the 'Strauss-type child' suffers primarily from a distortion of body-image and hence a perceptual handicap in his dealings with his environment. The most feasible interpretation is that there is a common factor of neural dysfunction in Inconsequence and motor disability which, as is characteristic of such dysfunction, may be more or less pervasive. In other words, some Inconsequent children are neurologically impaired only as regards a failure to inhibit primitive physical impulses, while in others the area of dysfunction extends to motor control. Similarly, some children suffer from specific impairment of motor function while others have more extensive neurological lesion which extends to the control of behaviour.

Hostility. There is a definite tendency for the most Hostile children to be motor-impaired (ratio of 1.60) and for the motor-impaired to be Hostile (ratio of 1.81). This suggests that in addition to the undoubted environmental factor in Hostility there is also an element of neural dysfunction which makes for inability to control rage-responses.

Over-all maladjustment. All the above comparisons understate the general relationship between maladjustment and motor impairment since children in the best-adjusted category for one type of maladjustment are not necessarily generally well-adjusted, and could even score highly in other types. Notably, the low scorers for Underreaction could be high scorers for Overreaction, and the other way round. It is therefore legitimate to use the total BSAG scores, even though for most purposes the heterogeneous nature of maladjustment makes them of limited application as a parameter. The adjustment categories chosen isolate, at one extreme, the 52 per cent of children who were well-adjusted in an all-round way (scores of 0–4) and, at the other extreme, the 10 per cent who accumulated a score of 17 or over in some type of maladjustment or other. In Table XI.5 the ratios a/b and c/d show respectively that three times as many of the maladjusted are motor-impaired as of those who are all-round stable, and 3½ times as many of the motor-impaired show maladjustment of some type compared with the well-coordinated. About a quarter of the maladjusted are motor-impaired compared with only some 9 per cent of the overall well-adjusted. And some 20 per cent of the motor-impaired are maladjusted in a general way compared with 6 per cent of the well-coordinated.

The Neurological grouping. The mean scores for this grouping show consistent rises with increase in motor-impairment score. The six behaviour items of which it is composed were not placed in any of the syndromes because they were at least in part involuntary or seemed to indicate 'nerviness' or other neural dysfunction rather than motivated act. Most of them were more closely associated with overreacting maladjustment. This is consistent with the closer association between the latter and motor impairment. The high ratios derived from the mean Neurological scores as shown in Table XI.2, that is, as between the motor-impaired and the well-coordinated, serves in some degree as a cross-validation for the assumption of a neurological factor in each. The Neurological grouping obtained remarkably similar ratios—for boys and girls separately and together—as did Inconsequence. Given all the assumptions made earlier, this could mean that Inconsequence ranks about equally with these behaviours, traditionally thought of as evidence of 'nerves', as regards a neurological component.

The closer relationship among girls. In Chapter Ten it was shown that, although girls suffered less both from the various forms of chronic ill-health and from maladjustment, the relationship between the two sets of conditions was more marked for them than for boys. The same applied in general to the incidence of motor impairment and its relationship to maladjustment. There was less motor impairment among the girls, but the ratios given in Table XI.2 show that, except for Hostility, its association with maladjustment was closer for them than for the boys. This confirms the tighter syndrome of multiple impairments among girls which was remarked upon in the earlier chapter. To instance the ratio of the mean scores for Inconsequence as between the poorly and well coordinated girls, at 2.30 it is the highest of all the ratios for either sex, although this form of maladjustment seems to be about six times more prevalent among boys. The runner up is that of 2.25 for the Neurological grouping, also among girls. If we can hazard an aetiological inference, this leads us to think in terms of sex-linked genetic factors. To ask what might have been the value for the human race to have evolved genes of an apparently contradictory differential lethality for each sex takes us into the realm of speculation. It is understandable in terms of population-control theory (Wynne Edwards 1962, Stott 1962b and 1969) that when a cut-back of population-numbers becomes urgent, the sacrifice of the males is less detrimental to subsequent recovery as conditions improve, since one male can fertilize a number of females. This would explain the far lower incidence of nearly all types of impairment, from health to behaviour, among that sex. One can only suppose that when the hardships consequent upon overpopulation reach a point when some females also have to be sacrificed, the job must be done more thoroughly.

12
Maladjustment and delinquency

The theory of adjustment to a sub-culture and the 'normality' of delinquency—previous findings of a relationship between maladjustment and delinquency—manner of identifying the offenders within the city sub-sample.

High mean scores for overreacting maladjustment among the offenders—but a significant proportion are well-adjusted in school—the concept of maladjustment as applied to lawbreaking—the mean scores by core syndromes—Hostility the highest—descriptions of the maladjusted behaviour most frequent among the offenders—mean maladjustment scores by type of offence—girl shoplifters no more 'normal' than other offenders—no consistent social-class differences in the amount of maladjustment among offenders—theories of cultural infection, social frustration or sub-cultural differences in norms of behaviour not confirmed as reasons for delinquency.

The 'normality' of delinquency

During the past generation it has been fashionable to explain delinquency along cultural lines and to deny or minimize the personal factor of intrinsic behaviour disturbance. Writing of the group delinquent, Shaw and McKay (1942), concluded that 'Within the limits of his social world and in terms of its norms and expectations, he may be a highly organized and well-adjusted person.' Mays (1954) maintained that the delinquency of inner-city youth 'is not so much a symptom of maladjustment as of adjustment to a sub-culture in conflict with the culture of the city as a whole'. His claim (1962) that 90 per cent of offences by juveniles are committed by those of stable personality is not based upon any behavioural assessment. Kvaraceus and W.B. Miller (1959) are somewhat more moderate in estimating that 'the preponderant portion of our "delinquent" population consists of essentially "normal" lower-class youngsters' and that not more than 25 per cent of all delinquents suffer from personal or emotional adjustment problems. Working from the theoretical standpoint of cultural infection as the chief cause of delinquency in lower-class youth, they hypothesized that the proportion of emotionally disturbed offenders will be relatively high in the middle class and extremely low in the lower class.

The acid test of a cultural determinant is that of incidence. If all or nearly all members of a sub-culture affect a certain type of behaviour it may be considered a cultural norm, but if it is only a small minority then individual determinants must be sought in addition. Even in the most overcrowded slum quarters of Glasgow only 22.3 per cent of youths were found to have been convicted of an offence between the ages of fifteen and eighteen years (Ferguson 1952). In the same city Stott (1960) found that of boys put on probation for the first time—78 per cent of whom were first offenders—only 23 per cent came in the 'best adjusted' group, as measured by a score of nine or less on the BSAG, compared with 72 per cent of the non-delinquent controls. Forty-six per cent of these delinquents, but only 8 per cent of the controls, met the criterion score of twenty for maladjustment. All illegal behaviour was excluded from the scores. Contrary to the hypothesis of Kvaraceus and W.B. Miller mentioned above, the mean maladjustment scores of the delinquents were very similar in all parts of the city, although the delinquency-rate varied with their socio-economic rating. That of the delinquents living in the most-prone, lower-class areas was 18.9, and that of those living in 'black spots', defined as having clusters of delinquent boys, was 18.3; in the middle-class areas, with lowest delinquency, it was almost exactly the same, namely 18.7. Even in the area of highest delinquency the mean for the non-delinquents was no more than 8.1. Thus, even these mostly first-offender delinquents scored twice as high as the general run of boys living in the same neighbourhood. Conger and W.C. Miller (1966) reached a similar finding in Denver—'despite the fact that delinquent/ non-delinquent pair members were of the same age and sex; had grown up in similar neighbourhoods (not infrequently the same block); had faced similar socio-economic problems; had, in the case of minority group members, encountered similar problems of discrimination and socio-cultural isolation.' Furthermore, 'they were less well-liked and accepted by their peers'. It is thus improbable that the 'group' or 'socialized' delinquency of Jenkins (1969) 'represents social group conflict more than individual psychopathology', or that it can be called 'adaptive' in any usual sense.

The delinquents within the City sub-sample

The survey of social adjustment reported in this monograph provided an opportunity to adjudicate upon these conflicting views in respect to delinquency in a North American industrial city. A list was drawn up from the court and police files covering the City sub-sample of all those who had been guilty of conduct bringing them into contact with the police over the preceding three years. The conduct in question consisted of offences of types which are usually classified as 'indictable'. It excluded 'technical' offences such as breaches of highway regulations. Behaviour leading to being brought to court as 'incorrigible' was included even though it did not constitute a breach of the law. Not all of the deviant occurrences resulted in a charge before a court, but for convenience they are termed 'offences'. The number and nature of each were recorded in respect of each juvenile. Among the 1940 pupils of the City sub-sample there were 133—105 boys and 28 girls—who committed such offences, and they are, for short, termed 'delinquents'.

High mean scores for overreacting maladjustment among the offenders. An over-all picture of the relationship between delinquency, as defined above, and social adjustment within the school setting is shown by the mean BSAG, Unract and Ovract scores in Table XII.1. They are given for non-offenders, and those with

TABLE XII.1 Mean maladjustment scores by number of offences

		Number of offences			
		0	1	2	3+
Boys	N	*884*	*65*	*14*	*26*
BSAG		7.91	10.78	15.57	16.88
OVRACT		4.80	7.74	10.93	13.46
UNRACT		3.11	2.95	4.57	3.38
Girls	N	*923*	*22*	*2*	*4*
BSAG		5.40	9.09	8.00	18.25
OVRACT		2.51	5.59	6.00	13.75
UNRACT		2.88	3.41	2.00	4.50
Both sexes	N	*1807*	*87*	*16*	*30*
BSAG		6.63	10.36	14.63	17.07
OVRACT		3.63	7.20	10.31	13.50
UNRACT		2.99	3.07	4.25	3.53

one, two, and three or more offences recorded against them (the last being referred to below as the recidivists). These means are depicted in the histogram of Figure XII.1.

It is seen that the mean total BSAG scores rise consistently with the amount of delinquency; that for the recidivists is never less than twice the mean for the non-offenders, and for both sexes combined is over two-and-a-half times as high. However, this total score disguises the true nature of the relationship, which is between delinquency and maladjusted behaviour of an overreacting type. The mean Ovract score for recidivists is nearly three times as high as the non-offender mean for boys, and over five times as high for girls. Even for first offenders the Ovract mean for both sexes is more than double that for the non-delinquents. In contrast there is no significant rise in Unract score with number of offences. The percentages of offenders in each Ovract score group are given in Table XII.2. Again we see regular increases with mounting maladjustment, which confirm the general relationship revealed by the mean scores.

The apparently well-adjusted delinquent

The above findings leave no doubt about the general relationship between delinquency and the overreacting forms of maladjustment. Nevertheless it is by no means perfect. One third of the boy offenders obtained Ovract scores in the well-adjusted category (0-3); and of these apparently well-adjusted boys 6.3 per cent had committed one or more offences. There would thus seem to be a class of occasional offender who remains otherwise well-adjusted, or whose behaviour disturbance is not apparent to his teachers. It may be that, in certain social settings, young people with only minimal tendencies to overreaction require the experience of being apprehended in a misdemeanor for social learning to take place. That only six of the twenty-nine offenders who came in the well-adjusted categories for both Unract and Ovract committed more than one offence lends support to this

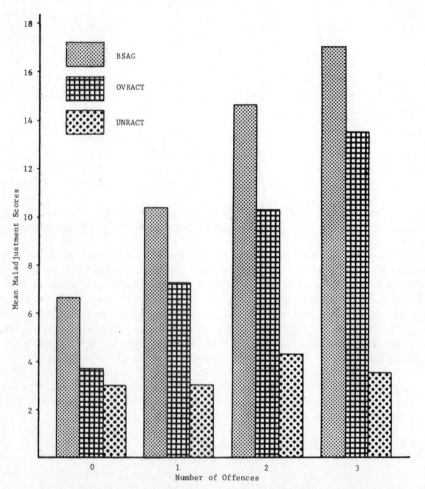

Figure XII.1 Mean maladjustment scores by number of offences (both sexes)

TABLE XII.2 Distribution of offenders within Ovract score groupings

Score grouping

	0-3	4-7	8-11	12-24	25+
Boys					
Total in group	557	158	104	148	21
Offenders:					
number	35	17	14	31	8
per cent	6.28	10.75	13.46	20.94	38.09
Girls					
Total in group	736	102	51	55	7
Offenders:					
number	15	3	4	5	1
per cent	2.03	2.94	7.84	9.09	14.28
Both sexes					
Total in group	1294	260	155	203	28
Offenders:					
number	50	20	18	36	9
per cent	3.86	7.69	11.61	17.73	32.14

hypothesis. Alternatively these apparently well-adjusted offenders could have reacted by delinquency against personal stresses without becoming maladjusted in their general life-style.

If we accept as a general criterion for maladjustment a tendency to act against one's own best interests, we have to ask why a well-adjusted boy should commit acts calculated to impair his relations with his parents and jeopardize his employment. Even though subjected to personal stresses or sensitive to pressures from his age-peers, he would be expected to obey the Law of Least Cost, that is to say, to resist the temptation to respond to stresses in ways which worsen his situation. Logically, therefore, we have to seek some personal weakness or aberrant motivation which, in certain circumstances, impels a boy to breach this fundamental law of adaptive behaviour.

In some apparently well-adjusted delinquents the Inconsequence may be of a mild type not observable in school but which reveals itself when the boy is anxious not to be left out of peer activities or cannot resist being dared into a delinquent escapade. Similarly, hostility generated by an unreliable family setting may not be transferred on to the teacher. These apparently well-adjusted delinquents need to be the subject of individual investigation before they can be claimed as examples of adolescent behaviour which is typical within certain cultural settings.

Mean scores for core syndromes

We can narrow down the relationship between delinquency and maladjustment by comparing the mean scores within the core syndromes for non-offenders and for

TABLE XII.3 Mean scores in core syndromes by number of offences

| | | Number of offences | | | |
		0	1	2	3+
Boys	N	884	65	14	26
Unforthcomingness		1.24	1.15	.93	.96
Withdrawal		.52	.57	.93	.85
Depression		.65	.75	2.07	1.19
Inconsequence		2.44	3.89	4.93	4.38
Hostility		.84	1.62	2.00	4.54
Girls	N	923	22	2	4
Unforthcomingness		1.57	1.77	0	2.50
Withdrawal		.30	.23	0	0
Depression		.34	.68	1.50	1.00
Inconsequence		1.18	1.64	2.00	7.50
Hostility		.59	2.14	1.50	4.25
Both sexes	N	1807	87	16	30
Unforthcomingness		1.41	1.31	.81	1.17
Withdrawal		.41	.48	.81	.73
Depression		.49	.74	2.00	1.17
Inconsequence		1.80	3.32	4.56	4.80
Hostility		.71	1.75	1.94	4.50

offenders with varying numbers of offences in the same way as was done in Table XII.1 for the main scales. The results are given in Table XII.3 and the histogram of Figure XII.2. Only for Unforthcomingness are the means lower for the recidivists than for the non-offenders, (the small number of girl recidivists makes their means unreliable). In contrast, those for the other two underreacting core syndromes, Withdrawal and Depression, are, for boys and girls combined, 78 and 139 per cent higher. Once again, Unforthcomingness marks itself out as a form of behaviour distinct from other forms of underreaction, making any general category of introversion or inhibited behaviour inaccurate.

Among the overreacting types of maladjustment Inconsequence likewise distinguishes itself from Hostility, but not to so striking a degree. The Inconsequential means are 2.7 times higher for the recidivists than for the non-offenders, while those for Hostility are over six times higher. Hostility would seem therefore to account for the greater part of delinquency.

Specific indications of delinquency-proneness

In Table XII.4 and Figure XII.2 the delinquent proclivity is brought down to specified items of maladjusted behaviour. Against each is given a scorer/non-scorer ratio, showing how many times more often the item was marked for delinquents than for non-delinquents. Listed are the twenty-five items for which the ratio exceeds three. Although the teachers were not informed which of the sample had

TABLE XII.4 Greater frequency of maladjusted behaviours among delinquents

	Number (del:non-del)	Frequency Ratio (del/non-del)
Inconsequence		
Shows off (clowns, strikes silly attitudes, mimics)	34:151	3.06
Borrows books from others' desks without permission	18:68	3.60
Hostility		
Will help (*teacher*) unless he is in a bad mood	26:82	4.31
Sometimes in a bad mood (*talking to teacher*)	23:93	3.36
Inclined to be moody	24:108	3.02
Seems to go out of his way to earn disapproval	8:30	3.62
Openly does things he knows are wrong in front of the teacher	23:75	4.17
Bears a grudge, always regards punishment as unfair	18:65	3.76
Becomes antagonistic	6:17	4.80
Has uncooperative moods	29:116	3.40
Has stolen in a way that he would be bound to be found out	3:7	5.82
Uses bad language which he knows will be disapproved of	12:22	7.41
Tries to argue against teacher	8:34	3.20
Squabbles, makes insulting remarks *(with other children)*	35:122	3.90
Non-syndromic Overreaction		
Sometimes a fluent liar	16:60	3.62
Mixes mostly with unsettled types	31:122	3.45
Damage to personal property	4:4	13.59
Foolish or dangerous pranks when with a gang	13:58	3.05
Damage to public property	7:7	13.59
Habitual slick liar; has no compunction about lying	10:36	3.77
Has stolen within the school in an underhand cunning way	7:17	5.59
Has truanted, or suspected of truancy	6:8	10.19
Bad loser (creates a disturbance when game goes against him)	25:110	3.09
Misuses companionship to show off or dominate	13:54	3.27
Bad sportsman (plays for himself only, cheats, fouls)	10:43	3.16

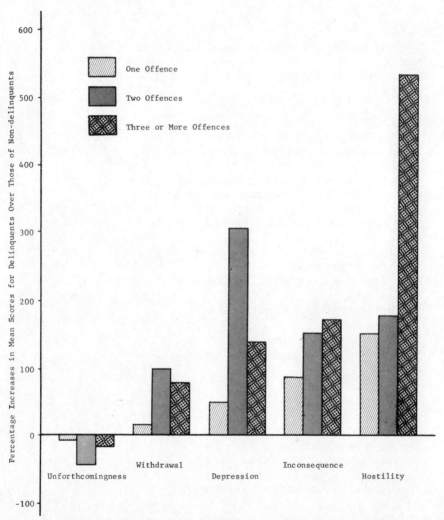

Figure XII.2   Excess of each type of maladjustment among delinquents compared with non-delinquents

TABLE XII.5 Mean Ovract scores by type of offence

	Breaking and entering	Theft	Incorrigible	Missing	Assault	Glue-sniffing	Vandalism	Shoplifting	Trespass	Non-delinquent
Boys										
Number	8	42	3	13	17	2	40	34	13	884
BSAG	14.9	13.8	23.0	18.5	15.7	17.0	13.9	12.9	13.8	7.9
Ovract	11.5	10.2	20.7	13.6	12.2	17.0	10.7	9.9	9.1	4.8
Girls										
Number	1	2	1	4	4	2	3	18	3	923
BSAG	20.0	11.5	10.0	10.5	19.8	13.5	11.0	10.5	6.7	5.4
Ovract	19.0	7.0	1.0	7.3	17.0	6.5	9.3	6.5	4.7	2.5

committed offences, it is evident from the ratios for the items referring to damage to personal and public property that the delinquent tendencies of the students in question had for the most part become known to them. The two items referring to theft within the school not surprisingly also gain high ratios, but offensive language has a higher ratio than either. Of the technically non-delinquent behaviour, truancy is most closely associated with delinquency, having a ratio of over ten.

In defence of the theory of cross-cultural conflict it might be claimed that the supposedly maladjusted behaviour recorded by the teachers was really an expression of the antagonism between the middle-class teacher and young people brought up in a different way of life. Against this is the evidence from the last three items in the Table, and the last under the sub-heading of Hostility, which point to bad relations with age-peers. The typical delinquent does not seem to limit his antagonisms to his relations with his teacher.

Maladjustment and type of offence

Some forms of lawbreaking carry a greater social stigma than others. Offences against speed limits or parking regulations carry little or none, and the only deterrence is the severity of the penalty. It has been claimed that, within the adolescent sub-culture of the city, this applies to certain forms of delinquency, notably shoplifting and vandalism. From his experience in a club for dockland boys in Liverpool, Mays (1954) observed that while breaking and entering were regarded as dangerous activities about which little was said, boys would openly brag about their shoplifting exploits and exhibit their trophies to each other. Shoplifting from large department stores has become so prevalent as to be regarded as a typical activity of inner-city youth, without implications of abnormality.

145

As a test of the validity of this viewpoint the mean maladjustment scores were calculated for those committing each type of offence. Table XII.5 reproduces the total BSAG and Ovract scores only, since those for Unract have little relationship to delinquency. Despite the small numbers of girls committing some types of offence, the means are given for the sexes separately in order to show the possibility of a different pattern for each. Since some committed an offence of more than one type, there is inevitably some overlap in the categories. For purposes of comparison the mean scores for non-delinquents are repeated from Table XII.1.

It is apparent that certain types of offence are more associated with maladjustment, especially of an overreacting type, than are others. The mean Ovract score for three boys brought to court as 'Incorrigible' is over four times that for the non-delinquents, but this is understandable considering that the behaviour which prompted such action would be generally regarded as highly maladjusted. The same could account for the high means for boys missing from home and those guilty of assault. The fashionable 'offence' of glue-sniffing is given a separate category, despite the small numbers, as the nearest to non-medical drug-taking (no data for the latter being available since it was dealt with by the Royal Canadian Mounted Police and not the City Police). The mean for the two male glue-sniffers is also high.

For the remaining classes of offence the Ovract means for boys vary from twice to two-and-a half times as high compared with those for non-offenders, except for trespass. Although the offences of vandalism and shoplifting show slightly lower means than those for breaking and entering, the difference is not large enough to confirm the impression that these are activities of typical adolescents within a City sub-culture. That for boy shoplifters is indeed exactly the same as for boys who committed miscellaneous thefts, and that for boy vandals is actually slightly greater.

Among the girls, shoplifting is seen as by far the favourite form of delinquency. The individuals concerned were nearly 2½ times more subject to overreacting forms of maladjustment than non-delinquent girls. Shoplifting cannot therefore be regarded as a normal feminine activity even among adolescents within a city. The Unract mean for girl shoplifters (not given in the Table) was 3.9, compared with that for non-offenders of 2.9. In short, the typical girl shoplifter, like her male counterpart, suffers from an overreacting more than an underreacting form of maladjustment, although she has somewhat more of the latter than the female non-shoplifter.

Only the most maladjusted girls entered into the masculine pursuits of breaking and entering (a record Ovract mean of 20), assault (17.0) and vandalism (9.3). The anomalous Ovract mean of 1.0 for the one incorrigible girl is due to her having suffered from severe underreacting maladjustment, with an Unract score of 9.0.

The outcome of the above analysis by mean maladjustment scores is that there is no class of offence, among either boys or girls, which is typical of the individual who is well-adjusted within the school setting. Nevertheless there was a significant proportion of offenders for each class of offence who came within the 'well-adjusted' score-category for Ovract. For both sexes combined, the percentages amounted to 11 for breaking and entering, 30 for miscellaneous theft, 25 for incorrigibility, 18 for being missing, 26 for vandalism, 39 for shoplifting and 31 for trespass. One of the glue-sniffers was well-adjusted in school. Shoplifting is seen to have the greatest proportion of well-adjusted perpetrators, but by no great margin.

146

TABLE XII.6 Mean Maladjustment scores by neighbourhood groupings

| | Socio-economic neighbourhood group | | |
	Upper and Middle	Lower-Middle	Lower
Total BSAG	12.48	13.12	11.73
Ovract	8.73	9.88	8.40
Unract	3.66	3.09	3.29
Hostility	2.32	2.79	2.09
Inconsequence	3.50	3.91	3.71
Number per group*	44	34	45

*Ten offenders attended schools which were excluded as serving mixed neighbourhoods

Social-class factors

There seems little likelihood that the relationship between overreacting maladjustment and delinquent behaviour was a cultural artifact because the difference between the means for recidivists and non-offenders was very much greater than that between the social classes as a whole. Nevertheless, to obtain an exact picture of the part played by cultural factors, mean scores were calculated by the social-class neighbourhood groupings of the schools as described in Chapter Nine. The six delinquents in the Upper class were amalgamated with the Middle. It is seen from Table XII.6 that there are no consistent trends in the means for total BSAG, or for overreacting or underreacting maladjustment. Those for the first two are slightly higher for the Lower-Middle group. For all three, the means for the Lower and the Upper are very similar. None of the differences between the means are statistically significant.

The general finding, in sum, was that the delinquents were equally maladjusted in an overreacting sense, irrespective of the neighbourhood in which they lived. As a test of the theory of cultural infection this grouping of delinquents by neighbourhoods was probably more appropriate than an attempt to assign them individually to social classes, since all those attending a particular school would be exposed to the same 'infection'. It is seen that the deduction from this cultural infection theory made by Kvaraceus and Miller (1959), that the proportion of emotionally disturbed offenders would be high in the middle class and extremely low in the lower class, is not borne out.

An alternative explanation in cultural terms—that of Cohen (1953) following the social theory of Merton—has been that lower-class youth, being handicapped educationally and economically in the attainment of the social goals of the upper class, free themselves from moral obligation to upper-class behavioural norms by resorting to hostility. The mean scores for Hostility were therefore included in the Table. It is seen that while the social-class differences are non-significant, there is

147

actually slightly less Hostility among the Lower than among the other two neighbourhood groups.

Yet another sociological explanation of delinquency runs that lower-class youth have different norms of behaviour, so that what is accepted among them may be regarded as deviant by the middle and upper classes. It is difficult to pinpoint the behaviours of which this could be true, but in consideration of the here-and-now nature of the lower-class culture, showing itself in greater impulsivity, the category of Inconsequence would probably contain them. It is seen that, once again, there is no significant difference in the amount of this type of disturbed behaviour as between the neighbourhood groupings.

The failure of the present study to confirm these popular sociological explanations of delinquency along lines of direct cultural infection, class antagonism or differences in behavioural norms must not be cited in justification of a purely psychogenic causation. The schools of sociology which have developed these theories did so deductively without any attempt at empirical verification. They assumed that the undoubted greater incidence of delinquency among lower-class youth was due to the direct impact of cultural influences on the youths themselves. It could also be a reflection of a higher incidence of behaviour disturbance of an overreacting type within disadvantaged groups due in part to inadequate nutrition, greater social stresses and poor health among pregnant women; or to the greater prevalence of family stresses during childhood which lead to anxiety and maladjustment. To these might be added a pattern of culture which favours tolerance of others' weaknesses rather than one which trains children to adhere to abstract moral principles. A combination of these three social-class differences—all of them cultural in the broad sense—would seem to be enough to explain the somewhat higher incidence of overreacting maladjustment and its delinquent expression among disadvantaged groups.

13
The follow-up after one year

Predictability implies a degree of constancy—the temptation to assume a constant 'essence' of personality—relatively constant situation-attitudes—hypothesis of greater constancy in expression of good than of poor adjustment.

Objectives of the follow-up—nature of the sub-sample—fall in mean scores in the follow-up—possible explanations—the 'therapeutic' effect of completing the schedule?—constancy of degree of maladjustment—considerable variability in the maladjusted—the well-adjusted largely remain stable—coefficients of reliability—constancy of type of maladjustment.

The concept of constancy in human characteristics

There is little point in making assessments of behaviour disturbance unless predictability can be demonstrated. We require to know whether the adjustment of pupils rated at one point of time within a given educational context resembles their adjustment at some later time in an inevitably somewhat different educational context. If there is little or no such resemblance we would be assessing the situation and not the individual. In so far, therefore, as we wish to measure the maladjustment of individuals, we need reassurance that on the test used there is a substantial measure of constancy.

However, as Hunt (1961) has pointed out with regard to the testing of intelligence, this requirement of constancy involves us not only in theoretical difficulties but in emotional conflicts arising from 'cognitive dissonance'. We like to feel that there is some immutable essence which justifies the construction and use of a test. If we accept such an essence as axiomatic, and conceive of the test as a means of measuring it, it follows that discrepancies between the original test and the re-test must be due to the failure of the instrument to eliminate chance factors.

In the assessment of behaviour disturbance we have to achieve a reconciliation between the scientific requirement that our observations are something more than purely ephemeral and haphazard, and the danger of being edged into the empirically unjustifiable position of assuming the existence of some sort of 'personality' essence. And this is rendered more difficult since the idea that every person possesses a basic character or personality is embedded in our culture.

When we try to translate the concept of an essence ('what we are trying to get at', 'what fundamentally the test measures', etc.) into causative factors, we are faced with a further threat to the comforting tenet of constancy: the relative strength of the determinants may change with time. To quote Hunt, 'it is no easy matter to distinguish essences which are in fact static from essences which are in fact changing.' This cryptic statement conceals a valid relativistic-developmental position which is also seen in his definition of intelligence as 'comprising strategies for processing information that develop in the course of the child's interacting with his environment'. We can apply the same philosophy in seeking a rationale for the predictability of behavioural adjustment. We have to ask what reasons there may be for postulating a *relative* constancy.

The concept of behaviour disturbance which ripened in the course of the present study was of some initial handicap—presumed to be based upon a neural impairment or immaturity—which may be aggravated by secondary complications or pseudo-adjustments, or alleviated by accommodation (conditioning) or maturation. Relative constancy would thus arise from the persistence of the neural dysfunction, or a limit to the degree to which recovery can take place or alternative neural structures brought into use. Some degree of constancy would also result from conditioning, that is to say, the acquisition of adjustments, whether or not truly adaptive in the long term. Such habits or, more accurately, *situation-attitudes* develop with a certain lawfulness, and should confer predictability provided the person continues to be exposed to the situations which evoke the system of conditioned responses.

In repeating behavioural assessments we have to reckon with a considerable variability because we cannot guarantee identity of the stimulus-situation. To quote Hunt again: 'Precise prediction requires knowledge of the future conditions under which the organism will live.' In the second assessment made after twelve months, reported below, the stimulus-situation remained the same in so far as the pupils' behaviour was observed in a school setting, but since they had mostly advanced a grade they were exposed to, and assessed by, different teachers. This difference would produce some intra-test unreliability since some teachers are better observers than others or are inclined to mark the items more freely. In addition, the general mode of interaction of each teacher to the class, and his or her attitude to particular maladjusted pupils, represent real differences in the stimulus-situation which would be likely to produce different reactions.

It has been pointed out by many authors that the well-adjusted child is much less situation-dependent than the maladjusted. Even if he finds himself in an unpleasant situation his better temporal integration will enable him to resist being provoked into responses which have disagreeable consequences for him. He obeys the Law of Least Cost, in other words he does not jump out of the frying pan into the fire. His relative imperviousness to aversive stimuli enables us to hypothesize the greatest constancy among the well-adjusted group.

Of the maladjusted, some may be suffering from persistent neurological handicaps which either reduce their ability to inhibit primitive first responses or deprive them of the positive motivation to cope with situations. In so far, however, as they learn to compensate for such weaknesses—by controlling impulsivity under certain conditions or by becoming familiar with a given environment—they will achieve a somewhat frail adjustment which is dependent upon the continuance of the standard stimulus-situation. But they may be taken unawares by an aversive or unfamiliar stimulus which they have not learnt to cope with. Moreover, the exact nature of the maladjusted situation-attitude may be a factor making for variability. A child with a strong tendency towards hostility may exercise it only on individuals whom he judges to be antagonistic to him; or he may transfer it on to individuals who remind him of some such person or on to all adults, or all persons whatsoever. From a record of hostility in one human context we cannot predict with certainty the degree of attitude-generalization that has taken place. In sum, we can hypothesize a greater variability on re-assessment among the maladjusted.

The follow-up sub-sample

The testing of the constancy of the results of the initial survey after the twelve-month interval sought answers to the following questions:

1 Did the maladjusted continue to appear as such, and if so, did they show the same type of maladjustment?
2 Did any significant intermediate group appear as maladjusted who were not so in the initial assessment?
3 Did the stable remain stable?
4 What systematic differences were there (suggestive of test-effect or other unreliability) between the initial and follow-up assessments?

It was felt that these questions could be answered by taking a stratified sub-sample, which was made up as follows:

TABLE XIII.1

Criterion		*Number meeting criterion*
1 All pupils rated as maladjusted on the basis of a score of either:		
14 or over in Ovract	180	
or 10 or over in Unract	172	
Meeting both criteria	5	357
2 Every second pupil by list in a middle score-range, namely:		
7–10 inclusive for Ovract		
or 5–7 inclusive for Unract		197
3 Every fifth pupil by list scoring 3 or less in Ovract and 2 or less in Unract, i.e. a well-adjusted stratum		189
		743

Of the above total it was possible to re-assess 634, or 85.3 per cent. The loss was accounted for primarily by the promotion of fifty-four pupils (7.3 per cent) to High School, where re-assessment was not feasible, and by the transfer of twenty-one pupils (2.8 per cent) to the other school boards. No assessments were requested in five cases because this would have involved the class-teacher in completing more than two BSAG's. A further five remained unassessed because of the non-attendance of the child or the absence of the teacher. There were only fourteen cases of failure (1.9 per cent) to make the return, which were not pursued owing to various special reasons apart from the child's adjustment.

The degree of bias due to the above losses may be gauged by the performance of the pupils in question in the initial survey. Apart from those promoted to High School, their mean scores were very similar to those of the rest of the follow-up sub-sample (for Unract 4.93 compared with 4.78; for Ovract 7.74 compared with 7.18). However, the fifty-four of the sub-sample who moved on to High School had a considerably lower Ovract mean (3.39) than did those who dropped out of school at this stage (5.28). On the other hand there was comparatively little difference between the corresponding Unract means (4.31 and 3.90).*

The fall in mean scores

The pupils included in the follow-up showed large falls in mean score compared with the initial assessment. Since they constituted a stratified sub-sample in which the high scorers were over-represented, a regression to the mean was suspected. The only way of counteracting this was to reduce the sub-sample so that it contained approximately the same proportions of maladjusted, intermediate and well-adjusted as in the original sample. In other words, four-fifths of the maladjusted and half the intermediate stratum had to be discarded. This was done by choosing every fifth pupil of the sub-sample who was maladjusted in the initial assessment, and every other pupil who came in the intermediate score range.

Rather than lose such a large amount of data, the opportunity was taken of inserting a reliability check: a second Reduced Sub-sample was made up of another fifth of the maladjusted (being the next names on the list after those of the first Reduced Sub-sample), the discarded half of the intermediate group, and the same well-adjusted group. We had thus Reduced Sub-samples (RS) I and II, each consisting of 304 subjects. The results are given for these alternative sub-samples separately.

Comparison was first made between the mean scores of the pupils in the initial and follow-up assessments. Table XIII.2 shows the percentage changes in mean score for Unract, Ovract and the five core syndromes, for boy and girls together and separately. It reveals an over-all tendency for the mean scores to fall, which cannot be due to a regression to the mean. For maladjustment as a whole (the BSAG scores) the falls average some 16 per cent, but are more pronounced among boys. This is accounted for by the much greater decreases in the Ovract scores among boys, averaging 24 per cent. The Unract scores also, however, fall consistently, but to a lesser degree—some 12 per cent for boys and 15 per cent for girls. Despite this general tendency to decrease in scores, a notable level of significance ($p < .025$) is reached only for the BSAG scores for boys and for both sexes together. Boys show a somewhat greater improvement in adjustment than girls.

The same general tendency towards improvement in adjustment over the year is seen in the core syndromes, although it is notably significant only for Depression in boys. The mean scores for Unforthcomingness actually increase for boys in both RS

---

*The import of these differences is that, at the end of the elementary school stage, it is a high Ovract more than a high Unract score that is associated with failure to proceed to High School.

TABLE XIII.2 Percentage changes in mean scores as between the initial and follow-up assessments

		BSAG	Unract	Ovract	Unforthcoming-ness	Withdrawal	Depression	Inconsequence	Hostility	Neurological
BOYS and GIRLS	I	−17.3**	−12.8	−20.5*	+ 2.4	−21.3	−32.0*	−20.0*	−29.5*	−25.0***
	II	−14.5*	−13.8	−15.1	− 2.4	−13.6	−23.3	−13.4	−22.6	−11.8
BOYS	I	−21.1**	−14.8	−24.4*	+16.0	−27.3	−50.8***	−20.8	−32.7	−33.3***
	II	−18.4*	− 9.5	−23.6*	+ 8.4	− 8.2	−29.9	−21.6	−25.0	−27.3
GIRLS	I	−11.1	−10.5	−12.5	− 9.5	−15.4	+11.8	−19.6	−25.4	0.0
	II	− 7.7	−18.9	+ 3.9	−10.7	−23.1	− 7.7	+ 6.0	−19.8	+16.7

I and II refer to each of the Reduced Sub-samples (RSI and RSII)

Levels of significance:
* .05
** .025
*** .005

I and II, but not to the level of significance. The greatest over-all improvement is in Hostility, which although only reaching modest significance for the sexes combined is consistent for both sexes in each of the sub-samples. A possible explanation of this is advanced on page 153.

The falls in scores over the year could not have been due to a spontaneous trend towards better adjustment. It was seen in Chapter Seven that there is no general tendency for scores to decrease with age. Indeed the Ovract scores, which showed the greatest fall between the two assessments, showed a slight tendency to rise. Moreover the effect of the losses at the follow-up, when the lower scores of those promoted to High School are taken into account, would have been to raise the mean scores, at least for Ovract. Nor does any practice or other intra-test effect seem feasible: a sharpening of the teachers' ability to identify symptoms of maladjustment, or a greater familiarity with the schedule, would have been more likely to increase the number of items marked.

The data were analysed by score-categories in order to discover whether the trend was more apparent among the mildly or the severely maladjusted. In Table XIII.3 this is expressed in ratios for Unract, Ovract and each of the core syndromes obtained by dividing the number in each score-category in the follow-up by the number therein in the initial assessment. A ratio of above unity therefore means that there were more pupils at the particular level of adjustment in the follow-up, and a ratio of less than unity that there were less. As before, the ratios are given for each RS separately. The score-categories are those for degree of maladjustment given in the fifth edition of the Manual to the Bristol Social Adjustment Guides.

It is seen that the ratios for the well-adjusted categories vary little from unity. In the most maladjusted category there is considerable variation as between RS I and II for the core syndromes, due no doubt to smallness of numbers. If, however, these ratios are reviewed conjointly with those for the Moderately Disturbed, a general tendency for the ratios to decrease from left to right of the Table can be discerned. This is most consistent in the Unract and Ovract scales. In other words, the falls in the mean scores were in the main due to an improvement in the adjustment of the more disturbed pupils. The trend is most marked for Hostility and Inconsequence, and also for Depression when the ratios for the two most disturbed groups are reviewed together.

Falls in score on re-assessment after one year had been reported by Lunzer (1960) with maladjusted children and by Morris (1959) in a study of backward readers. Stott (1966b) suggested that 'the intervention of the research workers and the use of an instrument in which bad behaviour was assessed in psychological terms might . . . incline the teachers to adopt a more understanding attitude to disturbed children so that the latter would in turn react less unfavourably to the school environment.' This explanation was based upon experience of the improvement of maladjusted children as a result merely of taking up the case and asking the teacher to complete a BSAG. In one instance a School Principal urged immediate attention to a hostile child, but at the next month's case-conference reported that the hostility had vanished.

The pupils were in the main assessed by different teachers in the follow-up because nearly all would have advanced a grade in the twelve-months' interval; nevertheless the great majority of teachers had completed a BSAG the previous year in respect of the pupils they had in their classes then, so that the above explanation could apply. It amounts to saying that merely asking teachers to complete a BSAG

TABLE XIII.3 Ratios of incidence at each level of adjustment in the initial and follow-up assessments*

		Well-adjusted	Mildly disturbed	Moderately disturbed	Severely disturbed
		0 - 2	3 - 5	6 - 8	9+
Unract	RSI	1.02	1.14	0.79	0.83
	RSII	0.98	1.70	0.72	0.77
		0 - 3	4 - 7	8 - 11	12+
Ovract	RSI	1.02	1.68	0.83	0.63
	RSII	0.96	2.00	0.97	0.64
		0 - 1	2 - 4	5 - 7	8+
Unforthcomingness	RSI	1.08	0.65	1.60	1.00
	RSII	0.99	1.07	1.10	0.43
		0	1	2 - 3	4+
Withdrawal	RSI	1.02	1.26	0.64	0.67
	RSII	1.02	1.09	0.69	1.00
		0	1 - 2	3 - 4	5+
Depression	RSI	1.05	0.95	0.28	1.40
	RSII	1.08	0.78	0.79	0.78
		0 - 3	4 - 6	7 - 10	11+
Inconsequence	RSI	1.05	0.86	0.82	0.50
	RSII	1.06	0.79	0.74	0.83
		0 - 1	2 - 3	4 - 7	8+
Hostility	RSI	1.03	0.96	0.94	0.33
	RSII	1.02	1.33	0.50	0.67

* The ratios = Number in follow-up / Number in initial

constitutes a form of situational treatment. The falls in the mean scores for Hostility are consistent with this 'therapeutic' explanation. It would suggest that the completion of the BSAG's by the teachers tended to make them regard undesirable behaviour more in terms of maladjustment than of 'badness' or as directed against them personally, with the result that they behaved in a more therapeutic and less punitive or rejecting manner towards the pupils in question. The very marked decrease in Depression among boys could be an improvement in students' motivation in response to changed teacher-attitudes. Nonetheless this interpretation of the fall in scores—being so surprising and having such large implications for teacher-training—must be accepted as only tentative until it is tested by an experiment designed in such a way as to demonstrate that a change in teachers' attitudes does in fact occur as a result of such intervention, and that the greatest improvements were found in those pupils who were exposed to teachers who changed most in a 'therapeutic' direction.

Opposite trends for younger and older children

The markedly different pattern of change as between the age-groupings may give further clues to the reasons for the tendency for the scores to decrease. It is seen from Table XIII.4 that the improvements in the Unract scores occur largely among the under-eights, amounting to between 20 and 32 per cent. This is moreover consistent for both sexes. Among the Underreactors of the 11-14-year group there is considerable variability as between the two sub-samples but little net improvement. In contrast there is a strong improvement among the 11-14-year group for Ovract of some 31 per cent, but none among the under-eights. These opposing trends give the impression that they are not test-artifacts but represent real changes in adjustment. If they are interpreted along the lines of the 'therapeutic' hypothesis, they indicate that inhibited children are more sensitive to improved teacher-attitudes at a young age, but acting-out children are more sensitive thereto around puberty.

Coefficient of reliability

As a formal measure of reliability, coefficients were calculated by Winer's method (1962). They are given in Table XIII.5. The average coefficients of 0.80 for over-all maladjustment, 0.74 for Unract and 0.77 for Ovract are satisfactory considering that real changes in adjustment may be expected to occur after an interval of a year, in different personal situations and rated by different teachers.

Constancy of type of maladjustment

Just as the value of measuring maladjustment depends upon being able to show that it has some degree of constancy, so the establishment of syndromes depends upon their persistence over a certain period of time in the individual case. The extent to which this occurred in the present study has already been shown. It is also important to be able to demonstrate a tendency for the syndromes to maintain the same relative strength. In other words, it has to be ascertained whether, if a person remains maladjusted, he is likely to do so in the same ways.

This aspect of constancy can be measured by examining changes in dominant syndrome. The comparison was of rank, rather than of score-level, so that it was unaffected by the problem of regression to the mean, and the whole sub-sample of 634 could be used. Since, however, one could not speak of syndromes where there was no maladjustment, only those pupils were included who exceeded the cut-off score for good adjustment in one or more syndromes. To overcome the variability in the means and standard deviations the syndrome scores were converted into percentiles. This made it possible to rank the syndromes as most dominant, second dominant, and so on, and to tabulate the shifts in rank. In effect, the last three

TABLE XIII.4 Percentage changes in mean scores for Unract and Ovract by age-groups in the initial and follow-up surveys

Age-group at initial survey	Number in sub-sample		Boys	Girls	Both sexes
	UNRACT				
less than 8 yrs	RSI	96	−30.9	−31.6	−31.1
	RSII	91	−25.9	−20.4	−24.3
8th to 11th birthday	RSI	111	− 8.9	−11.2	− 9.8
	RSII	109	− 1.5	− 5.2	− 3.4
11th to 14th birthday	RSI	88	− 9.4	+12.1	+ 0.3
	RSII	91	+12.3	−28.7	− 9.9
	OVRACT				
less than 8 yrs	RSI	96	−2.5	− 7.4	− 3.6
	RSII	91	+ 5.8	− 6.4	+ 2.6
8th to 11th birthday	RSI	111	−36.5	+10.5	−18.9
	RSII	109	−32.6	+20.9	− 8.9
11th to 14th birthday	RSI	88	−26.4	−45.0	−32.3
	RSII	91	−35.0	−18.1	−30.4

TABLE XIII.5 Reliability coefficients as between initial and follow-up assessments for the two reduced sub-samples

BOYS AND GIRLS

	RS I (304)	RSII (304)
Over-all Maladjustment	0.78	0.82
Unract	0.71	0.76
Ovract	0.74	0.80
Unforthcomingness	0.68	0.67
Withdrawal	0.45	0.50
Depression	0.43	0.64
Inconsequence	0.70	0.73
Hostility	0.62	0.73
Peer-Maladaptiveness	0.55	0.67

ranks had little meaning owing to the low or non-existent scores in the weakest syndromes. For practical purposes what we require to know is in how many cases the same pattern of maladjustment persisted, and in how many it was reversed. These results are given in Table XIII.6. If it can be accepted that remaining in the first or second place or in the last two places is a measure of reasonable consistency, and

TABLE XIII.6 Relative dominance of type of maladjustment in initial and follow-up assessments

Syndrome	In 1st or 2nd place in both	Remained in 4th or 5th place	Dropped from 1st or 2nd to 4th or 5th place	Rose from 4th or 5th to 1st or 2nd place
Unforthcomingness	59	103	9	22
	22.3%	39.0%	3.4%	8.3%
Withdrawal	75	20	29	18
	28.4%	7.6%	11.0%	6.8%
Depression	49	42	25	18
	18.6%	15.9%	9.5%	6.8%
Inconsequence	87	79	21	14
	33.0%	29.9%	8.0%	5.3%
Hostility	84	97	23	15
	31.8%	36.7%	8.7%	5.7%

that movement between the top two and the lowest two places a measure of inconsistency, the relative constancy of each type of maladjustment may be summarized as in Table XIII.7.

Unforthcomingness showed the highest constancy as a type of maladjustment, over five times as many cases maintaining a high or low rank as shifted from the one to the other.

Inconsequence and Hostility were nearly as constant. In Withdrawal and Depression only somewhat over twice as many cases remained constant as shifted. It is justifiable to assume that the indications of each of these syndromes were more easily confused by the teachers who completed the schedules than were the more compelling indications of overreacting behaviour.

The formal coefficients of reliability for each syndrome and associated grouping separately may be expected to be less than for the main scales, and this is seen to be the case in Table XIII.5 The Overreacting syndromes tend to have higher coefficients than the Underreacting, which once again points to the difficulty of distinguishing between the various types of inhibited behaviour.

Theoretical interpretation of the results

The global picture of the extent of constancy given by these findings must be reviewed against our theoretical background. Behaviour is a means of drawing advantage from situations and of avoiding disadvantage. By definition maladjusted behaviour is that which fails to secure such advantage or avoid the disadvantage. The failure will probably not extend to all situations. In so far as it is confined to some only it becomes a maladaptive situation-attitude, or a particular vulnerability to situations of a certain class. On the other hand, an intact behavioural system is likely to be adaptive in all normal situations. Hence the concept of constancy has

TABLE XIII.7 Relative constancy of types of maladjustment

	Reasonably constant	*Inconstant*	*Move from extreme to middle position*
Unforthcomingness	162 *61.4%*	31 *11.7%*	71 *26.9%*
Withdrawal	95 *35.9%*	46 *17.4%*	123 *46.6%*
Depression	91 *34.4%*	43 *16.3%*	130 *49.3%*
Inconsequence	166 *62.7%*	35 *13.3%*	63 *24.0%*
Hostility	181 *68.6%*	38 *14.3%*	45 *17.1%*

two aspects, according to whether we refer to maladaptive or adaptive behaviour. This, in sum, is the picture which emerges from the present study.

The behaviour evoked by an intelligence-test situation is no exception to the above reasoning. It tends to be more constant than the responses to the situations of real life because the testing situations are more uniform than the latter. Hence we cannot expect so great a 'reliability' in the assessment of real-life behaviour as we can that of 'intelligence'. In essence the result of a so-called intelligence test is a function of the particular situation-attitude used by the subject in certain kinds of problem-solving. We have also to recognize that the requirement of reliability is built upon an expectation of sameness in the subject's behaviour over time. It would be incorrect to expect a test to show a greater constancy than obtains in real life.

14
Summary of findings

Classification based on biological and evolutionary concepts

The primary objective of this study was to advance our knowledge of the nature and the natural history of behaviour disturbance by empirical procedures.

Every science begins by the observation of regularities which become organized cognitively as concepts. The first step in bringing order into a mass of observations is to classify them according to their similarities (or predictable regularities) and differences. In applying this method to the study of behaviour we have to face a difficulty from which the chemist, the physicist or the biologist is saved. This is the intangibility of our data. They cannot be weighed or measured in any physical way, and attempts to classify acts by their outward physiological similarities miss the whole point of behaviour.

We have in fact to be clear about the nature of behaviour in order to classify it meaningfully. Behaviour was seen theoretically as a means by which animal organisms have been able to establish more advantageous relationships within their environment. This axiom provided us with a biological-evolutionary definition of maladjusted behaviour as that which, immediately or over time, is disadvantageous to the agent. It also provided us with a principle of classification. Behaviours were regarded as similar when they resulted in a similar type of relationship between the

160

organism and its environment. In adaptive human behaviour we can infer a motivation, or 'intention' to achieve a given result from a reasonable expectation of what the result will be. In maladjusted behaviour this process is interrupted by some dysfunction, such as a failure to take account of the probable consequences of an act, and the result is disadvantageous to the agent.

In human beings and other social animals much behaviour is directed towards establishing certain relationships with others of their kind. These relationships are achieved—by a sort of biological economy—through signals of attitude or intent which save the organism from actually attacking or, alternatively, allow it to communicate an attitude of friendliness. Such signals can be read unambiguously by congeners, and this happy biological arrangment enables us human beings to record the intent or motivation, at least of children, with reasonable objectivity. The observations which were to be the units of our classification could thus be either physically observable results (child. falls off chair) or attitude-signals (child refuses to greet).

Reasons for the failure of previous attempts at classification

Previous attempts at the classification of maladjusted behaviour yielded inauspicious results mainly for three reasons. The first was a failure to establish reliable observational units. They were for the most part single-word trait descriptions borrowed from popular characterology with its dichotomy of 'good' and 'bad', acceptance and rejection, which reflected the attitude of the informant. It was the latter rather than the investigator who made the decisions about how to classify the behaviour. The second reason for previous failure stemmed from the tendency of behaviour disturbance to be maladaptive by either overreaction or underreaction. Consequently the technique of factor analysis that was mostly used identified two major factors, with very little of the variance left over for any further classification. This would have been in order if each of the two major factors were homogeneous; but evidence is adduced in this monograph to show that this is not the case, and indeed common observation shows us that, within the overreacting 'factor', there are important differences between innocent impulsivity or attention-seeking and 'bloody-minded' hostility; or within the underreacting 'factor' between the inhibition that comes from apprehensiveness and that which comes from depression or other lack of motivation. At a more theoretical level, factor analysis presents us with a model of apparently independent 'factors'— whatever these may be—each of which is responsible for the intercorrelation of a group of items—whereas the real state of affairs seems to be one of complex interaction of dysfunction. The only way of handling it empirically is by inductively building up an understanding or model of these interrelationships, not taken 'off-the-peg' but tailored to their own structure.

The third defect in most previous attempts at classification was the use of specialized clinical samples. There is a high degree of selection in referral to clinics or committal to correctional schools for delinquents. To a large extent the decision to refer or to charge with an offence is a function of the tolerance-limit of the adult who has to bear the brunt of the maladjusted behaviour. Teachers are much more likely to refer children whose presence in the classroom is stressful or frustrating than those whose maladjusted (i.e. personally disadvantageous) behaviour is unobtrusive or possibly even attractive. Children who are undisciplined, an active nuisance or hostile are over-referred; the Unforthcoming who sit meekly and obey all the rules are under-referred unless their avoidance of the learning situation is so extreme as to give the appearance of mental retardation. Children who are physically attractive or with winning mannerisms can 'get away with murder'; when an attractive child does get referred or committed, the receiving institution usually has a grave problem to deal with. In short, it is impossible to assess the full range of disturbed behaviour except in a sample representative of a child population. In addition there is a class of behaviour traditionally regarded as indicative of maladjustment—notably sleep disturbances, expressed fears, nailbiting, temper tantrums—which are not necessarily personally disadvantageous. They may indeed be symptomatic of the emotional instability which accompanies some types of maladjustment, and their abnormality can be judged only by their incidence within a given population. In some cultures fears are inculcated as an instrument of discipline, and temper tantrums are tolerated as a means by which the child gets its own way.

Parenthetically, it should at this stage be stated that the present study is concerned with *behaviour*, not with what people think or say how they behave, nor about how they describe their feelings and attitudes. Data of these latter sorts form a distinct area of study and require a somewhat different methodology. Nor have we been concerned with adaptive behaviour or its variants—except theoretically to relate the dysfunctions which are seen as maladjustment to the normal operation of the human behavioural system.

Methodology of the present study

Our study is the latest stage in an ongoing process over some eighteen years, bringing computerized methods of data treatment to bear upon an earlier inductive classification without such facilities. As the years went by the Day-School edition of the Bristol Social Adjustment Guides, the diagnostic instrument developed from this work, became increasingly out of date. This was notably the case with regard to hyperactive behaviour, which was treated purely phenomenologically. Following studies which validated the concept of Inconsequence (failure to inhibit first reactions involving a lack of cognitive rehearsal of the consequences of an act) it became of prime importance to review the whole classification.

The present study consisted in the use of an experimental revision of the BSAG into which were incorporated a number of new items formulated as a result of classroom observation. This revision also included a small number of items inserted after the last of the earlier validations, in 1956, and not subsequently tested. The schedule consisted of descriptions of behaviour arranged by situation but scrambled as regards their indicating good or poor adjustment. It was completed by the teachers of 2527 children aged in the main from five to fourteen years, but with a smaller proportion over fourteen. The sample consisted of those born on the 15th or 16th of any month who were attending public elementary schools in a fairly large industrial city, an adjoining rural county and a network of schools administered by the Dutch Reformed Church throughout Ontario.

The first step in the treatment of the data was to conduct a validation of the 150 items by the criterion of their incidence among children scoring twenty or more (the 'maladjusted') compared with that among the stable and near-stable (those scoring nine or less). In addition it was decided to reject items which had an overly high incidence among the latter category, even though the ratio of maladjusted to stable was satisfactory. The great majority of the items had already been subjected to a similar type of validation on two successive samples prior to the first publication of the BSAG in 1956. It was nevertheless gratifying that, in a somewhat different cultural and school environment, it proved necessary to reject only twelve items at this stage on the above grounds. Six of these had been added subsequent to the last of the earlier validations—which is an object lesson in the difficulty of formulating reliable descriptions of disturbed behaviour. The new items derived from classroom studies and inserted in the experimental revision on the whole stood up well. For all 150 items, good and bad, the mean ratio of more frequent occurrence among the maladjusted amounted to 18.35.

During the subsequent stages of the data treatment other items were deleted for several reasons. The smaller the number with which the degree and type of maladjustment could be ascertained, the more efficient the resulting instrument would be. Consequently those items which did not 'pull their weight' on either of these counts were removed. The same was done with a small number against which methodological objections might be raised. These included some which invited too much teacher interpretation or attitudinal bias, and some where a cultural factor might be involved. We were finally left with 110 items.

The second stage in the improvement of the instrument was the testing of the syndrome-membership of the indications of maladjustment (the 'items') and their transfer between syndromes until the best possible clustering emerged. Basically it was a matter of finding out whether the cases for which the item was scored showed more than a chance number of the other items of the syndrome. The goodness of the syndrome-membership of the item, calculated in this way, was expressed as a scorer/non-scorer ratio. A review of these ratios for all the items of the postulated syndrome showed whether it 'held together' compared with the distribution of its component items over all the cases in the sample. It corresponded to a loading in a factor analysis, and gave no information about how specific any item was to any one syndrome. Many items in effect achieved high scorer/non-scorer ratios in two or more syndromes vis-à-vis a chance distribution. Nevertheless this treatment served as a first step towards the confirmation of the syndromes, because no syndrome would be possible without an adequate number of component items with scorer/non-scorer ratios significantly in excess of unity (unity indicating a chance distribution).

By calculating the scorer/non-scorer ratios that each item would have obtained if it had belonged to each of the other syndromes, it could be seen by inspection which was, statistically, its best syndrome. Later, as better syndromes were established, syndrome-specificity ratios were calculated by dividing the scorer/non-scorer ratio of the item in its own syndrome by that which it obtained in the next-best syndrome.

The syndromes of maladjustment

Of the 1956 BSAG classification, the three syndromes of underreaction—*Unforthcomingness, Depression* and *Withdrawal*—stood up well, with only a small number of items requiring transfer from one to the other. A few more items had nearly equal ratios in two or, in one or two instances, in all three of these syndromes, and were later placed in a grouping of *Non-syndromic Underreaction.*

Two overreacting core syndromes were identified, the first of these being

163

Hostility. About half of its items came out as very specific—these being its moody, sullen, defensive aspects—but the other half—the aggressive and provocative aspects—had good runner-up ratios in Inconsequence (which see below). This was regarded as theoretically important and confirmatory of the observation made independently by a number of investigators: the Inconsequent child, by exceeding the tolerance-limits of the adults who are responsible for him, excites rejection and hostility, thus destroying the security of his own social affiliations, to which he in turn responds by hostility. The vicious circle of worsening child-parent and child-teacher relationships fails to appear only when the adults in question have temperamentally a very high tolerance-threshold or are assuming a therapeutic role.

The earlier 'K' syndrome, representing an unconcern for approval and an insensitivity to the maintenance of social affiliations, with the consequent release from social obligations, failed to emerge as a distinct syndrome. The items in question in effect achieved high scorer/non-scorer ratios in their own syndrome, but all except three had nearly as high, or higher ratios in Hostility or Inconsequence. Moreover, three of them—describing an indifference to a good relationship with the teacher—had a cultural taint, and were later rejected for this reason. The K syndrome was thus dissolved. This does not mean that it does not exist as a form of dysfunction of the behavioural system, but that—within the limits of discrimination of day-school teachers—it could not be differentiated from other types of anti-social behaviour. In attempting to isolate this type of maladjustment we again run into the complication that it tends to generate disadvantageous social relationships, which in turn generate other types of maladjustment. In a residential or other intimate setting the K-type of individual exposes himself to his associates by his failure to observe the rules of human fellowship and decency, and can no doubt be successfully identified.

Inconsequence, which had been proposed in an interim revision of the diagnostic system of the 1956 classification, was confirmed as the second of the overreacting core syndromes. However, its items failed to get high specificity-ratios owing to the tendency, referred to above, for one type of maladjustment to generate another, in this case Hostility, by interreaction with the social environment. Many of its items, although descriptively containing no hint of Hostility or any kind of anti-social intention, actually obtained ratios nearly as high or even higher within that syndrome. A further reason for the apparent overlap of these two syndromes is that both the Inconsequent and the Hostile child resort to primitive attack-responses, but with quite different motivations—the first because he deals with frustration in an aggressive way without weighing up the consequences, the second as a vehicle for his resentment. For these two reasons an overlap between Inconsequence and Hostility is predictible. For further analysis, five 'Inconsequent' items which were relatively free of Hostility were retained as a core syndrome against which to measure the specificity of the remainder.

The outcome of this stage of the analysis was to make us question the traditional model of a series of independent syndromes, and to work towards concepts of basic forms of dysfunction which might interact—through their environmental effects—upon each other.

Anxiety not a class of behaviour

The syndrome of Anxiety for Adult Attention failed to differentiate itself from the new syndrome of Inconsequence. Previously such attention-seeking behaviour had been interpreted as symptomatic of anxiety, but the present results showed it to be a variety of inhibitional failure. It is the Inconsequent child who persists, despite adult discouragement, in making impulsive bids for attention.

The dissolution of this grouping left no syndrome representative of anxiety, and in retrospect this is explicable on several grounds. First, anxiety is not a motive in the strict sense .of some sought-after change or goal, nor does it constitute a class of behaviour. It is rather a feeling-state, arising when the individual is unable to initiate an executive-response in order to rectify the disadvantage, either because he does not see himself as coping with the problem or threat, or because all feasible responses seem to him to incur further disadvantages (i.e. a conflict-situation). Hence anxiety is often associated with inaction or avoidance. There is undoubtedly much feeling of anxiety associated with an inability to conquer the apprehensiveness of new situations which is the basic characteristic of Unforthcomingness, and it is no doubt the retreat from such anxiety-creating situations which sometimes causes the Unforthcoming child to adopt a defence of mental slowness.

On the other hand anxiety is often associated with overreaction. At its normal and adaptive level of function, it has biological value in forcing the organism—by its unpleasantness and near-intolerability—to deal urgently in some way or other with the disadvantageous or dangerous situation which is its cause. Hence the ill-considered and irrational, and therefore maladaptive, character of some of the actions which are associated with anxiety. Thus, besides avoidance or withdrawal, anxiety is associated with overreacting maladjustment. The Inconsequent child who finds that his guessing strategies are ineffective may react aggressively against the learning-situation. As a response to the intolerable anxiety of a threatened breakdown of a love-relationship the Hostile child will either, by provocative acts, set out to antagonise the presumed disloyal one, or, by flight, banish himself from his or her physical presence.

In sum, anxiety pervades most maladjustment, whether it be of an underreacting or overreacting type. It cannot therefore be used as a category in a taxonomy, such as that attempted, based upon observed behaviour. This does not mean to say that it cannot be used as a form of cross-classification. But in doing so the investigator has to face the fact that, since anxiety is a feeling-state, the collection of his data requires access to how his subjects feel. This involves techniques for self-report which were outside the scope of a study of maladjusted behaviour such as could be observed by classroom teachers.

Testing the consistency of the syndromes over age and sex

Before proceeding to a further trial classification it was necessary to find out whether the syndromes as we had them were consistent over the complete age-range of the study. The children were divided into three main age-groups, with the over-fourteens (those who had failed to gain promotion to secondary school) in a further category. Scorer/non-scorer ratios were then calculated for the item within each age-group separately. Complete consistency was registered when, within all three age-groups, the item obtained the highest ratio within the same syndrome. This was found to be the case for 75 per cent of those items with a minimum marking of ten cases in each. A further 22 per cent of the items showed reasonable consistency, defined by having the highest ratio within the same syndrome in two age-groups and the second-highest in the third. Only one per cent of the items gave a quite inconsistent indication of maladjustment at different ages. This gave us the assurance that the descriptions of maladjusted behaviour could be interpreted as indicating by-and-large the same types of maladjustment over the whole age-range.

The same test of reliability was then carried out as between the sexes. It transpired that only eleven of the 122 items treated had highest scorer/non-scorer ratios in different syndromes for boys and girls. The items are thus in the main diagnostic of the same type of maladjustment, irrespective of sex as well as of age. This degree of reliability encouraged us in the view that the syndromes represented basic forms of dysfunction of the behavioural system.

A two-tier classification

At this stage in the classification we had five syndromes forming 'cores' of satisfactory component items. These were, on the underreacting side, Unforthcomingness, Withdrawal and Depression; on the overreacting side, Hostility and Inconsequence.

The unresolved problem in the classification was the large number of overreacting items which had high scorer/non-scorer ratios in the two latter. These were provisionally placed in a number of further groupings, namely Norm Violation, Peer Maladaptiveness (as later called), Peer-Group Deviance and Attention-Seeking. Their relationship to the core syndromes and to each other was then tested by the above criteria of scorer/non-scorer ratio and syndrome-specificity.

Norm Violation failed to stand up as a syndrome, nor was there any consistency as between boys and girls. Deviance has a diversity of motivations and can be the outcome of various types of behaviour disturbance. Peer-Group Deviance, isolated for special treatment in view of the part that it had played in earlier classifications, had such high ratios for Hostility and Inconsequence as to destroy its value as an independent behavioural mode. The notion that gang-delinquents are essentially stable in their personality was found to be definitely untrue. Norm Violation, Peer-Group Deviance and a small number of specifically 'delinquent' items in a legal sense were amalgamated to form a grouping of *Non-syndromic Overreaction*. One might say that the behaviours in question were culturally-suggested modes of realizing a number of different motivations. Although the outward result is the same, e.g. the commission of a crime, the conscious or unconscious intent of the agent might be to effect a breach in a love-relationship, secure his removal from an anxiety-creating situation, keep in favour with his pals, or to gain some material or personal advantage without adequately calculating the consequences.

The outcome was a two-tier classification consisting of five core syndromes, and a complex of associated groupings. The latter contained considerable elements of the core syndromes, and could be conceptualized as particular forms of defence, compensation, pseudo-adjustment or temporally unintegrated means of achieving goals. There was in addition a 'Neurological' grouping, whose items were satisfactorily associated with each other. Although some had good ratios in the core syndromes they had to be placed in a separate category because they seemed to be indications of neural impairment rather than motivated behaviour.

166

Underreaction and Overreaction

The emergence, in concordance with previous taxonomic studies, of two broad types, of underreacting and overreacting behaviour, raised the question of whether we can use a unitary over-all measure of maladjustment. When those children who scored low in both types, that is to say, were uniformly well adjusted, were removed, inverse correlations of from .3 and .4—according to sex composition— were obtained between the overreacting and underreacting behaviours (which we abbreviated into 'Unract' and 'Ovract'). This does not necessarily mean that these must be regarded as fundamental 'dimensions', as is suggested by such terms as Introversion and Extraversion. The concept of Introversion as a homogeneous pattern of behaviour was notably not confirmed: the Unforthcoming items followed a statistical pattern distinct from those of Depression and Withdrawal, and all three syndromes were differentiated by the specificity ratios. In short, Unract was not a fundamental 'dimension', since there could be different reasons why a child showed an underreacting form of maladjustment. Diverse origins can likewise be seen for 'Extraversion' (overreaction, when it is a matter of maladjustment). On the one hand there is the impulsivity and hyperactivity which spring from a failure to take account of the consequences of proposed behaviour. On the other there is the activation, by environmental stress, of tendencies to overreact to real or presumed disloyalty by hostility.

The fact remained, however, that the interaction between the various types of maladjustment occurred almost exclusively within these two broad divisions. Pragmatically, therefore, they offered the means of establishing general scores by which, in the first place, the discriminatory value of the items as indicators of maladjustment could be assessed. The relative frequency of each item among the maladjusted compared with that among the reasonably well-adjusted children was re-calculated in terms of Unract and Ovract scores. By this means we avoided the artificiality inherent in the earlier item-validation of accepting as a criterion of the discriminatory value of an underreacting item its frequency among overreacting children, which would be expected to be small in any case, and conversely the frequency of overreacting items among the underreacting. This calculation showed that the Unract items were on average between 28 and 30 times more frequent among children in the highest general score-category for *underreaction*, and the Ovract items were on average between 32 and 40 times more frequent among those in the highest score-category for *overreaction*.

Sex differences

The Unract and Ovract scores were used, in the second place, as convenient epidemiological parameters. Notably, they made possible a finer analysis of the incidence of maladjustment in each sex. Its great preponderance among males was found to be restricted entirely to the overreacting forms. In Unract the small excess among boys did not reach statistical significance. In Ovract, however, the mean score for boys was nearly twice that for girls.

Sex differences were further explored by calculating a sex-ratio of incidence for each item and averaging these by syndromes. Unforthcomingness was the only one more prevalent among girls, although the two other forms of underreaction— Depression and Withdrawal—were twice as prevalent among boys, once again underlining the heterogeneity of Unract.

167

In Ovract, Inconsequence showed itself to be highly characteristic of boys, with a high consistency across all its manifestations. Highest of all were those forms of male overreacting behaviour associated with aggressiveness and deviance. Neurological symptoms were on average twice as frequent among males.

Age differences

Analysis by age-groups showed, as regards Unract, hardly any trend by age for either sex. In Ovract, the scores for boys show a regular rise from the age of eight years, accounted for in large part by an increase in Hostility—which is as would be predicted of a form of response which is activated by adverse environment. The associated groupings in Ovract also showed a marked rise which is paralleled in the rise in delinquency rates up to the age of fourteen years.

Our data afforded the opportunity of finding out to what extent the main types of maladjustment were manifested in similar behaviour over the age-range of the sample. This was tested in two ways—first by shifts in the relative prominence of items within each syndrome as between the age-groups, and second, by differences in absolute frequency of the items (that is, of the manifestations of disturbance) at each age. By both tests the Unract items showed a remarkable constancy. The only trend among them was a higher incidence of indications of timidity, passivity and social isolation below eight years, which may be seen as immaturity and the understandable reaction of a young child to moving into a strange new environment.

In Ovract the manifest picture also changed less than would be expected as far as the items of the core syndromes were concerned. The exceptions were that overreacting children seem to learn to get on better with their age-peers and to control aggressive responses to frustration. But, no doubt owing to the advantage of size, they resort more to peer-dominating behaviour and are more prone to express hostility in a provocative, aggressive manner.

Of the 110 items covering the whole range of maladjustment, excluding the neurological, only nineteen moved with age from the top third to the bottom third in the ranking of their relative frequency within syndromes, and five of these showed no consistent trend. The reason for this constancy, it may be averred, is that the manifestations of maladjustment used reflected primitive stress-responses or basic forms of dysfunction which are relatively independent of age.

Social-class differences

The Unract and Ovract parameters were used in the ascertainment of social-class and other ecological differences. In the City sub-sample, which was some 77 per cent of the whole, the schools which its members attended were divided into four socio-economic neighbourhood groups. Once again the Unract scores showed no appreciable differences, either for boys or girls, as between those who resided in the most desirable or least desirable districts. In Ovract there was a steady rise in score the lower the socio-economic status of the neighbourhood; but it reached a bare level of significance only as between the highest and the lowest. This greater amount of overreacting maladjustment in lower-class districts was largely confined to the most severe category, among both boys and girls. If it had been the result of a conflict between the norms of behaviour accepted in their home environment and that expected of them in school, one would have predicted a *general* tendency to overreaction among them. It pointed rather to the existence, in a less favourable environment, of more factors predisposing to maladjustment. These can be congenital, in the same way that disadvantaged social groups show more mental retardation and neurological conditions. They may at the same time be postnatally environmental, as instance an unstable family background. In favour of a congenital or early-life hypothesis is that the greatest social-class difference was found among 5-8-year-old girls, whom one would not think to be affected by conflicting cultural norms.

The general picture, in this sample drawn from an industrial city with a well-marked socio-economic structure reflected in residential demarcations, was of surprisingly small socio-economic differences in the prevalence of behaviour disturbance. Such greater incidence of maladjustment as there was in the poorest socio-economic neighbourhoods was not widely enough distributed even within the latter to be explained as the conformity and adjustment of lower-class youth to a pattern of culture at variance with that of the city as a whole.

Urban-rural differences

The Rural were better adjusted than the City children in both Unract and Ovract. The mean differences in scores reached significance only for Ovract in boys, but they were consistently in favour of the Rural, as were also the smaller proportions of rural children in the most severe Unract and Ovract categories. There is evidently something in the traditional idea that country children are more stable than city children. Our finding could not be accounted for as a social-class difference, because rural incomes would be lower on average than city incomes, and rural/city differences in test-intelligence, which follow social-class trends, go in the opposite to the observed direction for social adjustment. The Rural children were indeed consistently, even though marginally, better adjusted than those of the highest socio-economic neighbourhood in the City.

The separate schools administered by the Dutch Reformed Church served a socially and economically homogeneous group. Nearly all the parents of the children in our sample had emigrated to Canada over a period of a few years immediately following the Second World War, and English was fairly generally spoken in their families. The Unract and Ovract scores for the Dutch sample were compared with those of the City and Rural samples. The usual constancy of the Unract scores in the face of social differences was once again apparent, but in Ovract the Dutch resembled the City children (being in fact themselves two-thirds urban). The picture was one of cultural assimilation rather than distinctiveness.

Maladjustment and ill-health

In earlier studies using the BSAG there had appeared a pronounced tendency for unhealthy children to be more prone to behaviour disturbance. It was found that children suffering from two or more morphologically distinct morbid conditions (illness, physical defect) were very much more maladjusted than those suffering from only one. This, together with the results of other studies demonstrating an interrelationship of disease, mental retardation and temperament impairment, led

169

to the formulation of a Law of Multiple Congenital Impairment. Although girls are less subject to each of the above conditions, it had also been found that, among affected girls, the interrelationship was closer than among boys.

Both these findings were confirmed in the present study. Scorer/non-scorer ratios in Unract and Ovract were calculated for the fifteen morbid conditions which were sufficiently prevalent to allow of statistical treatment and such as could be observed by teachers (respiratory conditions, other chronic ailments, speech defects, bad eyesight, poor muscular coordination, poor hearing, etc.). These ratios showed the extent to which each morbid condition was associated with each broad type of maladjustment. Of the sixty ratios—in Unract and Ovract for boys and girls separately—all except one were greater than unity, demonstrating a consistent relationship between all the morbid conditions and both underreacting and overreacting types of maladjustment. The highest ratios were those for speech defects and poor motor coordination, suggesting common origins for both of these defects and the behaviour handicap. By applying the procedure to each type of maladjustment separately, it was found that every one of the five core syndromes was associated with morbidity. Apart from the Neurological grouping, that of Depression was the most closely so, no doubt because of the depressive effects of certain illnesses, but the consistency of the picture among the other types of maladjustment suggested a more fundamental explanation to this maladjustment/morbidity relationship.

The hypothesis of multiple impairment was tested by arranging the fifteen morbid conditions into nine presumably distinct types of illness or defect, and calculating the mean Unract and Ovract scores for healthy children and for those suffering from one, two, three, and four and over (the highest number being five) of them. The result, for both forms of behaviour disturbance, was a striking increase in mean maladjustment score the larger the number of distinct types of ill-health from which a child suffered. Those boys and girls with four or five morbid conditions showed on average over three times more underreacting maladjustment than the healthy. For overreacting maladjustment the scores of the boys in the 4—5 disease-category were over twice, and those of the corresponding girls over four times, as high as those of the healthy of the same sex. In Ovract the gradient was much steeper for the girls, but only marginally so for Unract. The girls in this sample manifesting an overreacting type of maladjustment were thus exceedingly disease- and defect-prone. The same consistent rise in mean score was observed for all the core syndromes as between the healthy and the multiple physically affected children.

What this multiple-impairment phenomenon meant in practical terms is shown by the proportion of the maladjusted, compared with the well-adjusted, who were unhealthy; and conversely the proportion of the unhealthy, compared with the healthy, who were maladjusted. In the present sample, maladjusted children were some five times more likely to suffer from multiple health conditions, and unhealthy children were between 3½ and 4 times more likely to be maladjusted. Consistent with the method of analysis by mean scores, this relationship was strongest for Depression, with the likelihood, mentioned above, of some direct cause and effect. Of the other core syndromes it was closest for Inconsequence, and least in evidence (but still present) for Unforthcomingness. In nearly all cases the ratios summarizing the closeness of the relationship between behaviour disturbance and ill-health were higher for girls, even though among them the incidence of the conditions was considerably lower. If, as has been suggested, a relationship of this type can be most feasibly explained by a common congenital origin to both the behavioural and the somatic impairments, this would imply a congenital determinant for each of the main forms of maladjustment (congenital being used in its strict sense of that which originates at or before birth, covering both genetic constitution and adverse intra-uterine environment).

We were led to enquire what the nature of the congenital common factor or factors might be. The behavioural system operates for the most part through neural structures. Although we tend to think of the respiratory and digestive as physical systems, they are in fact also regulated by a network of nerves in the form of reflexes. It follows that common ailments in these areas may arise from neural dysfunction. An example is the bronchial infections to which mongoloid and other mental defectives tend to suffer, these being due to the failure of the reflexes controlling the ciliary hairs which clear the bronchial tubes. It is therefore not improbable that the common factor producing the relationship between behaviour disturbance and physical illnesses is one of neurological dysfunction. This, however, is a logically deduced inference which requires empirical confirmation.

Maladjustment and motor impairment

Motor impairment was chosen as a means of estimating the probability of a neurological factor in behaviour disturbance. The test used had been developed independently over some years for this purpose, all other feasible determinants of poor performance in its items having been reduced to a minimum. It was administered to a sub-sample of 713 children drawn from the City schools in a way to make them representative of the socio-economic neighbourhoods which these schools served. By the criterion used, some 15 per cent of the boys and 10 per cent of the girls were motor-impaired. The excess of the former is in conformity with the findings for maladjustment and ill-health, and suggests the same pattern of congenital determination.

There was a consistent upward trend in the mean Unract and Ovract scores with increasing motor impairment. For Unract the motor-impaired showed 40 per cent more maladjustment, as thus measured, than the well-coordinated. In terms of numbers, 83 per cent more of the motor-impaired than of the well-coordinated suffered from Underreacting types of maladjustment; and 73 per cent more of the children suffering from the latter were motor-impaired compared with the not-underreacting.

Overreacting maladjustment showed an even closer relationship with motor impairment. The mean Ovract scores were twice as high among motor-impaired children. About 2½ times as many overreacting as not-overreacting children were motor-impaired.

Among the core syndromes, Unforthcomingness was the only one showing virtually no relationship to motor impairment. Depression, on the other hand, was found to be closely related thereto—at the rate of an 84 per cent excess in mean scores, 68 per cent more Depressed being motor-impaired, and 151 per cent more motor-impaired being Depressed.

Inconsequence had the closest relationship of all with motor impairment. The mean scores for the impaired were well over twice those for the well-coordinated. Over three times as many Inconsequent as Not-Inconsequent children were poorly coordinated; and of the poorly-coordinated over four times as many were Inconsequent.

Especially in respect of Inconsequence the above findings enhance the probability of a factor of neural dysfunction at some stage of the child's development. The motor disability cannot be considered a necessary part of a general condition which includes Inconsequence, since only 31 per cent of the Inconsequent children were motor-impaired, and only 24 per cent of the motor-impaired were Inconsequent. This limited degree of overlap, while indicating a statistical relationship, suggests in aetiological terms a degree of communality in predisposing factors which operate in certain cases only. In short, the neural dysfunction appears sometimes to affect both motor function and the ability to inhibit responses, but more often—on average in 69 per cent of the cases—is specific to the one or the other.

To sum up what general conclusions can be drawn from the use of the Test of Motor Impairment, it appears, first, that motor disability conforms to the Law of Multiple Congenital Impairment in that it is associated stepwise by degree of severity with behavioural and physical handicaps. Second, these relationships are characteristically closer among girls, although the incidence of each condition among girls is lower. This complex of interrelationships points to common origins for all the conditions studied. And since, of them all, motor impairment is the most indicative of neural dysfunction, the findings heighten the probability of some sort of neurological factor in the others.

Maladjustment and delinquency

All those within the City sub-sample (105 boys and 28 girls) who had come to the notice of the police as having committed a delinquent or other deviant act were identified from official records. They differentiated themselves from non-delinquents by scores for overreacting maladjustment, the means for which rose consistently with the number of offences committed. The mean Ovract score for those who had three or more recorded against them was nearly three times that for the non-offenders among the boys, and over five times among the girls. Even for first offenders the Ovract mean for boys and girls together was twice that of the non-delinquents. There was on the other hand no significant difference in underreacting maladjustment between the delinquents and the non-delinquents.

These findings went counter to the theory that the typical juvenile delinquent is a well-adjusted boy conforming to the norms of his inner-city sub-culture. A breakdown of the mean Ovract scores by the social-class ratings of the schools failed to confirm the prediction, based on this theory, that delinquents from well-to-do neighbourhoods would tend to be very maladjusted, while those from poor neighbourhoods would on the whole be well-adjusted. In effect, the mean Ovract score for the former was very similar to that of the latter. Although the incidence of delinquency is greater in the lower-class neighbourhood, it would appear that its onset is associated with a fairly constant level of overreacting maladjustment, irrespective of social class. Nevertheless a significant proportion of the delinquents fell into the well-adjusted category; it was suggested that this group needed closer study before generalizations can be made about them.

Of the five core syndromes, Hostility stood out as being most characteristic of delinquents, with a mean score over six times higher than that for the non-offenders. Next came Inconsequence with a mean 2.7 times higher. As would be expected, there was less Unforthcomingness among the delinquents; on the other hand there was considerably more Withdrawal and Depression.

Twenty-five items occurring three or more times more frequently among the delinquents than among the non-delinquents were listed. They could serve as a means by which the delinquency-prone could be identified with a view to preventive treatment. Twelve of them fell within the syndrome of Hostility, two in that of Inconsequence, and eleven in the grouping of Non-syndromic Overreaction (which is a combination of Hostility and Inconsequence).

Contrary to the current acceptance of certain types of offence as part of the growing-up of the ordinary boy and girl in the inner-city sub-culture, those who committed shoplifting or malicious damage had Ovract means which were over twice as high as the non-delinquents' and only slightly less than the means of delinquents who had committed thefts and breaking and entering. The most maladjusted in an overreacting sense were the young people brought to the notice of the authorities as incorrigible or missing from home.

The follow-up after one year

One year later teachers completed a second BSAG for two sub-samples drawn randomly from the initial sample. In both there was a general tendency for the scores to be lower. For the BSAG scores as a whole this amounted to some 20 per cent for boys and 9 per cent for girls. Among the boys the improvement was again about twice as great in Overreacting as in Underreacting maladjustment.

These improvements could not have been due to losses on the follow-up because they were of a type that on balance would have raised the mean scores. They could not have been due to a regression to the mean because the sub-samples contained the same proportion of high-scorers as the original sample. Nor could they be attributed to any tendency of the scores to be lower in the higher age-groups, because there was a fairly good age-constancy. Such slight age-trends as there were—rises in the means for Ovract and in particular for Hostility—went in the opposite direction.

One explanation of the improvement over the year would be that the completing of the BSAG's led many teachers to see as maladjusted a range of behaviour which they had previously thought of as directed against them personally or as a threat to their discipline. The more objective approach might then have enabled them to handle the maladjusted children with greater tolerance and acceptance, so that the latter in turn reacted better to the more favourable situation.

The improvements were in fact confined to the more maladjusted pupils, which is consistent with the above 'therapeutic' explanation.

There was one indication that the improvements were real rather than test-artifacts. Analysed by age-groups, they were most marked among the young Underreactors. For those under eight years they were between 20 and 32 per cent. The oldest group of Underreactors, those between eleven and fourteen years, showed no consistent improvement. In contrast, the young Overreactors showed no improvement, while the oldest group improved by some 30 per cent. If we accept the therapeutic explanation, then it would appear that inhibited children are more sensitive to improved teacher-attitudes at a young age, but acting-out children are more sensitive thereto at around puberty.

Despite these tendencies to improvement in maladjustment, and the instability of the scores for the most maladjusted, the coefficients of reliability as between the initial and follow-up surveys were reasonably satisfactory. Averaging them for the two follow-up sub-samples, they were .80 for over-all maladjustment, .74 for Unract and .77 for Ovract.

Implications for the causes of maladjustment

When we come to sum up the aetiological implications of the study we have to bear in mind that no one empirical investigation can do more than add strength to certain probabilities, and possibly generate further hypotheses. Proof has no part in empirical science, because it implies the final rejection of every other explanation—but this we can never do since we are not omniscient and cannot reject what we are ignorant of. How unaware we can be of possible explanations 'round the corner' has been seen in the common assumption that 'environmental' means 'postnatal', as far as the determinants of behaviour disturbance are concerned—as if gestation were a period of biological hiatus during which the unborn child was granted a moratorium against noxious influences. If, as some studies already show (Stott 1957, 1959; Pasamanick and Knobloch 1960), the unborn child is susceptible to the mother's excessive exposure to stress to the extent that it incurs a greater risk of physical defect, chronic illness and behaviour disturbance, then we should expect to find a greater incidence of these conditions (in so far as this is not counteracted by higher mortality) among lower-class children. The higher risks of stillbirth and of prematurity, with the latter's associated handicaps, consequent upon extramarital conception (Stewart 1955, Stewart *et al.* 1958) point in the same direction. Drillien (1964) has further shown that congenital hazards confer not an absolutely greater probability of behaviour disturbance, but one which is contingent upon additional postnatal stresses. The congenital determinants of maladjustment would seem therefore to be in the nature of predispositions, that is, a heightened vulnerability to ill-health and/or behaviour disturbance. The greater risk of postnatal stress for the lower-class child due to poverty, poor living-accommodation, a less ordered way of life, broken families, etc., means that this vulnerability is more likely to be actualized in maladjustment. The social and cultural determinants of the latter can thus be very real, but of quite a different character than commonly supposed.

In the present monograph attention has been drawn from time to time to evidence for a congenital factor in maladjustment. It was further argued that primary forms of disturbance could, by interaction with the environment, generate secondary maladjustments. The most striking example of this was the association of Inconsequence, as the prime mover, with Hostility as the secondary reaction to the rejection which the nuisance of Inconsequence induces. A further example is the defensive retreat of the Unforthcoming child into mental incompetence.

The observed sex differences in maladjustment cannot be explained along the fashionable lines of conformity to culturally determined sex roles. Overreacting maladjustment, it will be recalled, was more in evidence among *young* than among older lower-class girls. The greater incidence of maladjustment among boys parallels their greater liability to all defects and non-epidemic illnesses except malformation of the central nervous system. These sex differences point in turn to a genetic determinant. There is experimental evidence with animal subjects (Frazer *et al.* 1954) that liability to prenatal insult, and the type thereof suffered, is determined by the genetic constitutions of the embryo and of the mother. In short, prenatal stresses can prove noxious by triggering off genetic predispositions.

It remains only to ask why such dispositions, with their obvious disadvantages to the individuals carrying them, have not only resisted elimination by natural selection, but are apparently still prevalent in normal populations. Why, in short, has a disease- and maladjustment-free race of human beings not been evolved? Instead we have an infantile mortality rate in uncontaminated primitive cultures of 50 per cent, and in advanced industrial cultures an incidence of maladjustment of some 13 per cent in boys and 7 per cent for girls. The suggestion has been made (Stott 1962b and 1969) that this biological inefficiency in the individual has had survival value for the group as a mechanism which adjusted population numbers to the available resources. The sorts of stress that overpopulation would impose are those which seem most productive of prenatal insult. Even the greater vulnerability of the male is compatible with this theory, since from the point of view of population-recovery the male is more expendable than the female. The theory could also account for the Law of Multiple Impairment further demonstrated by the present findings, since a complex of stresses occurring in one pregnancy could trigger off a number of genetic dispositions to impairment.

These speculations have carried us far beyond the empirical content of the present study. At its most parsimonious level, it was an exercise in classification, the first means of attack by a young science upon an array of phenomena not yet molded into a scientific discipline. But man is curious, and all nature is of a piece, so our minds cannot be stopped from ranging beyond what we can demonstrate.

Research applications

Up to the present, psychology and the life sciences in general have been unable to provide accepted and reliable phenotypes of behaviour. This means that the variables most central to their discipline have remained ill-defined. The effects of this neglect can be seen in the disappointing progress that has been made as regards the determinants of behaviour. It avails little to explore possible types of genetic transmission until the behaviours in question can be objectively identified. The same applies to that vast unexplored yet critically vital field of knowledge, the effects of prenatal and perinatal influences upon behaviour and personality. How little thought has been given to the establishment of behavioural phenotypes is seen, in experimental psychology, by the common practice of equating 'emotionality' in rats with frequency of defecation. 'Emotionality' is a vague and unjustifiably inferential term which prejudges the conclusions drawn from the findings; and defecation is a single behaviour which must be subject to important physiological variables.

In the psychology of humans we find a similar lack of methodological sophistication. Whereas researchers go to great lengths in the choice of measures of 'intelligence', when it comes to the assessment of social adjustment all too often an *ad hoc* check-list is thrown together and used without validation. It is not too much to say that practically every issue of child and adolescent development depends upon the quality of a behavioural taxonomy. Those of brain damage, early deprivation and the effects of the contemporary home situation upon social adjustment provide notable instances.

When it comes to deviant behaviour, the relative lack of interest of other than clinical psychologists in the topic has meant that little account has been taken of the variable of individual adjustment. At the same time this variable has been regarded as a threat by sociologists who claimed the right to explain delinquency within their own discipline.

It has been overlooked that—whatever general formative influences can be traced, whether these be genetic, congenital or cultural—they result finally in variations in the behaviour of individuals. The penultimate stage is the formation of the individual's behavioural repertoire. This term embraces his readiness to respond in certain ways to different types of stimulus, and may be conceptualized as an array of situation-attitudes. The identification and measurement of such of these as are liable to maladjusted expression constituted the goal of the present study, and should be part of the methodology of any study in which the social adjustment of individuals is a variable. Defined in terms of situation-attitudes which are the repository of the effects of many influences, the variable of social adjustment does not exclude or compete with the variables of the sociologist or geneticist. It is merely the last in a hierarchy of determinants of which the genetic, early-developmental and cultural are the earlier, and indeed the more fundamental.

Use of the classification in clinical diagnosis

The types of behaviour disturbance identified in this study could form a basis for some degree of consensus in clinical diagnosis. Here the word *basis* must be stressed, because the clinician must rely upon his experience and intuition in order to deal with individual variations. Nor must it be forgotten that the present study used as its data observations made by teachers of students in the school setting. The clinician must obviously go further than this, and will often be dissatisfied with broad categories which emerge from a statistically induced classification. As was pointed out in the text, the syndrome of Withdrawal could not be refined beyond a grouping together of behaviours which seemed to indicate impairment of social attachment motivation. It would thus cover presumably constitutional deficits which go under the name of autism, and defensive resistance to the formation of attachments arising from continued exposure to traumatic deprivation. Due in part also to the nature of the data, the anxiety-concomitant of behaviour disturbance was also left out of the classification. Yet in a family or residential setting, objective indications of anxiety for human affiliations—in the form of trying over-hard to win approval or indiscriminate efforts to make attachments to strangers—can be differentiated from the anxiety-free attention-seeking of Inconsequence. Inconsequence itself is theoretically and (in so far as the indications of our syndrome are unambiguous) operationally a clear-cut concept, namely that of the failure to inhibit the primitive physical response-modes which have temporal primacy in the hierarchy of problem-solving strategies. Because, in Inconsequent behaviour, the hypotheses for action are tried out in actual behaviour rather than in the mind, the result is a greater amount of activity; and there is a tendency to explore the possibilities for gratification presented by each stimulus as and when they are perceived. The observed hyperactivity and distractibility are resultants rather than fundamental traits, as witness the rapidity with which the Inconsequent child can sometimes be taught to attend and concentrate by a conditioning procedure. The clinician has to be prepared to find quite other reasons for hyperactivity and distractibility, and to learn to recognize the particular characteristics of each. They may, for example, represent a life-style built up of displacement activities, the object of which is to avoid recall of traumatic events. (Children in distressing family situations may show this type of substitutive avoidance hyperactivity.)

All these refinements of diagnosis must be reserved for a clinical monograph. Nevertheless clinical diagnosis needs its system. Above all it needs agreed baselines in the form of the principal types of behavioural dysfunction. These, if clinical psychology is to stand up as an applied science beside the practice of physical medicine, must be subject to empirical verification by accepted experimental methods. Perhaps the gulf between the clinician and the experimenter will be narrowed by quantitative studies such as the present one, in which the data—in the form of actual behaviours observed within the contexts of life—are also those which the clinician uses in individual diagnosis.

References

ACKERSON, L. *Children's behaviour problems Vol. II* Chicago: Univ. Press, 1942.

ADER, R. and BELFER, M.L. 'Prenatal maternal anxiety and offspring emotionality in the rat', *Psychol. Rep.*, 10, 711-18, 1962.

BARKER, R.G. and WRIGHT, H.F. *Midwest and its children: The psychological ecology of an American town* New York: Row, Peterson, 1955.

BIRCH, H.G. 'The problem of "brain damage" in children.' In H.G. Birch (Ed.), *Brain damage in children: biological and social aspects.* Baltimore: Williams and Wilkins, 1964.

BIRCH, H.G., BELMONT, I. and KARP, E. 'Excitation-inhibition balance in brain-damaged patients', *J. Nerv. Ment. Dis.* 139, 537-44, 1964..

BOWLBY, J. 'Forty-four juvenile thieves', *Int. J. Psycho-Anal.* 25, 19, 1944.

BRONFENBRENNER, U. and RICCIUTI, H.N. 'The appraisal of personality characteristics in children.' In P.H. Mussen (ed.), *Handbook of Research Methods in Child Development* New York: Wiley, 1960.

BRYAM, C. *Longitudinal study of aggressive and self-assertive behaviour in social intention.* Honours thesis, Radcliffe Coll., 1966.

CHAZAN, M. 'Maladjusted pupils: trends in post-war theory and practice', *Educational Research*, 6, 29-41, 1963.

CHAZAN, M. 'Symposium: recent research in maladjustment', *Brit. J. Educ. Psychol.*, 38, 5-7, 1968.

CHESS, S., THOMAS, A. and BIRCH, H.G. 'Characteristics of the individual child's behavioural response to the environment', *Amer. J. Orthopsychiat.*, 29, 791-802, 1959.

CHESS, S. 'Genesis of behaviour disorder.' In J.G. Howell, (ed.) *Modern Perspectives in Intl. Child Psychiatry* Edinburgh: Oliver & Boyd, 1969.

CONGER, J.J. and MILLER, W.C. *Personality, social class and delinquency* New York: Wiley, 1966.

DRILLIEN, C.M. *The growth and development of the prematurely born infant* Edinburgh: Livingstone, 1964.

EISENBERG, L. 'Behavioural manifestations of cerebral damage in childhood.' In H.G. Birch (ed.) *Brain damage in children: biological and social aspects* Baltimore: Williams and Wilkins, 1964.

EMMERICH, W. 'Continuity and stability in early social development', *Child Develop.*, 35, 311-32, 1964.

FERGUSON, T. *The young delinquent in his social setting* London: Nuffield Foundation and Oxford Univ. Press, 1952.

FRAZER, F.C., KALTER, H., WALKER, B.E. and FAINSTAT, T.D. 'Experimental production of cleft palate with cortisone, and other hormones', *J. cell. comp. Physio.*, 43 suppl: 237-59, 1954.

GÖLLNITZ, G. *Die Bedeutung der frühkindlichen Hirnschädigung für die Kinderpsychiatrie* Leipzig: Thieme, 1954.

GÖLLNITZ, G. *Revision of the Oseretzky Test of Motor Ability.* Neuropsychiatrisches Institut, Rostock, German Democratic Republic, 1961.

GROUP FOR ADVANCEMENT OF PSYCHIATRY *Psychopathological disorders of childhood: theoretical considerations and a proposed classification. Vol. 6,* Report No. 62, June 1966.

GLIDEWELL, J.C. and SWALLOW C.S. *The prevalence of maladjustment in elementary schools. Report prepared for the Joint Commission on the Mental Health of Children.* Chicago, Ill.: Univ. Chicago Press, 1968.

HEWITT, L.E. and JENKINS, R.L. *Fundamental patterns of maladjustment: the dynamics of their origin.* State of Illinois, 1946.

HUNT, J. McV. *Intelligence and experience* New York: Ronald, 1961.

JENKINS, R.L. *Diagnoses, dynamics, and treatment in child psychiatry* Amer. Psychiatric Assn. Psychiatric Research Report No. 18, 1964.

JENKINS, R.L. 'Psychiatric syndromes in children and their relation to family background', *Amer. J. Orthopsychiat.,* **36**, 450-7, 1966.

JENKINS, R.L. 'Classification of behaviour problems in children', *Amer. J. Psychiat.,* **125**, 1032-8, 1969.

JENKINS, R.L. and GLICKMAN, S. 'Patterns of personality organization among delinquents', *Nervous Child,* **6**, 329-39, 1947.

KAGAN, J. 'Information processing in the child.' In P.H. Mussen, J.J. Conger and J. Kagan (eds.) *Readings in Child Development and personality* New York: Harper & Row, 1965.

KAGAN, J. and MOSS, H.A. *Birth to maturity* New York: Wiley, 1962.

KAGAN, J. 'The three faces of continuity.' In D.A. Goslin (ed.) *Handbook of Socialization Theory and Research,* Chicago: Rand McNally, 1969.

KANNER, L. *Child Psychiatry* Springfield, Ill.: Charles C. Thomas, 3rd ed. 1957.

KOBAYASHI, S., MIZUSHIMA, K. and SHINOHARA, M. 'Clinical groupings of problem children based on symptoms and behaviour', *Int. J. Soc. Psychiat.,* **13**, 206-14., 1967.

KVARACEUS, W.C. and MILLER, W.B. *Delinquent behaviour: culture and the individual* Washington, D.C.: Nat. Educ. Assn. of the U.S., 1959.

LAPOUSE, R. and MONK, M.A. 'An epidemiological study of behaviour characteristics in children', *Amer. J. Pub. Health,* **48**, 1134-44, 1958.

LASHLEY, K.S. 'Dynamic processes in perception.' In J.F. Delafresnaye (ed.) *Brain Mechanisms and Consciousness* Oxford: Blackwell, 1954.

LORENZ, K.Z. *King Solomon's Ring* London: Methuen, 1952.

LORR, M. and JENKINS, R.L. 'Patterns of maladjustment in children', *J. Clin. Psychol.,* **9**, 16-19, 1953.

LUNZER, E.A. 'Aggressive and withdrawing children in the normal school', *Brit. J. Educ. Psychol.,* **30**, 1-10, 1960.

MARSHALL, A.G., HUTCHINSON, E.O. and HONISETT, J. 'Heredity in common diseases: a retrospective study of twins in a hospital population', *Brit. med. J.,* January, pp. 1-6, 1962.

MARSTON, N. and STOTT, D.H. 'Inconsequence as a primary type of behaviour disturbance in children', *Brit. J. Educ. Psychol.,* **40**, I, 15-20, 1970.

MAYS, J.B. *Growing up in the city* Liverpool: Univ. Press, 1954

MAYS, J.B. 'The influence of environment.' In *Delinquency and Discipline* London: Councils and Education Press, 1962.

MORRIS, JOYCE. *Reading in the PRIMARY School: An Investigation into Standards of Reading and Their Association with Primary School Characteristics* (National Foundation for Educational Research in England and Wales) London: Newnes Educational Publishing Company, 1959.

MURPHY, L.B. *The widening world of childhood* Chicago: Basic Books, 1962.

MURRAY, H.A. 'Toward a classification of interactions.' In T. Parsons and E.A. Shils (eds.) *Toward a General Theory of Action* Cambridge, Mass.: Harvard Univ. Press, 1954.

NISSEN, H.W. 'The nature of the drive as innate determinant of behavioural organization.' In M.R. Jones (ed.) *Nebraska Symposium on motivation*, 281-321. Lincoln: Nebraska Univ. Press, 1954.

NISSEN, H.W. 'Axes of behavioural comparison.' In A. Roe and G.G. Simpson (eds.) *Behaviour and Evolution* New Haven: Yale Univ. Press, 1958.

PASAMANICK, B. and KNOBLOCH, H. 'Brain damage and reproductive casualty', *Amer. J. Orthopsychiat.*, **30**, 298-305, 1960.

PETERSON, D.R. 'The age generality of personality factors derived from ratings', *Educ. Psychol. Measur.* **20**, 461-74, 1960.

PETERSON, D.R. 'Behaviour problems of middle childhood', *J. Consult. Psychol.*, **25**, 205-9, 1961.

PRECHTL, H.F.R. and STEMMER, C.J. 'The choreiform syndrome in children', *Dev. Med. and Child Neurol.*, **4**, 119-27, 1962.

PRINGLE, M.L.K., BUTLER, N.R. and DAVIE, R. *11,000 Seven-Year-Olds (First Report of the National Child Development Study)* London: Longmans, 1966.

QUAY, H.C. 'Personality dimensions in delinquent males as inferred from factor analysis of behaviour ratings'. *J. Res. Crime and Delinq.*, **1**, 33-7, 1964.

QUAY, H.C. and QUAY, L.C. 'Behaviour problems in early adolescence,' *Child Devel.*, **36**, 215-20, 1965.

QUAY, H.C., MORSE, W.C. and CUTLER, R.L. 'Personality patterns of pupils in special classes for the emotionally disturbed', *Except. Child.*, **32**, 297-301, 1966.

QUAY, H.C. 'Personality patterns of pre-adolescent delinquent boys', *Educ. Psychol. Measur.*, **26**, 99-110, 1966.

QUAY, H.C. and PETERSON, D.R. *Manual for the Behavior Problem Checklist* Champaign, Ill.: Children's Research Center, Univ. of Illinois, 1967.

RUTTER, M. 'Classification and categorization in child psychiatry', *J. Child' Psychol. Psychiat.*, **6**, 71-83, 1965.

RUTTER, M. and GRAHAM, P. 'Psychiatric disorder in 10- and 11-year-old children', *Proc. Roy. Soc. Med.*, **59**, 382-7, 1966.

SHAW, C.R. and MCKAY, H.D. *Juvenile delinquency and Urban areas* Chicago: Univ. Chicago Press, 1942.

SHEPHERD, M., OPPENHEIM, A.N. and MITCHELL, S. 'Childhood behaviour disorders and the child-guidance clinic: an epidemiological study', *J. Child. Psychol. Psychiat.*, **7**, 39-52, 1966.

SONTAG, L.W. *Fetal behaviour as a predictor of behaviour in childhood.* Presentation to Annual Meeting of the American Psychiatric Assoc., 1962.

STENGEL, E. 'Classification of mental disorders', *Bull. World Health Org.*, **21**, 601-63, 1959.

STEWART, A.M. 'A note on the obstetric effects of work during pregnancy', *Brit. J. Prev. Soc. Med.,* **9,** 159-61, 1955.

STEWART, A.M., WEBB, J.W. and HEWITT, D. 'Observations on 1,078 perinatal deaths', *Brit. J. Prev. Soc. Med.,* **9,** 2,57, 1958.

STOTT, D.H. *Delinquency and human nature* Dunfermline, Fife: Carnegie United Kingdom Trust, 1950.

STOTT, D.H. and SYKES, E.G. *The Bristol Social Adjustment Guides* London: Univ. London Press; Toronto: Gen. Pub. Co.; San Diego: Educ. Test. Serv., 1956.

STOTT, D.H. 'Physical and mental handicaps following a disturbed pregnancy', *Lancet* 18 May, 1006-12, 1957.

STOTT, D.H. 'Evidence for prenatal impairment of temperament in mentally retarded children', *Vita Humana,* **2,** 125-48, 1959.

STOTT, D.H. 'Delinquency, maladjustment and unfavourable ecology', *Brit. J. Psych.,* **51,** II, 57-70, 1960

STOTT, D.H. 'An empirical approach to motivation based on the behaviour of a young child', *J. Child Psychol. Psychiat.,* **2,** 97-117, 1961.

STOTT, D.H. 'Evidence for a congenital factor in maladjustment and delinquency', *Amer. J. Psychiat.,* **118,** 781-94, 1962a.

STOTT, D.H. 'Cultural and natural checks to population growth.' In M.F.A. Montagu (ed.) *Culture and the Evolution of Man* New York: Oxford Univ. Press, 1962b: reprinted in A.P. Vayda (ed.) *Environment and Cultural Behaviour* New York: Natural History Press, published for the American Museum of Natural History, 1969.

STOTT, D.H. 'A general test of motor impairment for children', *Dev. Med. and Child Neurol.,* **8,** 523-31, 1966.

STOTT, D.H. *The Social Adjustment of Children* (manual to the Bristol Social Adjustment Guides). London: University of London Press, Third Edition; Toronto: Gen. Pub. Co.; San Diego: Educ. Ind. Test. Serv., 1966a.

STOTT, D.H. *Studies of Troublesome Children* London: Tavistock Publications; New York: Humanities Press; Toronto: Methuen Publications, 1966b.

STOTT, D.H., MOYES, F.A. and HENDERSON, S.E. *Test of Motor Impairment* Guelph, Ontario: Brook Educational; Windsor: National Foundation for Educational Research in England and Wales; Victoria: Australian Council for Educational Research, 1972.

STOTT, D.H. Manual to the Bristol Social Adjustment Guides, 5th edition. London: Univ. London Press, 1974

THOMPSON, W.R. 'Influence of prenatal anxiety on emotionality in young rats', *Science,* **125,** 698-9, 1957.

TINBERGEN, N. *The herring gull's world* Glasgow: Collins, 1953.

UNDERWOOD, J.E.A. (Chairman) *Report of the Committee on maladjusted children* London, H.M. Stationery Office, 1955.

WHITE, R.W. 'Motivation reconsidered: the concept of competence', *Psychol. Rev.,* **66,** 297-333, 1959.

WINER, B.J. *Statistical principles in experimental design* N.Y.: McGraw-Hill, 1962.

WOODWORTH, R.S. *The dynamics of behaviour* New York: Holt, 1958.

WRIGHT, H.F. 'Observational child study'. In P.H. Mussen (ed.), *Handbook of Research Methods in Child Development* New York: Wiley, 1960.

WYNNE EDWARDS, V.C. *Animal dispersion in relation to social behaviour* Edinburgh: Oliver and Boyd, 1962.

Index